D1459177

Salmon

Salmon

ARTHUR OGLESBY

Queen Anne Press
Macdonald & Co   London & Sydney

First published 1971
New edition 1974
Second impression 1976
Third impression 1980
New edition 1983

Published in 1983 by Queen Anne Press,
a division of Macdonald & Co (Publishers) Ltd,
Maxwell House, 74 Worship Street, London EC2A 2EN

ISBN: 0356 07916 3

Typeset by Waterlow Ltd, Dunstable

Printed in Great Britain by
Biddles Ltd, Guildford, Surrey

Designer
Anne Isseyegh

CONTENTS

Arthur Oglesby with ten salmon taken on 3 November 1982 on the Upper Floors beat of the Tweed near Kelso. This catch is the heaviest weight of fish the author has taken in one day. The fish weighed 7lb, 6lb, 13lb, 13lb, 15lb, 16lb, 17lb, 18lb, 18lb and 22lb – an average of 14½lb per fish.

PREFACE

Writing a book, any book, involves a certain amount of vanity. The writer has to presume that he has something important or interesting to say, and then he must be sufficiently conceited to think that someone will read it. Back in 1969 I wrote the bulk of the text for the first edition of *Salmon*; it was published in 1971 and was subsequently enlarged slightly in 1974. By most commercial yardsticks the book has been a success, and it was well received by anglers; but certain events have now made it out of date. Therefore, rather than let the publishers do another reprint, I thought it prudent to redraft some of the text and rewrite the rest. Inevitably certain chapters bear great similarity to what was written before, but there are amendments and additions – for it would be grossly arrogant to imply that in 1969 I knew all there was to know about salmon fishing, and that the intervening fourteen years have taught me nothing more.

For instance, when writing about rod-making materials in the first edition, I commented that I was too old to be wooed away from split-cane. Such rods epitomised the full extent of the rod-maker's art. They were created in an era when craftsmanship was a proud British boast. Even before my book was in print, however, I found myself enjoying a courtship with rods made of fibreglass, and it was not too long before my cane rods were put into full retirement. The mid-seventies saw the advent of carbon fibre. I was one of a few anglers who were involved in the testing of prototype carbon rods, and, eventually, I allowed my name to be linked with the rod-making firm of Bruce and Walker Limited. My motives were diverse. Firstly, I felt that Bruce and Walker were, and are, making the finest rods on the British market. Secondly, Jim Bruce and Ken Walker are two of the greatest sportsmen and nicest people with whom to be involved. The third and not least important reason was that, by commissioning me to make a series of angling films, they offered me the opportunity to ally my skills with fishing rod and movie camera. *Game Fishing*, the first of these films, had its premiere in London in February 1980. And before this book gets anywhere near the bookstalls, I am hopeful that my second film, *Fly Casting*, will have made its debut.

However, all films involve a team and I am ever grateful to Hugh Falkus and film editor Roger Cawood, who together steered me through some of the pitfalls involved in professional film production. Additionally, Hugh has been a tower of strength in helping me with words and commentary. Now, it is my ambition to make this new version of *Salmon* as definitive a textbook for the salmon angler as Hugh's *Sea Trout Fishing* is for those who enjoy the midnight hours with splashing sea trout. I realise that I have set myself a daunting task. During the last ten years it is doubtful if I have added more than three hundred salmon to my previous total, which just topped the one thousand mark. But there is never a day spent by the riverside when I do not increase my knowledge of this fascinating sport. I hope that I shall have the wisdom to continue to learn, for there is no place for a closed mind in salmon fishing.

Although all types of angling are in a continual state of metamorphosis, change comes slowly to the world of the salmon fisherman. Methods we have inherited tend to stick, while many books on the subject have come and gone. Some have left their mark while others have not. Very few have provided the reader with *facts*. It is a shattering admission that, so far as the salmon is concerned, we are still comparatively short of facts. Fancies there are by the million, and I am not alone in having my share of these. My aim is to explore such facts as are known, but also to speculate on my fancies, and on those of well-known authorities of past and present. It may be that I shall not produce any great revelations for you, since the only safe route to successful salmon fishing is through one's own experience.

It is still true to say that one of the important factors affecting successful salmon fishing is the size of the angler's bank balance. Those who can afford the best beats, at the best times, usually have a head start on lesser mortals. In some instances, where these anglers have the services of a good gillie or boatman, they may well catch fish which have not been fully earned by their own skill. They return home with tales of monster catches and are credited for being expert anglers, when, had they been left to their own devices, many might have hit the river at the wrong time, enjoyed inclement conditions, or generally made a poor showing.

Although I have now caught in excess of thirteen hundred salmon, I am well aware that this number may be considered dismally small when compared with the vast totals amassed by some earlier writers on the subject. Therefore I approach my task with the appropriate humility, in the knowledge that there are many with greater experience than myself; many, indeed, who go quietly about their task and never commit a word to print, shunning the consequent limelight. I console myself with the thought of those 'instant' salmon fishermen, whose plentiful utterances are characterised by dogma and pedantry, drawn from their vast, or in some instances (believe it or not) limited, experience.

I was born in 1923 and started fishing at the age of eight. In those distant days, trout of the rock-girt streams near my home in northern England were the main quarry. Pike and roach came to the net from nearby ponds and rivers. Worms and maggots were the most used baits and it was not until the end of military duty in the second World War that I took to the fly rod. For the next ten years I became preoccupied with dry-fly fishing for trout. Salmon were fish I occasionally caught, usually by accident; and I became convinced that there could be no sane approach to salmon fishing. Gradually, this outlook changed as more opportunities for salmon fishing presented themselves. Success bred success as I began to realise that there were more factors involved than pure luck. I was to discover that there was even a vague formula – one that could barely be defined or proved. It was very basic, with many variable permutations, and the words *never* and *always* had no place in it.

As experience increased, my confidence grew. Inevitably I went into print. The printed word has a great aura of truth and this has made me aware of the many responsibilities of the writer. Eventually my writing led to wider horizons and brought introductions to well-known names. Opportunities to fish more exotic waters came my way; and further experience brought more successes because, to a large extent, the two are interdependent. I say to a large extent, because mere experience cannot be the final hallmark. There are some who either cannot, or will not, learn from experience. My grandfather may well have driven more miles than the current world champion racing driver, but there can be little doubt which of them is or was the most experienced – and, for reason of that experience, the better driver. The champions of most sports achieve their acclaim while they are young men. Only in the field of match angling does the angling world acclaim the youngsters: most angling accolades are not due until senility approaches, a time when cynicism and dogmatic views may be noted. Although it gets ever nearer, I have not yet arrived at this destination. Accolades and acclaim are not my aim. But for the past thirty years I have enjoyed wide and varied salmon fishing experience. I have learned what it pays to do; and what, sometimes, it pays not to do. I have also learned when it helps to fish hard; and when it seems preferable to sit and watch or go home.

I have caught salmon by every legitimate method and a few the other way. I have listened to the pundits and read their writings; but, a more important factor, I have fished – and fished diligently. I have learned the mechanics of casting from the tournament experts and how to tie flies that catch fish, even though not all my flies might catch fishermen! I have perfected the method of tailing fish from the water with my bare hands, instead of stabbing them through vital organs with a gaff. My general fishing activities have taken me to exotic places like Scandinavia, North America, Spain, Africa, India and Pakistan. They have introduced me to a hundred and one friends – and, I hope, few enemies! They have brought me immense enjoyment, fulfilment and some treasured memories.

Little success could have been possible without intimate friends. In the immediate post-war years, I had the good fortune to meet the man who was to have the greatest influence on my angling life. I refer, of course, to that controversial figure, the late Eric Horsfall Turner. We spent many happy days together and I am ever grateful for his guiding companionship. It was through him that I met many of the well-known names in angling. Perhaps the man who was to have the greatest influence on pure technical ability was the late Captain T.L. Edwards. Tommy was a tough teacher demanding nothing save the best. Not only did he teach me how to cast to a reasonably high standard, but he also gave me an insight on how to teach others. In my opinion, he was the greatest professional angling tutor we have ever had. No man, in a lifetime of angling, can ever learn all there is to know about it. It might take several reincarnations to enable the angler to reach even the threshold of full knowledge. To think like the fish we would have to be as dimwitted as the fish! We may never understand their ways; nor fully accustom ourselves to their environment. We are merely hunters, after the style of primitive men of old, but with the difference that, instead of fishing to live, we are merely concerned with the challenge of outwitting creatures from another environment by the most sporting methods. If some of the facts in this book help the reader to a greater understanding of salmon fishing problems, and some of the fancies show the worth of a trial which brings success, then my object will have been achieved.

Thanks are due to the editors and publishers of *The Field*, *Field & Stream*, *The Shooting Times and Country Magazine* and *Trout and Salmon* for permission to reproduce, either wholly or in edited version, some of my articles that have appeared in these journals. Thanks are also due to Reg Righyni for being such a constant and knowledgeable fishing companion throughout the sixties and early seventies; to my good friend Odd Haraldsen, for all his past kindness and his never-wavering promise to invite me annually to fish Norway's famed Vosso river at Bolstadøyri; to Ken Morritt, the founder of Intrepid reels, for his kindness and for the pleasure of his wit and company; to Hugh Blakeney, himself a great salmon fisherman and Factor of the Strathspey Estates, for his great assistance in securing for me access to good fishing on the Castle Grant waters of the Spey; to the Strathspey Angling Association on whose waters I do most of my instruction; to Lady Pauline Sykes, daughter of the late Countess of Seafield, on whose estate I have enjoyed so much wonderful sport; to Gerald Panchaud, owner of the North Harris Estate, for his gracious hospitality on those wonderful Hebridean lochs near Amhuinn-suidhe Castle; to Kirsty Ennever, formerly managing editor of Queen Anne Press, and Caroline North for all their meticulous attention to detail with my script; to my son Paul, Brian Bowman and Ray Burrows for the line drawings; to that talented photographer and dry-fly trout fisherman, Roy Shaw, for some of the pictures, and to photographer and film cameraman Keith Massey for others. Lastly, I bow to my wife, Grace, herself a keen and talented salmon angler, who has given me every encouragement throughout the tedium of writing and who occasionally filled my glass with Scotch!

Arthur Oglesby
Harrogate, 1982

Note: Fly Casting *and* Game Fishing *are available on one videotape obtainable from Video Image Productions Limited, 51 Burton Stone Lane, York.*

Most salmon anglers agree that when we come to comment upon anything to do with the question of salmon, we are very short of the full facts. We know that, at times of their own choosing, salmon move in from the sea and are only able to negotiate those rivers with the requisite water chemistry and dissolved oxygen content. We know that they move upstream as conditions permit, and then, in the autumn of the year, the hens shed their eggs, to be fertilised by the males, in a 'redd' or bed of gravel. With sweeping movements of their tails the hen salmon cover the redds with fist-sized stones; and the rest is left to nature. Exhausted, the hen salmon drop back into quieter water. Now known as kelts, both the males and females are in a weak state. Some males stay on the spawning grounds to fight off intruders. Perhaps there is little wonder that the bulk of male kelts perish and that only a few females survive to make the return migration all over again.

Meanwhile, in the sanctuary of the gravel, new life is being formed. Depending on water temperatures, the young embryos slowly undergo their strange metamorphosis until, in the early spring, the egg cases fracture and young salmon fry take to their fins. Small yolk-sacs, still attached to the fry, sustain them until the time comes to squirm out of the gravel and find natural food in the broad new world of the river. Here, of course, they are subjected to a high level of predation. Young fry of this size make an appetising meal for trout, herons and kingfishers. There will be massive mortality before they reach the parr stage and are better able to fend for themselves.

Varying factors then influence the period of residence in fresh water. Water temperatures have significant effect, as does the amount of

A kelt and a fresh salmon from the Tweed at Upper Hendersyde.

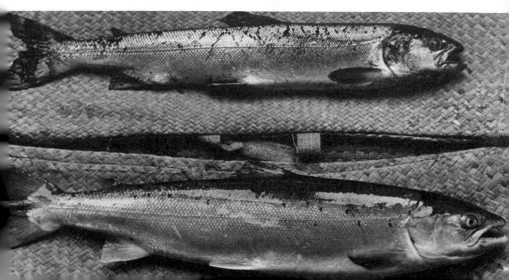

A complex fish pass on the River Leven at Newby Bridge, Cumbria.

available food. There may be other factors, but at the end of about two years the young parr don a silvery coat and become known as smolts. Now they develop a strange, nomadic instinct. Nature is telling them to drop downstream to face whatever fate awaits them. On this outward migration the fish are subjected to many trials. They have to negotiate weirs and possibly the turbines of hydro-electric schemes. They have to face the risks of pollution from industrial or urban communities' effluent near the estuaries. They have to run the gauntlet of the varying predators awaiting them in the sea. At this stage they become a bit of an unknown quantity. We lose our knowledge of the full facts and a few fancies take over. Not all is man's fancy, however. In his never-ending quest to reap a harvest from the sea, he finds certain sea-feeding grounds (notably those in the vicinity of Greenland) where it has been established that grilse-sized salmon may be netted in prolific numbers. A similar fishery was established by the Danes and Faroese on the high seas; and also by the Danes and Swedes on one of the migration routes of Norwegian salmon. But, as most of these latter fish were thought to be kelts returning to the sea, the greater concern was shown for the devastating number of fresh salmon which were taken off Greenland in the sixties by heavy commercial fishing.

With our increasing knowledge of some of the sea migrations, further information concerning the salmon sea diet continues to come to light. An article published by T. B. Fraser in the Canadian *Atlantic Salmon Journal* during the summer of 1968, and entitled 'Atlantic Salmon in Northern Latitudes', claims that salmon eat herrings, alewives, smelts, capelins, sprats, eels, small mackerel, haddocks, shrimps and crustaceans, and follow gatherings of such fish in their migrations. Seawater temperatures are said to have great bearing on where the shoals move; and it is stated that it has been scientifically proved that salmon can navigate by the sun. This comment is based upon the assumption that they can sometimes *see* the sun in northern wintry latitudes! Anglers interested in salmon navigation are recommended to read *Homing of Salmon – Underwater Guideposts* by Arthur D. Hasler of the University of Wisconsin.

Academic knowledge does not solve our problem. We lose our small smolts from our estuaries and do not hear of them again until they have acquired a weight of some 4-10lbs off Greenland. Even then, we are still uncertain whether the entire migration goes to Greenland; but if there are other selected destinations, such as the Faroes, it is a merciful blessing that some have not yet been discovered. Atomic submarines are alleged to have recorded shoals of salmon feeding under the Arctic ice. Their location has never been fully divulged and, if this is the feeding zone to which the bulk of them go, it is fortunate that the ice affords them protection from the destructive urges of the commercial fishing world.

Tagging experiments give us the next fact. After varying periods at sea, the salmon make every endeavour to get back to the rivers of their birth. Having found an abundant larder somewhere in the depths of the ocean, sufficient to take them from mere fingerlings to fish around 5-7lbs in their first year of sea feeding, some may well return during the summer following the year of their first migration. These young fish are termed 'grilse'. Salmon may, however, prolong their marine feasting and feel no urge to return until the second or third year at sea. By this time they are mature salmon, and may weigh anything between 12 and 30lbs. The greater part of their sea life behaviour, therefore, is unknown. Many fancies and just a few facts have been put forward; the most notable fancies, perhaps, coming from the pen of Richard Waddington in his book, *Salmon Fishing*, where he claimed that salmon followed the eels on their migration to the Caribbean Sea.

It has been well established that salmon return to the rivers of their birth for the prime purpose of meeting the natural instinct which leads to reproduction of the species. Somewhere, way out at sea, the urge comes upon them. They stop feeding and, like homing pigeons, begin their long and often arduous pilgrimage back to fresh water. Certain migration routes have been discovered by man; and drift netting with nylon nets reaped a rich reward until banned by law in Scotland. Off the north-east coast of England this form of netting is still permitted and one wonders just how long such indiscriminate cropping may be allowed to continue.

SALMON

Other predators lie in wait near the coast. Packs of seals, for instance, indulge in salmon feasts as the main run makes for the estuaries, where other commercial fishermen lie in wait to operate their various legal and illegal netting devices. The salmon have to negotiate polluted estuaries, with a high risk of mortality, in order to find upstream water of great purity. But slowly, as spring turns into summer, the rivers fill again with fresh-run fish who anxiously seek little more than peace and quiet until the autumn, when they find a mate and fulfil the requirements of species regeneration.

We know that as far as feeding for full sustenance is concerned, the mature salmon, unlike parr, do not feed in fresh water. People who continue to maintain that they do are like Flat Earth Society members who, despite having seen actual space pictures, still maintain their tenets. The digestive organs are said to cease to function upon entry into fresh water, but the full facts are not known. There is a deal of evidence for the theory that salmon then become *incapable* of feeding in fresh water; but some eminent authorities have expressed the view that should the salmon have the inclination to feed there is no reason why the digestive process should not continue to operate. Which comes first, therefore, the chicken or the egg? Does the stomach occlude and become inoperative due to fasting, or does the occlusion compel the fish to fast? Writing on this topic in his book, *The Atlantic Salmon*, Lee Wulff comments:

The underside of a fresh-run Norwegian salmon showing sea lice (near the anal fin).

'It is logical to conclude that the salmon's hunger leaves him and he has no essential need of vitamins or food. He shrinks in size, changing physically. The shrinking of size alone is fairly convincing. Salmon do not try to avoid it or retard it by foraging in the manner typical of feeding fish. They do not make a practice of cruising the pools to round up minnows. They cling to the safe and comfortable waters without foraging in the more productive shallows that hold the bulk of the river's sources of food. If they were seriously interested in the river's food supply they could be depended upon to make a systematic search for it. No fish eager to feed would allow so large a share of the available food to remain untouched.

'Salmon entering rivers from the sea are sometimes infested with tapeworms. Salmon are caught with tapeworms in them soon after they reach the rivers, but when salmon reach the fresh water, the tapeworms soon starve to death. They may be seen on occasions partly ejected and trailing behind as the salmon swims. We kept salmon captive in a small dammed-up pool at the Portland Creek camps. Salmon that had been caught on fly and released there for the guests to watch ejected several such starved-out tapeworms which were either picked up off the bottom or taken from the fish. When parasites cannot live on what a salmon eats, it is certainly not enough to support the fish himself. All logic points to a loss of appetite or nausea which nature induces for the benefit of the species and adjusts for in her own special way. To this moment, it is beyond our understanding.'

All authorities seem to agree that salmon do not feed in fresh water in the full sense of the word, and that they are maintained by the built-up fat and protein in the body tissue. The entire period spent in fresh water is a process of wasting away. The eggs or milt have to be formed from natural reserves: hence the salmon lose their girth while scale readings also show a recession in growth. The flesh loses its natural fat and by the time a spring-run fish faces the rigours of spawning, it is a sorry-looking creature. But even after completion of the sex act, the Atlantic salmon (unlike its Pacific cousin) is not necessarily doomed to die. As I have intimated, many females drop back into quieter water while the males search vainly for another mate or stay and guard the redds. While many do, in fact, succumb and die, a good proportion make their way back to the sea as kelts. Even though a high percentage of these kelts may fall to hungry marine predators, there is evidence that a worthwhile percentage at least survive to make the journey again.

Richard Waddington argued that for reason of birth location the salmon is basically a freshwater fish. The specific gravity of the salmon egg would cause it to float in salt water. This doubtless induces freshwater spawning; but by reason of feeding habit, salmon may be classed as sea fish. Assuming this to be a fact, why is it that salmon will sometimes take our flies and baits while they are in fresh water? What prompts them to do this? Is it the memory of their younger days in the river, as parr, when they

A salmon showing damage inflicted by a seal.

fed on every available morsel the river could produce? Is it the latent memory of their rich sea feeding? Is it anger at having the peace and tranquillity of their freshwater lie shattered by a wobbling spinner or a fluttering fly? Or is it purely reflex action, as Waddington postulated? Might another factor even be the great competition between salmon and salmon for a good lie? When the salmon finally finds a good lie, is the taking of a lure a show of resentment at the intrusion, not only of some other salmon, but of some other form of natural life? Could it be that the salmon shares an affinity with a half-sleeping cat? The cat knows that fluttering leaves are not edible, and there are many times when it will permit them to be blown on the wind without any let or hindrance. Just occasionally, however, the cat will jump up and chase a fluttering leaf and dab it with a paw. It does not want the leaf as food, but a particular moment has come when it cannot resist the opportunity of exercising its basic predatory nature. What prompts it to do this at certain times and not at others?

The fact is that we do not *know* why a salmon takes our lures. It may be any, or all, of these influences; but if one or more worked all the time we might catch every salmon known to run the river. Why is it that only at some periods are they on the take and at others there is nothing which will induce them to move? Why is it that fresh-run fish are easier to catch than the, presumably, more hungry, stale fish which have been in the river for a much longer period? Why is it that sometimes a fish will grab any fly, bait or spinner as though it represented the last meal of its life – which well it may do? The fact is that we do not *know* and to think that we do is mere fancy. The angler, of course, is perfectly entitled to his fancies. The facts are so desperately obscure that unless fancies had been there to fall back on, there would have been no progress at all in the techniques of salmon fishing. (This comment is based on the presumption that there has been some progress – which, in the full sense, I doubt!)

If an angler was asked to catch a fish of which he had never heard before, one of his prime questions would be, 'What does it feed on?'. Armed with this knowledge, he would then be able to devise the necessary lure, whether fly, spinner or bait, and sally forth with a modicum of confidence. He would, with some assurance, obviously present the appropriate type of lure to try to induce the fish to take it. We already know, however, that the salmon neither feeds nor takes food for nutrition in fresh water. Yet over the past decades man has devised lures galore which will take salmon under varying conditions. Have we yet arrived at a definite conclusion that any one of the various designs we adopt for salmon fishing is the best formula to induce a take? Might there not be some lure, undiscovered as yet, which will hook more consistently? We don't know, and as the fish does not take food, it is reasonable to suppose that it would occasionally take a spinning wristwatch just as well as the most beautifully contrived lure! I have never tried one, nor a wobbling carrot, nor any other such lure, for the simple reason that the salmon is never likely to encounter such things in its normal life. We realise, of course, that as great predators they must feed heavily on natural food in the sea. But have we, as yet, any firm knowledge of their staple diet? We have a deal of information on their infant feeding habits while in fresh water. We know that they take flies and small aquatic insects; we know them to be close relatives of the brown trout, who are among the most intensive of predators. Dare we assume, therefore, that the salmon's general behaviour is very similar to that of the trout? We know, for instance, that certain types of trout have accustomed themselves to a sea-going migration and have thus earned the term 'sea trout'. We know these fish to be great predators; so it seems reasonable to accept that the salmon are very similar in most of their moods.

It is not difficult, therefore, to understand the reasoning of the salmon angler of earlier years. If the small fly catches trout, then a large fly should catch salmon. It seems reasonable to assume that the first salmon caught was probably hooked entirely by accident when the angler was wet-fly fishing for trout. With the fine horse-hair casts or leaders of those far-off days, the fish could easily have been lost. But such experiences would, at least, bring some clue about what a salmon is occasionally prepared to take; and the flies, spinners and baits in use today doubtless owe their evolution to these primitive findings, rather than to knowledge of the salmon's staple diet. It could be argued that the old-fashioned types of lure would be equally effective on our salmon rivers today; and that it is purely fancy which makes us believe that our modern patterns have special qualities earlier lures did not possess. Have we, in fact, made any progress at all? We are little nearer full knowledge as to why a salmon takes our lures; and although it cannot be logical to fish with a spinning wristwatch, who is to say that it will not be as effective as modern designs of the Devon Minnow? The movement of a Devon through the water is surely most illogical, for nothing in nature moves in such a fashion. Yet I have caught far too many salmon on this lure to discard it lightly as a take-inducing one. The Devon has been the standard spinning lure for successful fishermen through many past decades; and although many of our lures have undergone minor changes over the years, it is only fancy which makes us prefer them to the originals. Does our half-sleeping cat deliberately select which leaf it will dab at and which it will leave alone? If so, what subtle influences affect its choice? We don't know.

We do know that, quite by accident, man has stumbled upon ways and means of catching salmon. We can only *assume* that we have found the better ways. Indeed, if better lures are there to be discovered, it could well be argued that they are best unfound; since their effective use would cause further depredations of our diminishing stocks. If the present ravages of legal and illegal drift and estuary netting, pollution, poaching, foul-hooking and acid rain continue unabated, then the prospect is indeed bleak. But so long as salmon remain, man will seek to catch them. Moreover, as anglers show the greatest concern about the future of salmon stocks, it is the anglers who have, logically, the greatest entitlement to catch them. Consider also the overall benefit to the economy. A salmon sent to market from commercial sources brings little benefit to the community in which it was taken. A fish caught by a visiting angler on rod-and-line, however, offers multiple benefits from its association with the hotel and travel trades, the employment of gillies, and other ancillary businesses.

In the meantime, while salmon continue to run our rivers, we know that they will take worm, fly, spinner, prawn and shrimp since they have been caught with all of these lures. We know that while in fresh water salmon do not take these lures for food. Let us now examine some of the old methods and some of the new. Many opinions will be based on fancy; but on a fancy born of experience and set against the yardstick of success.

2   SEASONS AND METHODS

We have already noted that salmon may be caught in fresh water with a great variety of lures. As yet, there is little more than pure speculation to guide the novice in his choice of season or method. It is, therefore, very important to have knowledge of several factors before a particular section of a river may be exploited to anywhere near its full sporting potential. Most land and riparian rights in Britain are held in private ownership. This means that each owner or his agent may negotiate with whoever he likes for access to those rights. Normally, he will impose no limit on the number of fish which may be taken, but there will be statutory times and seasons – not to mention methods – which he or the governing body might impose. These rules tend to be very complex, and there are marked differences in them between salmon rivers all over the Northern Hemisphere. Once the tenant has accepted the rights for a specific week or period at an agreed rental, it is normal practice for the owner or his agent to offer the same period to the same tenant for the following year. This means that a lot of the best fishing is regularly taken up by 'sitting' tenants, which is why the casual visitor seems to face a blank wall whenever he tries to find access to good water.

It must not be assumed, however, that an offer of access to water will automatically coincide with good fishing conditions. Most beats or stretches of water – even on the finest rivers – have specific times of the year when they will fish better than others. Such periods are often booked well in advance by other anglers, and the week on offer may merely represent a spare patch which the landlord seeks to let in order to gain maximum income from his capital investment. In order to understand this it is important to comprehend the diverse ways of salmon on the varying river systems. For an example, let us look at the river Tweed, one of the most prolific salmon rivers in the country. It is governed by a body known as the Tweed Commissioners, consisting of riparian owners, their agents and specialist salaried employees. The salmon begin to enter the river shortly after the New Year. Angling is permitted to start, with fly only, on 1 February. This is to appease the netsmen who do not begin their legal operation until 15 February. Thereafter bait fishing is allowed until 15 September – the date on which all legitimate netting ceases – when a 'fly only' rule is imposed again on the angler until the season ends on 30 November. 'Fine', you might think. 'Let's take a beat of the Tweed in February and catch all those lovely fresh-run fish!' Sadly, it is not quite as easy as this. Firstly, there will be grave problems finding suitable access on the best places and, secondly and more importantly, there is the question of how the early run of fish will disperse themselves in the river, and where they will offer the best chance of capture.

During the early and colder months of the year it is a fact that where

Grace Oglesby surveys the Tweed at Upper Hendersyde during a frosty February.

salmon do run they will generally concentrate into the lower and deeper reaches of the river. Only when the weather gets milder and the water a bit warmer will they move out of the lower beats and into the middle and upper reaches. This means that there are specific times of the year when certain beats will hit their peak in holding and catching potential. On the Tweed, for instance, and in a severe winter, the bulk of the good fishing will be concentrated on the river downstream of Kelso. By the month of May it could be that those lovely beats below Kelso have been virtually vacated and that all the fish have moved upstream. Much information about a beat or section of river may be gleaned from the price asked for it at a specific time. The highest prices usually reflect the greatest potential. It would not be unusual, for instance, to find a lower beat of the Tweed offered on these terms:

February	£200 per week per rod
March	£250 per week per rod
April	£150 per week per rod
May	£50 per week per rod
June	£25 per week per rod
July	Not let
August	Not let
September	£150 per week per rod
October	£200 per week per rod
November	£250 per week per rod

While my figures are fictitious and escalating all the time, they roughly represent the scale of charges involved for a good beat on the Tweed downstream of Kelso. They imply, of course, that the main spring run of salmon enters the river in February and March; that there is no worthwhile summer run which stays in the lower beats, and that the autumn run does not start until the first rains of September. If you hear, therefore, that *Hendersyde* is one of the best beats on the Tweed, this statement must be qualified by adding the time of year when it might be so.

Conversely, it is another fact of life that a beat in the vicinity of Melrose and Galashiels may be of little use to the angler during the very early months, but that it might be among the best on the Tweed at its own appointed moment. Even then the exercise of reserving salmon water anywhere is one of the greatest lotteries in which it is possible to indulge. The river might be in heavy flood from melting snow or recent rain. In the early season it might even be frozen over and of little more use than a skating rink. Whatever the conditions, the tenant has a legal obligation to pay the rent. It is not the landlord's fault if the best laid plans go sour. In order to find the best fishing, therefore, much research is required. Specialist sporting agencies will put their expertise at the disposal of clients. Much of my early time as a salmon angler was spent finding the good places and discarding the bad. Because of my experience as an angler, you might think that the most frequent question I am asked involves fish-catching techniques: not a bit of it! Hardly a week passes when my mail does not contain an enquiry about the best places to find good salmon fishing.

Throughout the sixties I was a regular tenant on the Upper Hendersyde water of the Tweed during the months of February and November. Examination of the records over a ten-year period indicated that these were the most productive times. In practical circumstances, however, there were years when, if there had been a very cold spell in February – as in 1963 – the fish would not run in strength until March. Alternatively, there were years when January had been very mild and when the bulk of the fish had already gone past us by the second part of February. Finding the beat full of fish on arrival was something which only happened to me twice. Needless to say we took full advantage of that situation when it occurred! One instance came when I had a tenancy on the water during February 1963. For the most part the river was an ice rink; but I was fortunate to have access again in March. By this time the thaw had arrived, and our pools were full of fresh-run fish.

It may be seen, therefore, that while it is wiser to take the same beat at a known good time, year after year, it will still give the angler fairly long odds against hitting conditions exactly right. Timing is always a gamble, and is made more so by the inclement weather we might expect at the beginning and end of a season. In an average year, by the time April arrives the beats below Kelso will be showing a shortage of fish. There will only be spasmodic runs until nearer the end of the season. A few fish might tarry long enough to get themselves hooked; but the lower beats will not produce any fish of consequence until, with the advent of autumn, the water temperatures drop. Then the autumn fish will slow down their pace of running and fill these lower beats once again.

The reason I have spent so much time outlining this specific instance of a salmon water is to demonstrate that knowledge of fish habits on a particular river can be fairly vital to the achievement of regular success. There will be little point in fishing with anything other than spinning tackle or a large sunk fly when water and air temperatures hover between freezing and the low 40s; and our flies and spinners should be fished as slowly as possible, well down in the water.

It is generally agreed that as soon as water temperatures rise to near the 50-degree mark, fly fishing with a floating line and smaller flies will come into its own. By such a time the fish could be well spread out in the middle and upper reaches of the river. Some may be losing their lovely silvery sheen. They may prove more difficult to tempt to the lure and there could be a period when they appear to be completely disinterested. Normally, however, I find that there are good early spells for the spinner and sunk fly, followed by an interesting season of floating line fishing in April and

A stale cock salmon caught in October from the River Lune at Newton, Lancashire.

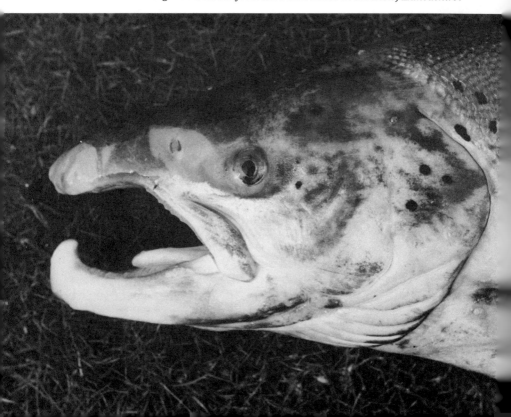

May. On many of the classic rivers, however, the end of May can see the start of the dog days. Prawning and worming may now save an otherwise blank day, but there should continue to be good evening times when fish will take the fly. On some rivers, prawning and worming are frowned upon; but they sometimes offer the angler the only opportunity of catching fish. This is not to imply that such methods act in magical fashion, but expert use of worm and prawn can bring successes which might not be achieved by other methods. It must be remembered, though, that indiscriminate use of the prawn can do general angling more harm than good. A water which has been heavily prawned might not provide good sport for the fly fisherman until fresh stocks of fish get into the river. Nowadays I refuse to use either of these natural baits when fishing in Britain; but I do occasionally use the prawn to good effect when requested to do so by my host on Norway's vast Vosso river.

There is an unsolved mystery about the times and seasons when salmon are likely to run our lesser-known rivers. More noted rivers like the Spey, Dee, Tweed and Tay all seem to have a good early run of fish; whereas other rivers will not see a glimpse of fresh fish until late spring or summer. Despite all attempts to induce a spring run, little rivers like the Yorkshire Esk rarely see fresh fish until June – dependent on rain and the consequent weight of water flow. I have seen dry summers there when the Esk fish have not been able to run until the season was virtually over. Again, what makes fish run the Tweed in February when they are not ready to spawn until November? What makes other fish run the same river in November when they are already on the threshold of spawning? Why are most Tweed springers small fish and the autumn ones much larger? Why are Eden springers the largest salmon likely to run the river during any year? Why won't the Esk fish go near the river until the first floods of summer? Doubtless the length of the river system has some bearing on these questions. The Tweed, Tay, Spey and Dee are all long rivers, whereas the Esk is barely 29 miles from source to mouth. It seems reasonable to suppose that the fish know when they must enter the river to reach their chosen spot by the time they are ready to spawn. The Argyllshire Awe gets a run of fish in April and May, but in times prior to the erection of the hydro-electric scheme, these fish were rarely caught in the Awe. Instead they went straight through the river, up into Loch Awe and thence into the Orchy. It was not until June that the Awe fish came in; but a lot of those habits have now changed.

There are many imponderables about the ways of salmon. The fact that any river has earned the label 'salmon river' gives little clue to the sport which might be expected from it. There are several factors, as we have seen, with which the angler must make himself aware before he can expect a river – or portion of it – to yield its best. On some of the lesser-known spate streams it is almost essential to be on the water at a precise hour of the day, when the gillie or a friend 'phones to tell you that the fishing is likely to be good. Again, the height and colour of the water plays an important role on all rivers, but is especially important on all spate streams. Having ascertained a reasonable assurance that there will be salmon in our beat during the time of our visit, we are better able to decide what tactics to adopt. It will also help to know whether the fish are likely to be fresh-run, while the height of the water will have a strong influence on the chances of a catch.

Over the years my fishing venues have been very varied. No spring was ever complete without an early visit to the Tweed. These days I tend to be more of a fair-weather fisherman, and the most anxiously anticipated moment is when I head north in mid-April for my annual six-week stint on the Spey at Grantown. As I am the chief instructor on the angling courses which are currently run from the Seafield Lodge Hotel, I only get a few opportunities to fish myself. When I do, I usually start with a sinking line and fly and then change to the floating line when water temperatures suggest a possibility of good sport with this method. Nowhere is the Spey a very deep river and the spin fisherman finds that a deal of his time may be spent retrieving stuck baits from the river bed. During early June I am back for a private session on the Spey and I am barely home for a change of clothes before I am winging my way across the North Sea in search of the giants of the Vosso. July will find me skirmishing in the Hebrides and then I do little more salmon fishing until the dying days of the season when I usually have a final fling on the Tweed.

With the notable exception of my visit to Norway, I have adopted a personal fly-only rule. No longer do I enjoy spinning, worming and prawning in British waters; but this does not prevent me from recognising the potential of these methods when responsibly used. Anyway, I share some conviction that on the Spey and Dee, the fly is the most effective lure and that it often only disturbs the water, and the fish, to indulge in other methods. Of course, there are occasions – at times of high water or flood – when other tactics are quite acceptable. Over in Norway, the Vosso will not experience the first snow-melt until late May or early June. This is the time when the river runs brimful of cold, clear water and when the giant salmon leave the fjords and make their ponderous way upstream. Many of the Vosso pools are deep, volcanic chasms and it requires heavy tackle and baits to get the lures down to where the fish might be interested in taking them. Just occasionally I catch a Vosso fish on a lead-cored fly line and the same monstrous-looking fly I would use on the Tweed in February or November. This then gives but a brief panorama of my seasons and methods. Let us now examine them in detail.

We have already examined the premise reasoned by earlier anglers that if a small fly caught trout, a larger one should catch salmon; and that the evolution of the salmon fly was based on little more than idle speculation. In 1850, 'Ephemera' (E. Fitzgibbon) in *Book of the Salmon* was giving detailed dressings, with lists of salmon flies, 'for every good river in the empire'! He was not to know how little 130-odd years would do for salmon flies, or that the Empire would be ground into ashes. In 1855, William Blacker gave us the *Art of Fly Making*, with many descriptions of how to dress flies for salmon: but it was not until 1895 that George Kelson unloaded his tome, *The Salmon Fly*, on the angling public.

Kelson claimed that salmon fed on butterflies, and attempted to model his patterns on that style. I find it strange that his work was taken so seriously. One presumes that Kelson was sincere in his supposition that the multitude of fly patterns he illustrated in his book all had their times and seasons – but, as I glance today through page upon page of colour plates, I am struck by the overall similarity of the illustrated designs. In my opinion, it is crediting the salmon with a great deal more intelligence than they possess to suggest that they have a preference for one fly on occasions and not for another. I think that Richard Waddington produces some logical thought in his postulation that salmon in cold water require a much larger fly than those in water over 50 degrees. Certainly my experience has been that, for early spring and late autumn fishing, there seems to be little point in using a fly less than two inches in length; and that the fly has to be fished well down, near the bed of the river. Balfour-Kinnear, in his otherwise excellent book, *Catching Salmon and Sea Trout*, did not appear to agree. He argued that, in his opinion, there was *never* a need to scrape the bottom, and that fish taken on the sunk line could be hooked well above the bed of the river. All experienced anglers and writers do seem to agree on the necessity for long casting. This helps the fly to get down to a worthwhile depth and enables it to be manipulated into a position where the fish will not have to travel a great distance in order to take it. In really cold water, I like my fly to be well down. If on the odd cast I scrape a rock or some protrusion on the bottom I feel a bit more confident of success. There is, of course, a danger of foul-hooking fish when manipulating the lure in this way; but salmon have to be thickly populated in their lies for this to happen. On some pools, when waters are well-stocked later in the season, weights of fly and hook sizes may be limited to inhibit this distasteful practice – indulged in by some as 'sport'. But, for the legitimate sportsman and angler, fishing in cold water, if the fly is at the right depth to foul-hook a fish it is also at the right depth to hook it in the mouth on a genuine take.

In order to be fully primed for all types of sunk-line fly fishing the angler should have at least two outfits. Ideally, I like to have three on hand; but most times the same rod will serve all purposes. Essentially the angler requires lines and flies of different weights and densities. This will enable him to cope with high or low water, and to be able to select the line and flies most suited to the conditions. Waddington was right when he wrote that for early and late season fishing there is little point in using flies less than two inches long. In days gone by flies were tied almost exclusively on single hooks; and those more than two inches long were not very good in hook-holding quality. There was a good deal of leverage with those big flies, which made it easy to lose a fish once it had been hooked. Nowadays the tube-fly or an adaptation of this style is more practical, since the triangle of hooks are usually articulated below the tube to prevent loss of fish from leverage.

My present-day tackle for sunk-line fishing may be chosen from one of three carbon fibre rods. My initial impulse is to opt for my all-round favourite double-handed rod – the 15-foot 'Walker' made by Bruce and Walker Limited. The advent of carbon fibre has meant that one can use a 15-foot rod all day with the minimum of fatigue, whereas to use a similar-sized rod of greenheart, split-cane or even fibreglass risks the possibility of feeling as though one has spent a day on the rack! Alternatively, I might choose the 17½-foot 'Walker' or the 16½-foot 'Walker'. All three rods are excellent for their purpose and give tremendous 'water command'. On smaller rivers, I might opt for the 14-foot 'Walker', but the ultimate choice depends on personal preference. By utilising a shooting-head portion of sinking line, instead of a full 30-yard line, there is no great advantage to be gained from a rod much over 15 feet, but the longer rods come into their own if the angler prefers a full line. What *is* important, is the choice of line to suit the task in hand. Most line manufacturers now make sinking lines in varying densities. The WetCel range, for instance, has a line of neutral density – which does just sink slightly. Then there is a slow-sinker, a fast-sinker, and the Hi-D (High Density). The last of these is most useful in very strong streams, but if the angler needs still more sinking qualities he can resort to one of the many lead-cored lines now on the market. For most of my early spring and late autumn fishing forays I have all types of sinking line on hand, for I am not to know the state of the water immediately on arrival. Some experimenting may be necessary to find the best one to suit the prevailing conditions. As I have stated, I do not now use a full-length sinking line: instead, I cut a double-tapered line in half, throw away about three yards of the middle (belly) portion, and splice the back portion to oval monofilament of about 25 to 30lbs test.

Many brands of oval monofilament are now on the market. Its main feature is that it does not curl like traditional monofilament, and it is particularly suited to match up with shooting-head lines and for certain applications with spinning or multiplying reels. The backing line lies limply in loose coils and is a better material to 'shoot' than ordinary monofilament or braided line. The combination of shooting head and oval backing gives me a line which is easily aerialised without stressing the rod too much. Then, with the backing suitably coiled on a line raft, in the bottom of the boat, looped in my hands, or on the bank, it is possible to make a long cast and shoot the backing to achieve maximum distance.

It is important to be able to make long casts when sunk-line fishing on a big river. The distance achieved will have great bearing on the depth at which the fly will 'swim'. Sometimes, in very heavy water, I have known occasions when, after making an exceptionally long cast, I have put the rod point under the water to facilitate 'fishing' the fly at a greater depth. Some experiment may be necessary to find the ideal length of shooting head to suit your rod, and it may vary with lines of differing density. Ideally, you should start with a portion of fly line which is slightly too long. It is then but a simple matter to cut small portions away until the ideal has been found. Sometimes it is possible to buy shooting heads already assembled. These are usually 10 yards long, which may not be quite long enough to 'load' the rod of your choice. Mostly I find that 12 yards (36 feet) suits me admirably.

Although many forms of sunk-line fishing tend to look untidy, it is sometimes possible to make a quick 'mend' in the line before it starts to sink. This helps in the presentation of the fly and enables it to get down to greater depth. The rod point should be held well up and at right angles to the current to get the shooting head and fly well down and to prevent the fly coming round too quickly (see Fig.1). Leading the fly round by altering the angle of the rod is to be discouraged, since it is likely to make the fly move too quickly. As soon as the cast is fished out, the backing is hand-lined in, slowly at first, and a further cast made. As much of this fishing may be done from a boat, the boatman will determine the distance

Fig. 1

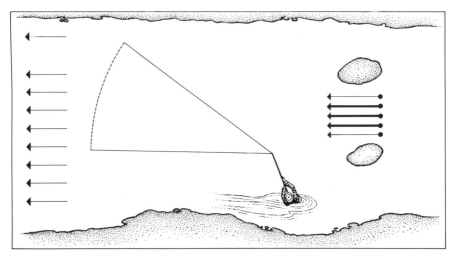

between consecutive casts. Boat fishing in this style is much easier, since the bottom of the boat makes a handy platform to hold the coils of monofilament backing until they are shot out in the final fore-cast. Even then this method of fishing can be a tedious business, but I still prefer it to spinning.

Although it is very important to select the correct density of shooting head to suit the conditions, it is equally paramount to select the right fly. Some flies are tied on aluminium tubes and have little more than neutral buoyancy. Others may be tied on brass tubes, and thus sink as deep as the tapered portion of fly line. It is possible to have additional lead weighting incorporated in the dressing of the fly and I have known exceptional occasions when I have put an extra spiral lead on to the leader to give a similar effect to that achieved when spinning a large bait in very heavy water. Of course, such contraptions are abominations to cast, and it may be that traditional casting techniques have to be modified to suit.

One of the basic problems lies in the assessment of what tackle to use for a given set of circumstances. Only occasionally, and where permitted, do I use a lead-cored line in British waters. They may be used to good effect in the deep waters of some Norwegian rivers, but most British salmon rivers are never quite so deep and there is a constant risk of getting the fly hung up on the bottom. The Hi-D line is frequently used when a river like the Tweed is running three feet above normal and when the water is very cold. My choice of fly may be determined by little more than the type of pool I am to fish. Having decided that the fly should be a minimum of two inches in length there is little point in altering the size of the fly to suit conditions, but there may be every advantage in selecting a fly of a different weight.

The sunk-line fisherman will not always find a high river at such times as he uses the sunk line. Hard February frosts quickly lower the water levels. Once the river is down to normal height, the Hi-D line might prove too heavy, causing the angler to get snarled up on the bottom as every cast comes round. In these circumstances there is a temptation to put on a *smaller* fly – it should be resisted. Obviously you will need a much *lighter* fly, while the Hi-D line may be replaced with one of lighter density. On such occasions I often discard the flies tied on brass tubes and resort to flies of the same length on aluminium tubes. Rod length may also be reduced, if it is thought desirable, but the necessity for long casting remains and the original choice of rod will usually suffice. The technique remains basically the same, but it will feel a bit more like fly fishing than it did when you were throwing heavy tubes on equally heavy lines. Also, the fly will not bang you on the head as frequently as the heavy one might do! Lower water should ensure that the fish are more settled in their lies too, since they are unlikely to run fast or far during a cold spell of lower water.

There are occasions when really low water greets the early and late season angler. Under such conditions it may be that the angler requires little more than a line of neutral density or even a floating line with a sinking tip. The fly size would normally remain the same as that used in heavy water, but it may be that the colouring of the chosen fly should be a lot more subdued, as visibility through the water increases. There are, of course, many other lines with slow-sinking qualities which would serve equally well, but to reach full potential the sunk-line fisherman should have, ideally, at least three alternatives of lines and flies. One should have fast-sinking qualities; another, medium-sink rate, and the third almost neutral buoyancy. A little experience will teach the angler, by a glance at the river, which outfit is likely to be the most effective for presentation.

In the main, I have so far dealt with circumstances which compel the angler to use the sunk fly, out of sheer necessity. In many of the conditions described the angler might have been better advised to spin. It can be argued, however, that a fly can be fished more slowly than a spinner, and thus be more effective. A skilful angler should have no difficulty in fishing both lures at the same pace; and although I do not now spin in British waters, I have never changed my original opinion that on high water in the spring or late autumn, spinning is frequently a more productive method.

To illustrate this we need only consider the recorded catches on a well-known beat of the Tweed, where, as I have said, the fly is mandatory until 15 February. When the regulation is relaxed, most anglers put their fly rods away and come out with their spinning rods. In a general year this change doubles the number of salmon caught. There is no certainty, of course, that this is due entirely to the spinner being more effective at all times. It may well be that preference is pure fancy; and that the salmon are only responding to a change of lure because, for the past fifteen days, they have seen nothing but flies. My own private opinion is that it may well be nothing more than the fact that the bulk of anglers are more skilful with their spinning tackle than they are with their fly tackle. I well recall one instance, however, after we had been spinning for about a week with diminishing catches, when I reasoned that the fish might well show some interest in the fly again. I had spun a pool down twice with different baits and taken nothing. 'Let's go down with the fly', said I to the gillie; and the fly promptly took two fish from that same pool.

Admittedly this does not *prove* anything. The fish were fresh-run, and might well have crept into the pool while we were changing to fly. They might have taken the spinner if I had gone down with it a third time. But at least we knew from observation of jumping fish that there had been a stock there all the time; and as they refused the spinner on two occasions, it seemed reasonable to show them something else. It might also be reasonable to assume that it was the change that brought the required reaction – although there are complex possibilities. For instance, the conditions might simply have changed for the better during those minutes when I was changing to and using the fly.

Most salmon anglers are well aware of the fickleness of salmon, when a blank day to, say, 3 p.m. may suddenly be transformed into a halcyon one, without change of method or style. We have already assumed, rightly I think, that salmon in fresh water require nothing more than a peaceful lie in which to idle their time away until the inclination to spawn comes upon them. We have speculated upon the various reasons which might induce a fish to take a fly, spinner or bait; but we are still little nearer a worthwhile solution. Some writers hold the belief that fish will not take until they are settled in a pool; others, that the fish must become unsettled before they will take. I have sufficent evidence from my own experience to show that neither view can be fully right or wholly wrong. If salmon take when they are both settled and unsettled we should catch a lot more of them. There must be some other factor which influences their taking habits, and I am convinced that both settled and unsettled fish will take on occasions. The running fish, for instance, might well take if and when it stops for a brief rest. The angler, of course, must be on a collision course with it, and his bait or fly must cover that fish – possibly in an intimidating manner – during the brief time it is resting. At other times I suspect that running fish do not take very well, particularly when they are actually moving. We must also remember our half-sleeping cat and its reaction to blown leaves: who dares predict when the cat might be brought to a point of full alertness and then chase after a fluttering leaf?

The oxygen theory was one which my good friend, Reg Righyni, speculated upon in his book, *Salmon Taking Times*. Even if it leaves the reader in some doubt about accurate prediction, the book is well worth examination. It will at least give him some clue to the identification of good conditions, and a reasonable guide to the selection of suitable tackle and lures. If we had sure knowledge of a definite taking time, there would be little point in fishing until this came. As it is, most salmon anglers are well aware that the salmon have not read our books. Most certainly they do not read my film scripts and are frequently quite unaware of the starring role required of them. They have an irritating habit of pleasing themselves, but the angler who fishes longest, in skilful fashion, is generally the angler who will catch most fish. He will catch them at what he considers a most unlikely time; and he may fail at a time when conditions look most promising. It is doubtful if even the fish know their exact responses at any given time. It might be helpful to have a field laboratory to predict their reactions. Nonetheless, the reading of *Salmon Taking Times* may help the angler to recognise some of the conditions under which he may, or may not, expect sport. Some of the experiments now being conducted on fish passes, where temperatures, pH values, barometric pressures and several other factors are assessed, indicate that some of Righyni's arguments are well-founded when it comes to his prediction about running salmon. Most experienced anglers have, quite unconsciously perhaps, learned to recognise times when to fish hard, and when to sit and watch or go home. Most of these times are extremely difficult to predict or determine, and it is impossible to lay down a sound formula.

As a general rule, and as we have seen, it is reasonable to assume that we shall not catch many salmon when they are running hard and fast. Experiences on the Awe, in earlier times, when the Orchy fish were running through, indicated that few tarried long enough to succumb to the angler's lure. Again, fish which become settled in a pool seem to become more uncatchable the longer they stay there. So, it seems reasonable to assume that the best taking conditions occur somewhere near the point when settled fish become unsettled or vice versa. The height of the water will have great influence on these factors, as will its movement up or down. But I will have more comments on this aspect in a later chapter. Doubtless there is something in the oxygen theory propounded by Righyni; and the conditions of light, temperature, barometric pressure and water clarity and chemistry must all play an important role.

Having commented that much of our early season fishing would be better done with a spinner than a fly, I must now go on to say that there are a few occasions when I would back the sunk-fly against any other method. Just as the early season trout fisherman is keen to change from wet-fly to dry-fly I think that, on large spring rivers, some anglers change to the floating line before conditions have reached their best. It has to be admitted that fishing with a floating line is less tedious than any form of sunk-line fishing, but this is not to imply that it is always more effective. The floating line is easily lifted off the water, whereas the sunk line has to be brought to the surface of the water before it can be lifted. Attempting to lift a long, drowned line for a backward cast is one of the most sure ways I know of smashing a good rod. A simple roll cast downstream should bring the line to the surface. It can then be picked up for a back cast before it has time to sink. Sometimes it is a good plan to make a false cast, in order to get a clean pick-up before the final cast is made. This method is not advisable on quiet, gliding water, since it may well disturb the fish the angler is hoping to catch.

Much controversy exists on the question of leaders. No longer are they referred to as 'casts'. For sunk-line fishing they are not over-important. It makes sense to have them stronger than normal. This is principally because we will be using heavier flies than normal and the stresses at the knot joining fly to leader will be greater. For early season fishing I use monofilament of about 18lbs test and 9 feet in length. I most certainly do not bother with the expense of tapered leaders, and merely carry a small spool of the appropriate line in my pocket. As I now rarely fish in February or March, quite a lot of my double-handed sunk-line fishing is confined to the month of April on the Spey below Grantown. The fish will already have seen a variety of spinners and one or two may have been caught on a smaller fly and floating line. The water temperature may fluctuate violently: one day it may be 44 degrees and a day or so later it could be up to 52 degrees. Shortly afterwards it could bounce down to 46 degrees. And, hard though it may be to believe, I have known the water temperature at that time of the year to vary by as much as 10 degrees in less than a week. Things will be in a state of flux; and on top of this the water may be rising or falling, settled or otherwise, depending on the state of the snow in the mountains or on the amount of rainfall. Days may be cloudy or sunny, with air temperatures higher or lower than the water. Consequently the angler may well be uncertain, as we all frequently are, of just what to do for the best. He may well have tried the spinning rod or the floating-line fly to no avail. It is at such times that I opt for the sunk-line fly. Fly sizes may be much the same as those I might use on the floating line, but generally they are slightly bigger.

I recall one occasion when I had spent an entire morning with both spinner and the fly on the floating line. The pools were well stocked and I felt that something ought to take. After lunch I put up a sinking-line outfit and the same No. 6 Blue Charm I had been using on the floater. In the space of 45 minutes I took three fish weighing 18lbs, 15lbs and 12lbs, and lost a fourth. Who knows? Conditions might have changed after lunch. I might have got these fish on the floating-line fly or on a spinner. Such days are one of the mysteries of the game, and I shall not pretend to give you any rhyme or reason for them. The fact is that I *did* make a change and I *did* catch three fish. Here again it might be reasonable to suppose that the change had some connection with my success. There are so many imponderables in salmon fishing that one can only speculate. And, as speculation is frequently more entertaining than full knowledge, we sometimes speculate to a point where we confuse theory with fact. The great bulk of salmon fishing literature has been based on speculation and assumption, so it leaves us with few alternatives.

In the type of mid-season fishing which we are examining, the depth at which the fly swims does not seem so important as it does during the early and late season. Indeed, if Balfour-Kinnear had confined his comment about fly depths to this type of fishing, I would agree with him that the fly only needs to be a foot or two under the surface to make it effective. Also, a river like the Spey is never very deep and to fish with very heavy tackle – except in the heaviest water – might induce the fly to spend more time on or in the river bed than it does 'fishing'. Perhaps we might also assume, as we do with so many tactics concerning salmon, that the large sunk fly and heavy spinner are too easily seen for what they are in clear water; and that the fly on a floating line is too near the surface for the fish to incline to take it. The medium-sized sunk fly is more of an elusive object, something that vibrates in mid-water and which requires less effort to take it. I realise that all these postulations are pure speculation and assumption, but they are bred from long experience.

In the days before the use of lines which floated and before the advent of spinning reels, nearly all fishing was done with a line that sank. Plenty of fish were caught. Why should they not be caught with that method now? What has changed? Certainly not the salmon. It is only the angler's fashions – although I do vaguely believe that different runs of salmon over different seasons may have distinct preferences for certain types of lure, and that a lure, be it fly, spinner or bait, which seems highly successful one season, may not prove to be so useful the next. Anyway, I do not want to diminish spinning or fishing with the floating line, but only to re-establish a place for traditional methods at a time when everything seems to have to be new or brighter than white.

Times to try the sunk line with medium-sized flies are difficult to predict. But if there are resident stocks of salmon in the river and they have seen a wide variety of spinners or small flies on the floating line, a trial with the sunk-line fly may do the trick. It may be used to good advantage in high summer even, but I will have more to write about that later.

Techniques for using the sunk line are basically the same as for all other methods of fly fishing. The fly should be cast across the current and then allowed to swing round to the angler's own bank. It may not be quite so vital to make the fly move as slowly as one might do in February or March, but it always pays to let the fly hang for a while at the end of a cast, in case a fish has followed it into shallow water. For the same reason it occasionally pays dividends to make an initial slow retrieve of the fly just before it is lifted for the next cast. The extra movement gives life to the fly in dead water and this may just induce the right response from a fish. Alternatively, I have known occasions when, by deep wading, I have literally hung a fly over a sure lie in the current for periods up to several minutes, and then had it taken when I least expected. Do not become wedded to a rigid drill. The salmon do not read our books or listen to our opinions.

A worthwhile alternative to the fully sinking line has presented itself with the advent of a floating line with a built-in sinking tip. These lines are well-established on the market, but after an initial, and quite ecstatic, love affair with them I have discarded them almost entirely. They consist of a main body of floating line, but with a 9-foot front taper of sinking line. While easier to lift off the water than a fully sunk line, they are not as pleasant to use as a full floater. They do assist in the presentation of the fly at a slightly lower depth than the full floater, but I find it simpler to use a slightly heavier fly on a fully floating line to achieve much the same result. In a really strong current they may be used in lieu of a floating line and light fly, since they will prevent the fly from skating on the surface – something which might occasionally happen with a full floating line. For general purposes, however, they do not quite fill my bill any more.

I suspect that sunk-line fishing forms a basis for our tactics with salmon; this is traditionally so, and the technique is still worthy of its place today. In some respects it is tedious and there are times when spinning is not only easier, but may well be more productive – depending on the competence of the angler. There are times, however, when the sunk line really comes into its own and its use should never be regarded as old-fashioned. Let us now look at the wide variety of flies which may be used with this method.

4   FLIES FOR SUNK-LINE FISHING

Having dealt with the vast potential available to the angler by the use of sunk-line fishing techniques, let us now turn our attention to the wide variety of flies which may be used.

I have already expressed an opinion that there is much early season fishing which might be better done with a spinner. Certainly it could involve less work; but because of certain bye-laws, there are some rivers – notably Tweed – where the fly is mandatory for the first two weeks of the season. It is not surprising, therefore, that the flies which have been evolved for this type of fishing bear a strong resemblance to the 2½-inch or 3-inch Devon Minnow. The Yellow Belly and Black and Gold are early season favourites and so flies have been constructed to look vaguely like these, a play of sorts to design a lure to resemble a silver or golden sprat. There are many professional makers of such flies, but many anglers prefer to dress their own. Over the years I have tried varying methods, from Waddington-type mounts to plain brass or polythene-lined aluminium tubes. The problem with the former is that if the hooks become damaged it is virtually impossible to replace them and the entire fly has to be discarded, whereas with the latter the hooks are separated from the fly and may be replaced as necessary. Most of my flies are now tied on standard tubes which are obtainable from Veniard's. I have a stock in both brass and aluminium, in sizes ranging from 1½ inches to 3 inches. In very heavy water it is possible – and sometimes desirable – to put two tubes on the leader and make the 'fly' a veritable monster. Dyed bucktail is generally used, but care must be taken to ensure that the bucktails are the best quality; goat hair is straighter, but it is largely a matter of personal choice which is used. I rarely bother to tie in any body materials these days and the flies are quickly constructed with varying shades of colour in the fibres. It is a good plan to have a wide variety of fly colours, with a ration of garish-looking creations for high and coloured water conditions. Yellow and hot-orange are popular, with one or two streaks of black or brown. For really low water, much more sombre colours seem to be effective, with plenty of black and brown. Some anglers prefer to use a 'keel' fly – a fly constructed with a small keel-shaped piece of lead tied under the main body. Because it always 'swims' keel down, the top part of the fly should be tied with dark fibres, the underbelly with lighter fibres. The object, of course, is to represent a small fish. Illustrated in the colour section are a few examples. It will be seen that there are many variables and the permutations are endless. Some anglers prefer to use aluminium tubes entirely and to have additional lead wire round the body to give a wider range of weights. I have already made the point that there is little to be achieved by using flies shorter than 2 inches for this type of fishing and that the weight of the fly may have more influence than its size.

Having built up or obtained our stock of flies it is a simple matter to thread the leader through the tube and tie on a triangle of hooks. At this stage a half-inch piece of polythene or rubber-valve tubing should be fitted to the rear end of the tube to keep the hook tight and in line with the tube. Care must be taken when dressing the fly to ensure that the wing fibres will flow far enough backwards to cover the hooks – but not too far beyond, to avoid the risk of their presenting incomplete entry into the jaws of a taking fish.

Many years ago I conducted a series of experiments with flies suspended on a leader to 'swim' in running water in a glass tank. The outcome of these experiments became the basis for an article I wrote for *The Field* (29 June 1961). The main disclosure of my trials was that the old-fashioned, heavily-feathered flies did not look at all lifelike. They were inanimate in the water and looked exactly like old salmon flies. By contrast, more modern dressings, with either heron, goat hair or bucktail winging, looked much more realistic and easily gave the impression of natural life. In this respect, therefore, I think it safe to assume that the modern tube-dressing is a definite improvement on the old, heavily-dressed, meat-hook type and that it represents a useful advance in lure design.

As we have already seen in Chapter 3, the flies mentioned are basically for those cold, early or late season days when the water temperature is unlikely to exceed the low 40s. However there are other conditions when the sunk-line is worth a trial where these flies would be far too big and cumbersome for successful presentation. For example, during the period of flux, before the fish show inclination to take the small fly on the floating line; or at times when they appear to be disinterested in everything later in the season. Here our flies need differ little from those we would use for fishing with a floating line; but there are a few alternatives worthy of mention. However, let us first speculate on the effectiveness of colour in our designs.

It is my fancy, and purely a fancy, that the smaller the fly, the less important the colour seems to be. The design of big flies has been suggested in a variety of colours, some garish. The purpose of these designs is to enable us to cope with differing heights and clarity of the water. Above all else we have made them so that the salmon should have no difficulty in seeing them and so that they fish at a depth where the salmon will have little difficulty in taking them should it have the slightest inclination to do so. When water temperatures climb towards the 50-degree mark, however, the big fly often loses much of its effectiveness. As we shall see later, it may be used to good effect at many times throughout a season; but, for most situations, the fish are now content with a much smaller fly. I suspect that it is the illusion of life in a fly, and not its startling colours, which draws their attention. As the fish should now be prepared to move out of their lies more frequently to take a fly, colour seems to be less important. Nevertheless, I think that the angler should have an eye for colour; and the fly should be dangled in the water and inspected against the river bed, so that the angler can assess its appearance and decide whether it looks in keeping with its new environment.

Several well-known writers have commented upon the value of pattern; but they have been referring principally to fly selection for fishing with the floating line. We shall examine some of these comments in a later chapter. For sunk-line fishing I do not think that pattern is of paramount importance, but it may be more important than with floating-line techniques. With a sunk line, the fly is being presented in such a way that the fish can take a more critical look at it than if it was to take a fly just under the surface. In this case, the fly is seen more in silhouette and the fish usually decides to take it long before it is near enough for critical examination. We are all aware, of course, that on occasions the head-and-tail rise to our floating-line fly appears to result in nothing more than a mere touch of the fly. In such cases, the fish may have seen some alarming feature as it came close. On this basis alone it seems reasonable to assume that pattern will be more important in the sunk fly, even if only slightly so. We do not know, as yet, why a salmon takes our flies at all; so there can be no known influence by so-called exact imitation as in dry-fly fishing for trout. There the angler tries to put on his leader the nearest artificial facsimile to the natural fly upon which, he presumes, the trout are feeding. The choice of salmon fly, on the other hand, is largely a matter of fancy – and in many cases the fancy of one angler is just as likely to be as effective as that of another. A great deal of mumbo-jumbo is talked and written about fly selection for salmon. Few facts or factors exist to assist the novice to make his own selection.

The basic influence on my decision as to which fly to use is the overall colour of the water and the river bed. On most rivers this is predominantly brown; but the water may vary in hue, depending upon the colour of any suspended matter or the quality of the light falling on it. Sometimes the water will demonstrate a faint yellow-green colour following a quick spate. At others it will show a strong blue tinge from the ultraviolet of the sun's rays. It is advisable to pay attention to the effect of sunshine, since the fish are likely to see the fly in greater detail in the absence of sunlight than under full sunlight. There are certain times when fish may be virtually dazzled, and if they see the fly at all, it will be as an elusive silhouette. Fly colour, in such circumstances, will be of minimum importance. We cannot, of course, predict the influence of light at the precise moment of a take; but the old contention that it is undesirable to be fishing when the sun is shining straight down the pool from upstream is sound common sense. On most of our easterly-flowing rivers the sun does not therefore present a problem until late afternoon, whereas westerly-flowing rivers present a problem in the morning. Sunlight over southerly-flowing rivers may well prove troublesome during early morning or late evening, but not during daytime fishing. Frankly, I dislike a lot of sun, particularly during the months of June, July and August. Earlier and later, a certain amount of sunshine may be advantageous; but even so, I like the suggestion of humidity in the air and I try to avoid those days when the entire landscape is visible for miles in sharp relief. Such days are better for photography or sun-bathing – anything rather than salmon fishing! Often, days like this are associated with high-pressure meteorological conditions, but may occur when a cold front is approaching or passing through. Wind direction also has some influence. Winds from the west are inclined to be damp after their long passage over the Atlantic, and are generally favourable. So are some winds from the south. East winds are notoriously bad; but not nearly so bad over western as over eastern rivers.

So much for my speculations on the general water and overhead conditions and their influence on fishing. Once again, I should like to remind you that the words *never* and *always* have no place in the jargon of the salmon fisherman. But the successful salmon fisherman quickly learns that weather and water conditions are among the most important considerations that he must take into account. Once he has decided that fishing is worthwhile, the next problem facing him is the choice of fly.

The smaller sizes of tube fly and those tied on treble hooks, as devised by Esmond Drury, are all worth consideration; but because of their limited size, their turnover tends to make them catch on the leader unless steps are taken to eliminate this risk. The solution to the problem in the case of tube flies is to a large extent the device of Thomas Clegg, mentioned earlier, of using a small piece of polythene tubing at the end of the tube. This will also release its hold from the tube or hook when a fish is in play, thus removing the risk of leverage by the complete fly which will cause the hook to come free from the jaws of the fish. Much mid-season sunk-line fishing is done with these flies and I have tied them to such patterns as the Logie, Thunder and Lightning, and Stoat's Tail. The sizes range from ½-inch to 1½-inch. The smaller sizes even make quite effective flies for fishing on the floating line. Normally, however, I prefer to have all flies for sunk-line fishing rather more heavily dressed than floating-line flies. A major advantage of the tube is that it lends itself to a good amount of flowing hair fibres and some very lifelike patterns may be made. I like to inspect all my flies in a tank of flowing water, paying scant attention to their colour and more to their action. Tube weights may also be varied, as for big flies, and some very effective mid-season flies have been tied on short brass or copper tubes, barely a ½-inch in length.

If the river is of sufficient height to warrant the use of a 1½-inch or 2-inch spinner, there appears to be good reason for putting on a fly which is only slightly smaller than the spinner length. We may assume, I think, that the fly will fish or move a little more slowly than the spinner and, therefore, that it does not need to be quite so large. Much will depend on the presentation ability of the angler and there can be no hard-and-fast rule. I dress many of my 'flux'-period sunk-line flies on low-water double hooks from size 4 to 8. The reason for the low-water hooks is that they have a slightly longer shank than normal ones, and this extra length may be used to continue the body dressing further than might be desirable for fishing with a floating line. But I am not sure that it matters too much! Occasionally I under-wind fine wire to add weight to the fly. It is my opinion that the entire secret of good sunk-line technique lies in having a wide range of flies for size and weight variation, so that the angler can adjust his tactics as water conditions dictate. I am not, as I have commented, over-concerned with pattern. And, as the flies get smaller, the colours need be no more than the brown-black suggestion with, perhaps, a tinge of blue or orange at the throat – as directed by the overall colour of the water. Many of the flies I use remain unnamed. They are made up at the fly-tying bench with any odd materials at hand. While most of them will catch fish on occasions, I suspect that few of them would catch many fishermen!

Illustrated in the colour section are some examples of the smaller flies used for sunk-line fishing. And, as we have now dealt briefly with the varying fly requirements for all types of sunk-line fishing, let us now examine one or two vastly different fishing occasions and analyse the methods used.

It was a cold November morning on the last day of the Tweed season in 1966. A watery sun struggled vainly to push through the early mists; but there was a sense of urgency awake in the river, as first one salmon and then another flung itself into the air with that gay abandon so characteristic of the salmon in its quest for the spawning grounds.

'Howaryer feelin' this morning, sirr?' greeted Wattie Lauder, our Tweed gillie. 'Bit woolly', I answered. 'Drank too much of your wine of Scotland last night. Anyway, how's the fishing going to be today?'

'Well sirr – if you and the other gentleman will fish hard, there are fresh-run fish to be caught.'

The other gentleman, incidentally, looking just as woolly as I did, was my old friend Colin Bell. A Scot by birth, he had spent the previous evening, as is the custom of many exiled Scots, in toasting absent friends. Despite his Scottish origins, he was destined to spend several years of exile in rural England and had never caught a salmon. He was, perhaps, keener than I to take advantage of the good conditions and was not long in making ready with his tackle.

Since he was a novice and a newcomer to the water I suggested that he go with the gillie in the boat, leaving me to fend for myself fishing from the bank. It was a piece of water which I had known and fished for years, so I knew many of the likely places suitable for wading or fishing from the bank. Colin, though, would need the gillie's care and guidance if he was to have any real chance. The river was running about a foot above normal – a good height for the beat – and as temperatures were in the low 40s, I reckoned I would need my medium-sinking line and a 2½-inch brass-tubed fly. A 9-foot length of 18lb test monofilament was utilised as leader, and a fairly garish-looking yellow bucktail fly tied on.

I had not been fishing for more than ten minutes when I heard a shout from upstream and turned to watch Colin playing his first salmon. Down the river I overheard odd snatches of the conversation as Wattie gave Colin a running commentary on how to play the fish. Some fifteen minutes later it was safely netted. A shout brought the news that it was a fresh-run fish of 18lbs – and, 'What the blazes are *you* doing messing about?' I felt delighted for Colin and continued casting in silence; but by that time was beginning to scrape the bottom a little too frequently. I was fishing a long line, casting the 36 feet of shooting-head line and about 60 feet of monofilament backing. Since I did not wish to shorten the length of my casting, I wound in and tied on the same size and colour of fly, but on a lighter tube. This had the desired effect. I felt confident that it was moving sufficiently near the bottom to interest any fish it happened to pass, yet not so deep that it would scrape the bottom. I fished the pool down carefully to no avail; and on my way back upstream, half-an-hour later, I saw Colin's rod point up in the air again as he played his second fish. He really was enjoying himself and dealt with this one in a much more masterly fashion than the first. It was soon on the bank and a grinning Colin looked up, as much as to say, 'Now who's the novice?'

Unlike some anglers who cannot bear the sight of someone else catching salmon, I was thrilled with his success; but felt that little bit of humility which I think does us all good at times. I started at the top of the pool once again, determined to concentrate every inch of the way. I even changed my fly again, and selected a slightly less garish one of the same size and weight. I was just about to break off for lunch when I felt the determined tug of a taking fish. It was a dour, heavy pull, and within seconds line was screaming from my reel as the fish made a strong run against the current. Salmon in cold water seem to fight more slowly than summer fish; but they still use their weight and power in attempts to shake out the hook. This spirited fish used every dodge in the book to try and outwit me. It did not expend its energy in long, determined runs, but instead bored relentlessly, shaking its head like an angry dog. Although I had now confined it to a quiet piece of water, it had no intention of giving up without a stout battle. The minutes seemed to tick by very slowly as the contest continued. Nearly twenty minutes elapsed before it lay on its side and let me lift it out by the tail. It weighed 22lbs and was gleaming silver, with the sea lice still on it.

By lunchtime, then, Colin had the advantage over me by one fish; and as November days in Scotland are short if not always sweet, I was anxious to have my turn with the gillie and the boat before the best of the day had passed. The weather, however, was deteriorating rapidly. All traces of sun had gone and a fine, cold drizzle added to the discomfort. My chances, I felt – even with the boat and the gillie – were fast diminishing. It would be dark by 4 p.m., and I would have to work hard and pull out all the stops of experience if I was to avoid a hiding on what I regarded as my own water.

Lunch quickly finished, Wattie and I made our way to the top pool of the beat. He quickly boated me into a position where my casts would cover the likely lies. I still had on the fly which had brought the earlier success, and I had not been fishing for more than five minutes before I felt the heavy pull of another fish. Cold water or not, this one definitely resented any notions of coming gracefully as it set off on a screaming run upstream. I thought at first that I must have foul-hooked it, since I was on to my backing in no time as Wattie sculled the boat after it as quickly as he could. A ding-dong battle ensued before I could subdue it; but Wattie's big net was under it eventually and my biggest Tweed fish to date, a 23-pounder, was on the bank. It was well hooked in the mouth, but had fought valiantly to gain its freedom.

The part of the pool we were fishing was not quite so deep as the pool I had fished during the morning; so, although I did not alter the size or the style of dressing, I made yet another change of fly to reduce the terminal weight. We were soon afloat again and lengthening out the casts. Five minutes later I was into another spirited fish; and then another, and another – and at the end of that short afternoon we trudged back in the failing light with our burden of five prime salmon. A more than adequate reward for perseverance and experience was to find that Colin had drawn blank, but was already toasting his earlier success with several fellow anglers! Between us, we had accounted for eight salmon from a small stretch of water on a day when less hardy types would have been huddled round a fire.

Conclusions? I am not sure that there are any. The six fish to my rod, and the two to Colin's, give little clue to the relative merits between a novice and an experienced angler. I like to think, however, that my knowledge of the water and the ability to change my tactics was responsible, in some measure, for my better catch. Of course, I may be fooling myself. If Colin had been in the boat that afternoon, with the gillie's help, he might have done equally well. The day did demonstrate, though, the effectiveness of big tube-flies; and that they are a very worthwhile substitute for spinners when legal requirements make some form of fly obligatory – and, maybe, of even greater value in their own right.

The next occasion when I was glad of the sunk-line fly was one of those exasperating late spring days when I didn't know what to do. There were plenty of fish in the beat, some of which were already so coloured that they might well have been there since the opening day. Other fish, however, showed every indication of having arrived only recently; and as the river was fining off after a nice rise, it seemed reasonable to suppose that a percentage of the fish could be absolutely fresh-run.

During the morning the river had been high enough to make spinning worthwhile; but I had tried both the small spinner and the floating-line fly to no avail. The day had dawned bright and sunny with a fresh, but light, breeze from the south. There was a slow build-up of some fair-weather cumulus cloud; and following lunch, the sky consisted of a higher percentage of cloud than blue sky. Fishing-wise, therefore, the day was improving. During the morning I had evidence of a little interest in both the spinner and the fly. A 1½-inch Black and Gold Devon Minnow had received a vicious pull, and I had noticed a nice head-and-tail rise to a No. 6 Blue Charm on the floating line. Following the first occasion, I had tried both smaller and larger spinners. I tried fishing them fast and slow, upstream and across, and downstream. None of these tactics brought a successful result. Despite the fact that the day was not quite right – to my mind anyway – I felt that with only a slight change of tactics, there were fish to be caught. It was an occasion long before the advent of salmon disease could have influence and I felt that only a slight tactical change was required to ensure a chance of catching fish. The movement to the fly had suggested some willingness on the part of the salmon to have a go; but although I tried further fly variations, I was still fishless.

During lunch I pondered over these problems. 'High time to take a bit of your own advice', I thought. 'You are always telling people not to discard the sunk-fly too lightly. Is this not one of those times when it might pay off?' My lunch quickly finished, I replaced my floating line with a slow-sinking WetCel line; and put on the same leader and No.6 Blue Charm which had been on the floating line. The cloud cover continued to increase, but the air temperature remained roughly the same and, as far as I could detect, the masking of the sunlight was the only variable factor involved. Doubtless there were others of which I was not aware; but as I waded into a favourite pool I began to get a vague feeling of confidence. The better feel of the day for fishing brought on this expectancy. Indefinable, this mood is something the angler feels rather than measures. There is certainly no formula for it, other than the sense created by the hard and bitter school of experience, which somehow tells you when things are promising.

I had not been fishing for more than ten minutes before I felt the determined tug of a taking fish. There were no doubts about this one; the fish took the fly firmly and made sure that it was no light touch. It came up immediately, made a splashy boil, and set off on a screaming run upstream. I was on to the line backing in no time; but followed the fish quickly and soon had all the backing back on the reel. As soon as I got opposite the fish, it ran again and was quickly wallowing about in the white water at the head of the pool. Once it was there I eased the pressure in the sure knowledge that this was the best place to tire it. There were a few anxious moments as it jigged and bored among the rocks and obstructions on the bed of the river, but after five minutes of this it began to move downstream again. Its slower movements showed that the bulk of the power had gone out of it and it was not long before I caught glimpses of its glinting sides. I was quite surprised to see that, far from being one of the fresh-run fish, it was somewhat coloured and had obviously been in the river for some time. Following a few more panicky rushes, it lay still and on its side. It was then but a simple matter to tail it and ease it up the bank. At 2.30 p.m. it was my first fish of the day; a fine, though slightly-coloured, 19lb cock fish, safely on the bank.

The floating-line pundits would inform me, no doubt, that this fish could have been taken on the floating line; and, for all I know, they may be correct. The fish might even have taken the spinning bait that I had been using during the morning. The point is that I just do not *know* – nor, I suspect, could anyone else *know*. The fact is that such methods had failed, but the sunk-line had succeeded. What was even more confusing was that I went on to take another two fish on the same sunk fly and had three further offers with which I failed to connect. By 4.30 p.m. I had fished the most likely water and could not interest any more fish. I was more than satisfied with my three, but there was still plenty of daylight left and even the chance of some sea trout from dusk onwards.

It was about this time that I thought that a quiet break at the local pub would make a pleasant interlude. I spent the next hour with a dram and some bright chit-chat with the landlord and the locals. Back at the river once again, my entire experience suggested that the floating line should be the ideal tactic. Fish were head-and-tailing all over the river. The light was soft and the breeze had dropped to a mere zephyr. The sun could be seen like a transparent globe with its light filtered through the high layers of alto-stratus and wispy cumulus. There were several layers of fine clouds which cast a yellow glow over the scene through their transparency. Apart from the bubble and sparkle of the streamy runs, all was tranquil. Instinctively, I knew that I should use the small fly on the floating line; but the plain fact is that I was too lazy to change. Instead I compromised. Throughout the day the river had fallen a good two inches. If my No.6 Blue Charm had caught fish at 2.30 p.m., would it not now be sensible to try a No.8? Then, as the light failed, a No.6 again, or even a No.4 as it got still darker? This was the way my primary reasoning worked. I put on a No.8 Logie – don't ask me why the Logie, because I suspect that it was the only No.8 that was handy, which is no reason at all. I started once again at the top of the favourite run. There was a slight eddy at the top of the pool and although it had always looked to me like a good resting place, I had never moved a fish in this particular spot before. I unhitched my fly from the rod butt and let it fall on the water in preparation for casting. Instantly, and to my complete surprise, a salmon swirled at it; then moved back to its lie. Incredible! The fish was lying not more than three yards from where I was standing and yet it had the cheek to make a pass at my fly. If it would do it once, perhaps it would do it again? I cast carefully with a mere rod length of line, so that the fly would pass again over the precise spot. The resulting action was like a slow-motion drama. The fly was within inches of my feet when up came the fish and gulped it down. The tension was quite uncanny and I had to restrain all my natural impulses to strike too quickly. After what seemed an age, the fish turned down, and as it did so I raised my rod tip and was fast into what appeared to be a more silvery fish than any I had seen all day. I will not bore you with all the details of the prolonged fight, but the fish turned the scale at 16lbs and was covered in sea lice. Number four went safely into the bag.

From then on followed a chapter of interesting incidents. By 7.30 p.m. I had changed back to my No.6 Blue Charm and in quick succession I had four offers with which I failed to connect. I did not know which course to adopt. Had the change from the No.8 to the No.6 been made too prematurely? Or should I really have already changed to the No.4? I decided to go for that course of tactics, tied on a No.4 Logie, and started fishing with it. There was no doubt about the next offer and I was soon playing another fish which was quickly beached. It was the smallest fish of the day, barely 8lbs and slightly coloured.

By any standards, to take five salmon in a day must be considered a good catch. I had enjoyed a wonderful day of sport and, for the moment, I was content. As the light failed, the air turned cooler, and since I was fully satisfied I decided to give the sea trout a miss and wend my way home.

Quite a few days elapsed before I began to reflect on that outing. Why had I been so complacent? What was there really to give cause for such satisfaction? It had been a day when I had received no less than fourteen offers to the various spinners and flies, and of those fourteen offers I had only succeeded in landing five fish. Surely, this was a poor showing? Where had I gone wrong? What variable permutations could have given fourteen instead of five? The plain fact is I don't *know*; nor does anyone else. It is feasible that some experienced angler would have adopted different tactics and might have taken more than I did. On the other hand, an equally experienced angler could have done things a slightly different way and finished with a blank day. He would, no doubt, have come back with great tales of the offers which had come his way, and his diagnosis might well have been that the fish were not properly on the take.

Having tried the floating line and spinner during the morning, I think that my tactical decision to change to the sunk fly was the right one. Apart from any other considerations, it did secure five fish for me. I may have been too idle to change back to the floating line after tea, when conditions looked good for that method, but who can tell me that it would have been more successful than the sunk line, which took two fish during that period? Such factors are, in my opinion, impossible to assess. I should need the perception of the Almighty to be able to predict accurately what to do during any one minute of the day. The odd fish might have responded better – if that be the right word – with a firmer take, to a 2-inch Black and Gold Devon Minnow at, say, four minutes past three, despite the fact that the same fish might take a No.8 Logie quite firmly at ten minutes past six. How could we predict such acute changes in reaction to fly or spinner? The fact is, we cannot! This doubtless provides one of the irritating imponderables in salmon fishing and gives power to the elbows of some who incline to scorn salmon fishing as purely a game of luck. This is not quite the way I see it, for the fish present a constant challenge to the angler. He cannot, and *never* will, find a suitable formula for *all* occasions; but being the questing soul that he is, he will continue his attempts to find one. Herein, perhaps, lies the greatest fascination in salmon fishing; its inducement of a search for a formula which the angler suspects does not exist and *never* (I use this word with caution) will exist. The sunk fly secured me five fish during a day which was half-spent with other methods which had been unsuccessful. Could there be any more justification for using the sunk fly at such times? Possibly, had I persisted, I could have taken more on the floating-line. But somehow I doubt it.

For another example in more recent years, I had occasion to revert to the use of the sunk line on a mid-July day. I was fishing the No.3 beat of the Castle Grant water of the Spey. I was with my wife, Grace, and some friends. We had started our week with traditional double-handed rods, light floating lines and small flies. On the Monday morning I had taken the right bank of a well-known Spey pool – Pollowick – while my wife and a friend laid siege to the left bank. In most situations the left bank is more productive than the right, but not always so. Over our first morning the female opposition took three fish to my two and we could do little in the afternoon but bask in the bright, recently-emerged sun and wait until evening. This was heralded by a short but sharp thunderstorm and we soon gave the fishing best until the next day.

Tuesday saw a slight rise in the water and a tinge of colour. Fish were jumping everywhere, but there was not a single one which would give as much as a tweak to our flies. Much the same pattern was observed on the Wednesday and by Thursday lunchtime I had become heartily tired of hurling out my fly for an absolutely nil response.

'What are we doing wrong?' urged my wife.

'Nothing, so far as I can tell', I responded. 'Maybe they might take a fly on a sinking line?'

And with that I grabbed my tackle bag and put on a sinking line. I selected a slow sinker and a large tube fly of the same type I might use on Tweed in February. Beginning at the head of the pool, I had not been fishing for more than a few minutes when I felt a fish take. By some miracle it turned out to be a fresh-run one of 13lbs and I promptly got back into the pool to try for number two.

By 5 p.m. that afternoon I had five lovely salmon on the bank and had decided that enough was enough. I was just removing my waders when my host, Hugh Blakeney, came down from his nearby office to see how we were getting on. Hearing of my success and the methods utilised, he was not long in making ready with his own sinking-line tackle and a similar sized salmon fly. He waded into the top of the pool and had not been fishing very long before I saw his rod bend into a hoop. He was into a salmon. The fish fought with great verve and tenacity, and at the end of fifteen minutes it seemed just as playful as it had been at the start. Catching odd glimpses of the fish in the water, we had already decided that it weighed in excess of 20lbs; but it was not until we got it nearly ashore that we reckoned it could be over 30lbs. Although I was still in my house slippers, I was bade to do the best job I could at gaffing the fish. It only occurred to me later that, had I been really helpful, I could at least have put my waders on again and showed more willing . . . but with good luck and management Hugh soon brought the fish within easy gaffing distance. By another stroke of luck, I did not miss and the fish was quickly on the bank. It had coloured up a little from its stay in fresh water, but it had no difficulty in bouncing the scales down to 36lbs. It was the biggest Spey fish I had seen and the biggest I had ever gaffed myself.

Following that, my host went on to catch another two fish before

Hugh Blakeney with a 36lb salmon he took from Pollowick, on the River Spey at Castle Grant.

dinner: and all this on a day when other anglers, up and down the river, had not received so much as an offer to their small flies on floating lines. But fishing with a floating line is a most fascinating form of angling and we should now move on to consider that form of sport in greater detail.

Most present-day techniques for fishing with a floating line stem directly from the methods which were developed and practised by the late A.H.E. Wood; and a brief examination of their origin might be interesting. On page 69 of Jock Scott's book *Greased-Line Fishing for Salmon – The Methods of A.H.E. Wood of Glassel,* details are given of the birth of Wood's idea while on an Irish river during July 1903. It seems the river was very low, and the fish were all lying close to the sill of an eel weir. Traditional methods had failed, but Wood detected that the fish were rising occasionally, and apparently taking a small white moth from the surface. Eventually he put a small artificial fly on his leader and dapped it over them. It evoked such interest from the fish that in the short space of a few hours he succeeded in landing six of them. He lost others and pricked more than he cared to count. Following this experience, he found himself fishing as near to the surface as he could and started greasing his line to facilitate this. Wood goes on to comment that from then on he became convinced that salmon either wanted the fly well down near the bottom, or as near to the surface as he could contrive it to move. He forsook his mid-water tactics from that day onwards. As I have commented in earlier chapters, however, I do not fully agree; although, on the waters that Wood fished, he may well have had reason for his confined tactics. The Cairnton beat of the Aberdeenshire Dee where he spent most of his time has always been one of the more prolific beats on that river.

From a brief description of the birth of this method, therefore, it would seem that instead of making a case for floating-line fishing as we know it today, Wood succeeded in showing that, in fact, what those salmon really

Fig. 2   Wood's method of leading or extending his cast.

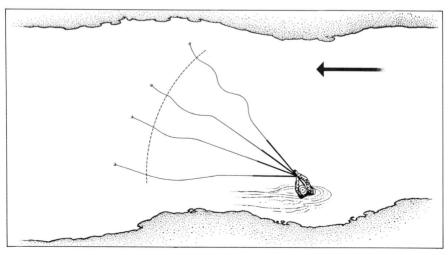

wanted that July afternoon in 1903 was a dry-fly dapped over them. There is no indication that present-day floating line methods would have worked any better for him on that occasion, than the traditional methods to which he was so accustomed. Further reading of this chapter also seems to give the indication that his technique was akin to dry-fly fishing, since he claims that he did not like drag to be imparted to the fly.

I find it difficult to reconcile Wood's comments with the type of floating-line fishing practised today. It would appear, or so it seems to the casual reader, that Wood liked his fly to float down, inert. Just how he would expect it to move across the pool from the far bank to his own without some form of drag is a mystery. Floating-line tactics these days are entirely dependent upon some form of controlled drag being imparted to the fly; otherwise, how could it possibly have the illusion of life? If the fly were carried down by the current in an inert fashion, it would look like little more than a piece of flotsam; and unless it represented some form of floating insect and brought a predatory response from the fish, as one gets in fly-fishing for trout, then it may hardly be called floating-line fishing as we now know it.

There is, of course, a deal of evidence that salmon will take a dry fly on occasion. The method is in frequent practice on the Atlantic salmon rivers of the Eastern seaboard of Canada, and has been tried with limited success on such lovely rivers as the Scottish Dee. American expert Lee Wulff frequently fishes in this style and has developed his ultra-fine tackle to the utmost of lightness, and catches many fish with it. Further reading of Wood's comments, however, implies that his method did, in fact, induce some drag; but that after making what he termed 'a slack cast', he liked to lead the fly round so that it did not describe a true semi-circle. In effect he used the slack line to give a slower draw than the current would induce to a taut line. Many anglers feed some slack line out following a cast, particularly in very fast water. I have yet to be fully convinced that this tactic has great merit, but I have tried it occasionally and caught fish. In this sense, therefore, while the fly is still dragging to some extent, it is not dragging at the same pace which would be achieved with a taut line. The fly will be travelling at a compromise speed, somewhere between the speed applied at full drag in the current and being motionless in its relation to that current. If the water speed were five miles per hour, it could be assumed that fly speed, relative to the current, and for part of the period, would be in the region of 2 to 3 miles per hour. Frankly, this still involves drag and, therefore, forms the basis for all our thinking in modern floating-line techniques. Wood's flies were constructed so that they had to drag to some extent before they could remotely resemble any sort of lure. They did not look even remotely like a dry fly; and, for the most part, were sparsely dressed on long-shanked single hooks. Wood even went to the extreme, on occasion, of painting the shank only. Such a 'fly' has to drag in the current in order to evoke interest and we must assume that some form of controlled drag is not only forced upon us, but is essential in all forms of wet-fly, floating-line fishing for salmon.

If we come to examine the background to salmon fly-fishing generally, it may be of interest to note that, in the early days, before the general use of plaited silk lines, lines were invariably made of plaited horse-hair. The question is, did those horse-hair lines sink as rapidly as the silk line? Could it not be, in fact, that the very early salmon fly-fishermen were using methods akin to those of Wood? Could it not be that Wood only succeeded in rediscovering the method by accident? The facts are very hazy on these questions. Nevertheless, it would seem that, following the changeover to silk lines, it became common practice to fish the fly deeply; and that Wood did not invent, but only rediscovered, a method to make the fly move nearer the surface.

Nowadays the greasing of a silk line in order to make it float is almost a thing of the past. Such lines still have great merit; but the continued greasing throughout a fishing day makes it a tedious business; and so most of us take the easy way out and use the modern floating lines. They do not always float as perfectly as the makers would have us believe, but they are very convenient and eliminate the possibility of getting line grease on the leader (something which inevitably happened in the old days) which causes the fly to skate on the surface of the water.

Modern floating lines are made in a wide variety of weights, contours and sizes. It is a simple matter to find the one best suited to you or your rod. Whether you decide on a line with forward-taper principles or the standard double-taper, is largely a matter of choice. You will possibly shoot more line with the forward-taper; but you will find it impossible to execute any worthwhile form of Spey cast. I like to have both on hand, so that I may choose a line best suited to the conditions of the day.

My floating-line outfits are much the same as those I have described for use with the sinking line. The 15-foot 'Walker' is a great favourite for April-May fishing on the Spey; but I might frequently use the 16½-foot 'Walker' which lends itself so admirably to double-Spey casting. Most times I use a double-tapered No.11 line with either of these rods. And, at the time of writing, I am involved in the development of a specific 35-yard No.11 line especially suited to Spey casting. Only in the late spring and summer do I resort to forward-taper lines, and then mostly on a single-handed rod.

Line colour has been a subject which has brought much controversy; white lines are very much in vogue today, on the basis that the under-belly of a fish is white, and that this colour is least likely to be noticed by fish swimming underneath. Though this seems a perfectly logical assessment, it must be borne in mind that, whatever the colour of the line, it will still cast as great a shadow as any other since it is no more transparent. A white line is certainly a joy to use. The angler sees it plainly and knows, at all times, the precise placing of his fly. There are times, however, when the

Spring on the Association water at Grantown on Spey.

short-tapered portion of the line sinks slightly below the surface. In these circumstances, I am not certain that white is the ideal colour.

I recall a favourite pool on the Lune, known as the 'Groynes' because of the number of man-made groynes put there to prevent bank erosion. In a good year, the pool used to hold a fantastic number of fish. But it was, in the main, a difficult pool to fish correctly, consisting of smooth, gliding water with many swirls and eddies. Vision for the fish was superb with that mirror-like, unbroken surface and they were frequently seen moving off their lies as the pool was fished down. Fishing this pool with a white line never produced more than the odd fish for me, yet a similar type in brown or green frequently produced good bags. This, of course, proves nothing – it is merely a fancy, but a fancy so long held that I rarely bothered to fish the pool with my white line, preferring to use the same line in a mahogany colour. On the clear waters of Norway, many gillies shake their heads sadly when they see an angler with a white line. 'White line – no good', they say. Such a remark may be born out of prejudice, but they might have a point.

However, I do not want you to think that I am condemning the white line out of hand. Most of my floating-line fishing has, in fact, been done with one, and I have used one in Norway with equally good effect. The fact is that if nature invested fish with white bellies then it is more than reasonable to suppose that a white line is less easily seen than one of any other colour; always provided, of course, that the entire line floats and is viewed from directly underneath. Normally the fish should not see the line at all: the length of leader should eliminate any possibility of this. But if a small portion of the head of the line sinks below the surface, it is possible that it may be more visible than a line of more subdued colouring. Most fish become accustomed to seeing reeds and weeds waving in the water. On gliding water, therefore, and on many lochs, where a certain amount of tip submergence is likely, I have felt some conviction that green or brown would look more natural. When we come to examine the question on streamy, popply water, we immediately find an ally in the fact that such water can hide a multitude of sins; and camouflage even the most garish-looking tackle. Much of our salmon fishing, though, will take place in streamy water, where the visual help of a white line far outweighs any other consideration. Of course there may still be a certain amount of tip submergence, but this fine detail is lost in streamy water.

I have never been able to determine to my own satisfaction the exact depth at which a floating-line fly should fish; and to some extent I feel that it is a factor over which the angler has little control. There are those, I know, who feel strongly on this topic. They argue that the depth at which the fly fishes is crucial. My good friend Reg Righyni argues in this fashion and his record of fish caught on the floating line, in the good years, make it difficult to disregard his contention. To me, however, it seems that we are again only dealing with fancies. Fancy born of experience is always worth a hearing and when fancy has stood the test of time in fishing it may be assumed by some to have become a fact. Troubles arise when we examine the differing circumstances while fishing one single pool of a river.

Perhaps the first consideration we should make in our floating-line fishing is the length of the leader. If the line is floating, and the leader is rubbed down with Fuller's Earth paste (a mixture of glycerine and Fuller's Earth powder) or detergent to make it sink, the length of the leader will have some influence on the depth below the surface at which the fly fishes – as will the weight of the fly. Bear in mind that we are dealing with a mere inch or so. If we incline to fish the fly deeper still, we should have to resort to a line with a sinking tip, or even a fully sinking line. The strength of the current will also have great bearing on the depth of the fly in the water. Obviously the fly will fish higher in the water in a strong, streamy current than the same fly would fish in a slacker portion of the pool. Whatever the circumstances, however, I have no hesitation in putting up the longest leader I can use comfortably – generally two feet shorter than the rod I am using, or even longer than the rod if I am using a single-hander. As with sunk-line fishing, I rarely bother with a tapered leader; and certainly avoid the knotted variety as an abomination. If there is any tendency for the fly to skate on the water, there may well be a series of 'wake forms' from each knot on the leader, and I know of little else more likely to put fish off the take. The simple fact is that no two casts could ever make the fly fish at precisely the same depth. There may be a certain amount of line-tip submergence on one cast that is not apparent on the next. One cast may result in the fly skating on or near the surface, while the next gets better entry and fishes correctly. Generally speaking, a skating fly is to be avoided at all costs, though I know of instances when deliberate skating has taken a fish, such is the unpredictability of salmon. North American anglers sometimes deliberately put in a 'riffling hitch' in order to make their fly skate. This consists of a half-hitch around the fly, after it has been tied on to the leader in the normal manner, so that it hangs at right-angles from the leader. This riffling or Newfoundland hitch was a device used by Canadian anglers, to get full use out of old-fashioned flies with gut eyes. Because of the weakness of gut eyes, the hitch was merely added for greater security when playing a fish. In due time the Canadians discovered that certain tactical benefits accrued from fishing a fly in this manner and the technique is highly regarded by many North American anglers. It is important to tie the hitch at the side of the fly which suits the side of the river from which you are fishing. There may be an advantage in trying this method on British waters, if only for experiment. The ideal position of the fly, for most forms of floating-line fishing, however, is just under the surface; and one of the best ways I know of controlling fly depth is in the careful choice of the fly.

It was Anthony Crossley, in his excellent little book *The Floating Line*

R.V. Righyni, a great advocate of feeding slack line to a taking salmon, fishes on the River Lune at Newton, Lancashire.

for Salmon and Sea Trout, who suggested correctly that if you need a No. 6 fly for the head of the pool it would be logical to put on a No. 8 for the quieter water downstream. Doubtless, he was referring to the visual impact of the fly on the fish; but there is also the question of the differing weights of the two flies, and the alternate depths – fractional though they may be – at which each would fish. Normally, weight of fly in floating-line fishing is of little consequence, while the amount of dressing the fly contains and whether it is dressed on single, double or treble hooks, is very significant. Contrary to popular belief, the double- or treble-hooked fly (because of its extra weight) does not always swim at a lower depth than a single of similar size. The multi-hooked fly, because of its extra bulk, causes more drag in the water than a single-hooked fly, and on strong, gliding sections of the river it is often difficult to avoid the undesirable result of the fly skating on the surface. The matter may be remedied by putting up a slimly dressed single to offer the minimum drag in the water. There are, of course, many occasions when the extra weight of the double or treble does make it fish slightly lower in the water than the single. Only long experience on a particular stretch of water will tell the angler precisely what to do, according to the conditions of the day. For most fishing we have to be content with the knowledge that our fly is somewhere just underneath the surface; not skating, and not fishing too deep. The precise depth is almost impossible to determine, since this will alter as the fly moves in differing strengths of current. If the fly still maintains a tendency to skate, simply feeding a little line will often effect a cure; but, failing that, the leader may again be rubbed down with Fuller's Earth paste or detergent. Sometimes the trouble will not be remedied until a change of fly has been made, or the angler has moved down the pool to flows of a different type from those at the top of the pool.

Having determined the length of leader, I cut off a level section of nylon monofilament line of around 13lbs test. The strength of the leader is normally determined by the height and strength of the water, or the weight of fish likely to be encountered. Over low water on the Lune, for instance, I may well use 7 or 8lbs strength; but I would rarely use less than 9lbs on the Spey, or 18lbs test on Norway's Vosso river. Apart from any other consideration, it is not a good plan to fish with small flies and thick leaders; nor is it common sense to fish with big flies on fine leaders. There is always the danger of cracking off a big fly while casting, while a small fly on a thick leader never seems to swim in a lifelike manner.

Let us presume that we have already decided that conditions are right for fishing with the floating line. The water is the right height and colour; water temperatures are in the 50s and the air is warmer than the water. It might well be the month of May, with pools already full of recently-run fish. The odd sign of a fish doing a porpoise-like head-and-tail rise will lend strength to our decision. So we tie on our fly and start fishing.

It is really amazing how an angler going trout fishing will take every care

Grace Oglesby playing and handtailing a salmon on the Garrapool of the Spey at Castle Grant.

to conceal his presence and stalk his fish: yet the same person, on a salmon river, throws caution to the wind, and barges in without a thought for stealth or river-craft. Salmon are just as shy as the wiliest trout – and a lot more so than some hatchery-reared monstrosities. The fact that salmon do not always scurry out of their lies does not mean that they have not been alarmed into a non-taking mood. In all types of salmon fishing, therefore, and particularly floating-line fishing, approach your chosen spot cautiously. Watch for shadows and vibrations on the bank. On at least three occasions I have taken fish while the fly was literally dangling from the rod point while preparing to cast. Had I bulldozed my way to the river bank, the fish would either have fled or moved slowly away.

Having approached the place from which you are to commence fishing, don't be in too much of a hurry to cast to the other side of the river. First let the fly dangle in the water. Make sure that it has life and movement in the current; and that the leader is straight, and free of wind knots or any tendency to coil. Stretching the nylon is the best primary method of rendering it straight and limp; while rubbing it down with Fuller's Earth paste, detergent, clay or soil will remove any traces of grease imparted previously by handling. The nylon monofilament should sink readily, and the fly should swim in a hook-down position. When you have satisfied yourself on these small points, start casting. Keep the casts short initially; and be careful to watch the area you know your fly to be in, to observe any response from the fish.

Tactics with the floating line differ slightly depending on the time of year and the height and temperature of the water. During the early season I think that deep-wading techniques may be used to good advantage. We do not want our fly to pass over the fish too quickly, so it is a sound idea to make our initial casts well downstream of a point immediately opposite our bank and to let the fly hang, as it were, over the most likely water. It is also a good plan to hold the rod well out at right-angles, so that minimum fly speed across the current is achieved. Any tendency to bring the rod point round might well cause the fly to move too quickly, and this rod movement should be deferred until the fly is on the dangle and ready to be cast again. It is a good tactic, too, to hold the rod point well up in the air. This maintains a minimum amount of line on the water and makes it less susceptible to influence from the stronger, central current which may induce a downstream 'belly' to be formed. It is a much better technique than what Richard Walker terms the 'despondent droop'. Perhaps, therefore, we may be permitted to label it as the 'expectant erection'?

Later on, as the water warms considerably, it may be sound policy to cast more squarely to the current and thus let the fly swim or move that little bit faster. It is a common mistake among novice anglers to disregard these points; but, if you think about it, you will appreciate that any tendency to ignore them will only result in your leading the fly round more quickly than it would otherwise travel despite the fact that, at this stage, you wish your fly to travel as slowly as possible over the lies. One of the causes of trouble, in all forms of across and downstream fishing, is the 'belly' formation in the line caused by the strong central current. If a cast is made as in figure 3a (a) to (b) it will not be long before the line has assumed the shape shown at a to c. If this were to go uncorrected, the fly would soon start moving at a faster pace than you want, and, for the first part of its travel, in a downstream direction. As we lengthen our casts, therefore, we have to adopt a method of preventing this 'belly' from forming as in figure 3b. This is best achieved by 'mending' the line, as it is termed; and is simply done by a slow-lifting action upstream just as the fly touches the water. (Other aids to good presentation will be examined in a

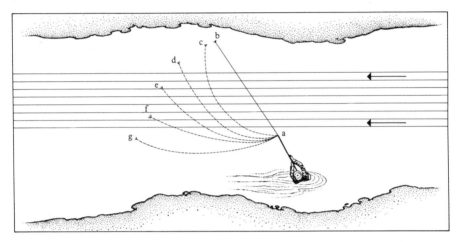

Fig. 3a   If the fly is cast from a to b and left to its own devices a pronounced line belly will be formed.

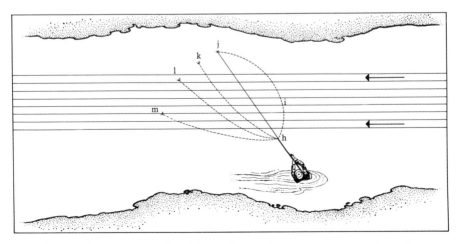

Fig. 3b   Following the cast h to j the angler should throw an upstream 'mend' to enable the fly to move correctly for the remainder of its path or arc.

chapter on casting.) It may well be necessary to make further mends in the line as the fly moves round in the current. The central current will frequently tend to form this downstream belly; and in order to make the fly fish correctly, the line should be smoothed out as the belly forms. When the fly has reached a point at roughly 45 degrees downstream of the angler, tradition suggests that this is the most likely taking place. A large proportion of fish certainly, are hooked in this area; but it pays to concentrate throughout the entire time the fly is fishing, and even to make a few slow pulls on the fly before lifting for the next cast.

By the time you have extended your casts so that they virtually cover the pool, it is quite likely that you will wish to cast more line than you can aerialise comfortably. The extra distance is best achieved by shooting line. At the end of a cast, a few coils of line are hand-lined in. The line is then picked up for the back-cast; then, as the power is applied in the fore-cast, the hand-held line is released. With practice, it is possible to shoot quite remarkable lengths of line, but take care not to fish a long line just to show off. Long-line tactics, while extremely useful on many occasions, should only be used as river conditions dictate.

Generally speaking, therefore, the foregoing tactics form a basis for floating-line fishing. Continue casting down the pool, trying all the time to cast the same length of line and in the same direction as at the start. You can move down the pool slowly or quickly as you wish, but personally I would rather fish a pool down twice, quickly, than once, slowly. There are those who argue that they would prefer to be the second angler down the pool, rather than the first. I think that this preference depends mainly on the nature of the pool and the experience of the angler in fishing it. I have few qualms about fishing first, second or third; but in the two latter cases, prefer to know that my predecessors are reasonably competent. Under ideal floating-line conditions, I sometimes prefer to follow an angler who is spinning, rather than another competent fly-fisherman. It is doubtful if the spinner will take fish; I hope that it serves merely to wake them up and act as a sort of advertisement for my fly! There have been a few times when I have fly-fished behind an army of spinners, on hard-fished association waters, and have taken fish when the spinning fraternity have gone home clean.

One of the most controversial questions is exactly what to do when a salmon takes the fly. Some writers argue that all the time one is fishing, a yard of slack line should be held between the reel and the butt-ring. When resistance is felt, the slack is allowed to slide through the rings; and the rod point is then drawn sideways towards the angler's own bank. Some say that the perfect take is when the line stops and the point slowly sinks. A one-two-three count is made; then the rod point is raised slowly to drive the hook home. Other writers think that the perfect take is when they see a porpoise-like head-and-tail rise at their fly, and they raise the rod slowly as in chalk-stream fishing for trout. My own experience and that of the late

Captain T.L. Edwards (who, incidentally, caught over 300 fish in one month alone on the floating-line fly) is that it matters little what you do. Perhaps, also, I could have no greater support for my argument than that of one of the greatest salmon fishers of the century, G.P.R. Balfour-Kinnear. In Chapter 3 of his book *Catching Salmon and Sea Trout*, he gives a very reasoned argument for *not* feeding slack line. Referring to the fact that the fly may be easily disengaged from a salmon's mouth, he says: 'If you do not want to hook the fish, then be as gentle as you can – even to the extent of throwing loose line at it . . . You may well say that all this is nonsense and that you catch fish this way. Of course you do. You would find that if you threw the rod into the water whenever you saw a boil and picked it up five minutes later, you would catch fish; but not so many as if you were more orthodox. I contend that throwing line to a fish has mistakenly become orthodox because so many fishermen follow a false teaching.'

In most instances, therefore, the fish is hooked – or it is not. No attempt should be made to strike at the rise; but, after a fish has been felt, then it has either hooked itself or it has merely pulled the fly. My own technique is to fish without any slack line at the reel, holding the line lightly between my forefinger and the second finger. Then there is usually sufficient 'sag' in the line, between the rod point and the fly, to cushion a particularly severe pull. So, if a fish head-and-tails at the fly, I wait for the pull; and, under slight resistance to set the hook, let a few coils of line be pulled off my reel. For this reason I frequently fish with a light ratchet on the reel; but I don't think it really matters. There are many times, of course, when hooking fails; but I cannot for the life of me see how any other tactics would work better. When a fish takes without the promising head-and-tail rise, the first thing one usually knows about it is a determined pull. Before there is time to do anything about it, the fish is either hooked – or not.

All the above comments refer, of course, to normal streamy or gliding water. There are occasions, during low water periods, when there will be very little flow in the river; yet fishing with the floating-line fly might be worthwhile. Because of lack of flow, the fly may sink deeper than in a normal current strength; and a stoppage of the line may well be the first indication that a fish has taken the fly. With a very small fly, however, it may still be sufficiently near the surface for the angler to see the head-and-tail rise, or a bulge in the water. Under these circumstances it would not be sensible to strike until the fish is felt; since, in most instances, a salmon will hang on to the fly for a lot longer period than a darting moorland trout. Even then, grilse as well as some salmon have a habit of taking quite quickly at certain times of the season; and the angler who dallies too long may not even feel the pull before it is too late. There can be no hard-and-fast rule. Certainly, salmon may be given more time than one would normally give to trout; but once the fish is actually felt, I see neither rhyme nor reason for delaying the strike. Perhaps the word 'strike' is misleading.

There should be no need to strike in the full sense of the word. If the angler has been fishing diligently, his line should at all times be under control; and there should be no s-bends, coils of line floating on the water, or excess slack line to be taken up before contact is made. The literal meaning of the word 'strike' should not, in fact, be applied to salmon fly-fishing.

If we assess the point at which an angler stands in the river to be almost in the middle of a clock face (provided he is fishing from the left bank): directly upstream will be three o'clock, and directly downstream, nine o'clock. Immediately opposite him, on the far bank, will be twelve o'clock. For normal floating-line fishing I like to commence with a cast to half-past ten, followed by a quick mend to bring the fly slowly through nine o'clock – the point where fish are likely to take – then to half-past eight, before the line retrieve is started and a fresh cast made. In slacker water, or later in the summer, I may well make a cast to half-past eleven, followed by one or two *downstream* mends before the retrieve at nine o'clock. In very strong water, however, it might pay to concentrate on fishing the portion between ten o'clock and half-past eight as effectively as possible when, by wading well out, the angler is able to make his fly fish very slowly through this narrow arc. It all depends on the angler's assessment of the best tactics to adopt. Only practical angling experience will reveal this.

There are times when, in very low water, hardly any movement by the current will be imparted to the fly. Casting upstream to one or two o'clock and hand-lining the fly back will sometimes work; as will the technique of what is termed 'backing-up' a pool. There the angler starts fishing at the bottom of the pool, and, following each cast, he takes a pace or two

Fig. 4

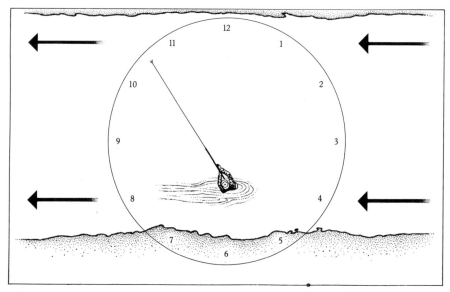

upstream in order to drag the fly over the lies more quickly than a stationary position would permit. The method has the disadvantage, however, of the probable showing of yourself or your line to the fish before you actually cover it with the fly; but it can be practised quite effectively on some waters. Other ways of increasing the pace of the fly may be made quite simply by fishing in the traditional way and either making downstream mends, or hand-lining back as the cast is being fished out. I have used the latter method on frequent occasions; and occasionally I prefer to fish with a larger fly and make it fish faster, than fish a smaller fly in the traditional manner. In very low water, a biggish fly hand-lined in very quickly will sometimes produce a take, as will the same technique when the fly has been cast upstream. Alternatively, I have known occasions in very fast water – say, at the head of a run – when a take may be induced simply by letting the fly hang in the current and making it move slowly downstream by paying line off the reel. There are many permutations to all these tactics; and when in doubt a bit of experimentation often produces a surprising result. Don't be fooled into thinking that you have suddenly found an answer to all salmon fishing problems. On one day, the fly dropped downstream may work; but thereafter it may be completely ineffective for several seasons. Much the same applies to the fly thrown upstream, and quickly retrieved. There is still no sound formula; but the experienced angler knows when best to try these tactics. They are, at best, only a poor alternative to traditional floating-line methods; but they sometimes have the advantage of saving an otherwise fruitless day.

Provided that the angler can recognise good floating-line conditions, and can cast to a reasonable level of competence with tackle suited to the job, floating-line fishing is possibly the easiest form of salmon fishing available. Perhaps a highly controversial task is that of deciding which fly to use and when. We shall move on, therefore, to examine some aspects of fly selection in our next chapter.

We have already examined the various techniques the angler may adopt in order to take salmon on the floating-line, and have pointed out the necessity for the angler to carry a wide range of flies if he is to be able to meet all the varying considerations likely to be encountered throughout a season's fishing. In Chapter 4, when examining the question of colour in salmon flies, I made the point that it was my fancy that the smaller the fly, the less important the colour. Let me begin this chapter with a brief examination of the colour question by referring to some of the well-known authorities of the past.

On page 41 of Jock Scott's book (referred to in Chapter 6), Wood is reported as having commented, 'As regards pattern I do not believe that this matters at all. Blue Charm and Silver Blue are my stock, simply on the principle that one is more or less black and the other white and so give me a choice.' Again, on page 144 of the same book, we read, 'I do not believe in the colour flash theory at all; in my opinion it is simply a case of the fly travelling – accidentally or otherwise – at such an angle that it arouses the curiosity of the stiff fish. No fisherman could make his fly travel in exactly the same way at each cast; and although he may *believe* that a different colour would flash and attract the fish, my idea is that it is the different way in which the fly is presented.' Yet again, on page 164, when comparing his methods with those of Crossfield, Wood comments, 'Except for a fly out of the ordinary, just for experiment, I see no object in changing unless you can convince me that fish are particular as to certain colours. I should be quite happy with one fly only – in various sizes; in fact, if I started all over again I should use just a Black Doctor and a Silver Doctor, the one dark and the other light.' Mr Crossfield responded to this with 'I am in absolute agreement with you about particular shades of colour being so much nonsense; but I do like to have a dark fly and also a light one.'

So far as is possible I have not quoted out of context; and I would not like it to be thought that, because of these quotes, such eminent anglers would have used gaudy flies in order to prove their point about the lack of importance of colour. I have already mentioned the importance of colour, to my mind, in big sunk-flies; but I am firmly of the opinion that the smaller our flies become, the more subtle and elusive the colours should be.

The question of colour has caused a rage of controversy throughout the years. Richard Waddington, one of our leading authorities, gave the subject a great deal of coverage in his excellent book *Salmon Fishing*. In my opinion, Waddington gave more thought to the entire question of salmon fishing than had ever been undertaken since books on the subject were first written. Though his book was first published in 1947 and advances in factual knowledge have proved him wrong on some counts, this in no way detracts from the value of his perceptive thinking: after all, every theory put forward waits for destruction. On the question of colour, however, there seems to be a little confusion; and a fine distinction must be made between the words colour and pattern. On page 112 of his book, Waddington comments, 'The question of the value of various colours and patterns of salmon flies is one that is constantly recurrent and one on which widely divergent views are held. I think that most fishermen have felt that to suppose that the salmon could differentiate between say a Black Doctor and a Thunder and Lightning was faintly ridiculous; and the more modern school of thought is tending, all the time, largely as a result of the experience of greased-line fishing, to the belief that colour is of little importance in the salmon fly.' Continuing to the bottom of page 115 we read 'Colour then, can have little effect, for it is the tone of the fly that is important . . .' etc, etc.

Waddington made these comments to support the argument for his own particular design of fly. Such flies have made a great contribution to any worthwhile advancement in salmon-fly design since the salmon fly was first invented. Personally, while using this design for some of my sunk-line fishing, I prefer the traditional treble, double or single hook for the floating line. In more recent years I have become quite addicted to the flies tied on the treble hooks which are marketed by Esmond Drury. They have excellent hook-holding qualities, are very easily dressed at the fly-tying bench, and require the minimum of materials to do so efficiently.

When we turn to page 211 of Waddington's book, we find what appears to be a minor contradiction. He writes, 'In greased-line fishing in the standard manner matters are very different. Probably as much as 50 per cent of one's luck depends on using the right size and *pattern* of fly in the right place.' Of course, 'size of fly' and 'being in the right place' are paramount considerations; but how can Waddington differentiate between pattern and colour? Surely these two are necessarily inter-related? On page 223 he goes on to comment, 'I used to think that the *pattern* (my italics) of the greased-line fly was of no importance and that anyone who fished at random for a whole season with but one pattern, chosen at random and tied in the various necessary sizes, would be every bit as successful as the angler who gave himself several choices . . . I am no longer of the opinion that the pattern does not matter. On the other hand, I am equally certain that small differences between one pattern and another very like it, are both unnoticed and unnoticeable by the fish . . . I do not think that colour, except in so far as it affects tone, is of the slightest importance.'

Waddington contradicts himself further on page 269, where he states, 'Nor do I personally very much mind what pattern of fly I use. I have known the time when nothing but the Blue Charm would do . . . I have seen seasons when the Silver Blue was my first choice – or a Logie or a

Jeannie. Today it appears to be the Hairy Mary. All these, and many other patterns, catch fish equally well and it is only wishful thinking that invests any pattern with magic qualities.'

To my mind, a pattern is a mixture of colours; and a tone is the result of such blending. Patterns of colours can be arranged to give a red tone; a sky-blue tone; or even the most garish green. So colour has some importance; but in my opinion the emphasis should not be laid on colour alone, but that colours should become more subdued as our flies become smaller. Presumably, to Waddington it is in this respect that colour is regarded as having no importance. If we had some vague idea of what the salmon take our floating-line flies for, we would then have some cause for making judgements on this vexed question of colour or pattern. But as we have seen in earlier chapters, we are still no nearer any such knowledge. Any guesses we make are mere speculation. Over the years, however, certain floating-line patterns have emerged which are more popular than others, while a few fancies have stood the test of time for so long now that they have established themselves factually as regular 'taking' patterns. These include the Blue Charm, Logie, Thunder and Lightning, Black Doctor or even a Silver Blue – though this is a fly I rarely use. One of our greatest catchers of salmon today, Major the Hon J. Ashley Cooper, stated in an article on salmon fishing, 'As to pattern of fly this appears to matter little providing the dressing is sparse'.

If we agree, therefore, that colour or pattern in the least defined sense of these words have little bearing on our fly selection, what are the factors to be considered before deciding which fly to use for a given set of circumstances? We have already examined the effects of slimly dressed singles and heavier dressed doubles and trebles in varying types of water currents; and, to a large extent, I let my choice of fly be dictated by these considerations. My favourite flies are difficult to name, since they are usually tied by my wife or myself; and, as neither of us is very expert, they tend to be of the simplest design and construction. I shudder to think of them ever acquiring such names as Oglesby's Orrer, Artful Arthur, Grey Grace or Gracie's Glory. Having a pattern of fly named after me is definitely something to which I do not aspire! In general, however, my favourite patterns roughly follow such well-known flies as Blue Charm, Logie, Thunder and Lightning, Stoat's Tail and Hairy Mary. Perhaps my real favourite consists of nothing more than a black silk body with fine tinsel ribbing, a touch of orange cock hackle at the throat, and some black or brown squirrel tail for winging. I make these in a variety of sizes; and with varying amounts of dressing on single, double and treble hooks. As they are, they resemble the Thunder and Lightning; but for an alternative I substitute the blue cock hackle for the orange, to give me a type of Blue Charm. My so-called Logie has a touch of yellow silk at the tail followed by a main body of claret silk, fine tinsel ribbing, a mixed blue and ginger throat hackle, and dark brown squirrel tail for winging. Another favourite is an all-black base with only fine tinsel ribbing to make the contrast. These, with the possible addition of some flies with an all-tinsel body, constitute my stock. I have already commented in Chapter 4, when writing of sunk-line selections, that I like to choose a pattern of fly which blends in with the overall colour of the water and the river bed. The fly should not stick out like a sore thumb, except in very turbid water; and should, therefore, be of subdued colouring and tone. Indeed, its design might suggest that I do not want the fish to see it too easily. Bear in mind, always, that the angler looks *down* at his fly while the salmon looks *upwards* at it – and, depending on the actinic value of the light and its direction, sees the fly either in bold relief or as an elusive silhouette.

As I have already stated, it is my opinion that the size of the fly and the amount of dressing it contains are vital; and, as a general rule, there is nothing much wrong with the formula that the higher the water temperature, the smaller the fly should be. It is essential, though, that this be related to river height, strength of current and colour of water. The late Ian Wood, a salmon angler of some note, argued that bright flies performed best on cold days and dull flies on warmer days; but water temperature by itself is no guide. In my early days of floating-line fishing, I took the water temperature religiously, and it is, of course, very important that the air should be warmer than the water. But actual knowledge of water temperatures is only a minor consideration in making an assessment of the fly to use. A. H. E. Wood argued, and I would not quarrel with him, that a No. 6 should be regarded as the basic size for floating-line fishing. However, a No. 6 fly heavily dressed is a vastly different proposition from a fly on the same hook which is lightly dressed. In fact, a heavily dressed No. 6 may well look larger than a lightly dressed No. 4.

My plan, therefore, is to concentrate on a range of sizes between 4 and 8, with the odd 10 for occasional use; and I have one set of flies lightly dressed with a second set heavily dressed. I tie these on singles, doubles and trebles; and thus finish up with around eighteen alternatives of any one pattern in sizes 4, 6 and 8. On a normal height of water, under good floating-line conditions, I would normally select a lightly dressed No. 6 as the fly with which to start. Choice of pattern is dictated by such considerations as overhead light, colour of water or river bed, pure fancy – or the fly that is most convenient in my fly box! If the day is bright, with a good sprinkling of blue sky and white clouds, then I might go for something on the lines of a Blue Charm. If the day is grey, with a tinge of peat in the water, then it would almost certainly be the Stoat's Tail, the Thunder and Lightning or the Munro Killer. A really bright day with low water might induce me to put up the Silver Blue instead of the Blue Charm. Basically, though, my selection would depend on fancy, and on nothing else – since, in the final analysis, there is little else to go on.

If conditions remain the same, I will persist with the fly of my choice for quite some time; but if no response is forthcoming from the fish, I would ultimately change to a fly of the same size with heavier dressing. I cannot tell you why I do this, nor give you any logical reasoning for doing so. If the river were dropping slightly throughout the day, as it does most times when sport is to be at its best, then it would seem logical to put on a smaller fly. I might well do this at a later stage; but not without an exploratory cast or two with the heavier dressed fly. What I am really hoping for is some response from the fish – not necessarily a take, but fish sometimes move to a fly that is more easily seen without actually taking it. If I get some sort of response, and fail to connect, I would promptly fish that same cast again with a sparsely dressed No. 8, in the hope of secure hooking next time. Just to add to the confusion, there are times when fish will make a pass at a fly presumably because it is too small. The real answer then lies in putting on a larger or more heavily dressed fly. Such are the fascinating variables in a day's floating-line fishing. Only rarely would I take into account the question of pattern, for with the patterns I have named the colour differential could hardly be discerned by the salmon; and, in my opinion, is of little consequence. It would be important, however, to know if the fish sought were fresh-run or stale. This could affect both my choice of fly and my tactics.

My most productive days with floating-line have often commenced with good spinning water. Rain in the hills has brought a rise of water and some fresh fish into the pools. As the river fines off, spinning becomes the order of the day; and undoubtedly a few fish are taken. Suddenly the fish seem to go off the spinner and, if I have my wits about me, I realise that it is time I started with my floating-line fly outfit. As the river falls so does my size of fly, until, finally, I am using lightly dressed No. 8s or 10s. There could come a time in mid-summer when I might use a fly even smaller than size 10. But as I have said, I do tend to regard a No. 10 as the minimum size for general spring fishing. My choice of a single, double or treble hook would be entirely dependent on the character of the water, and not necessarily on the consideration that the double or treble might give me better hooking qualities, which they may well do! In the preceding chapter I have outlined the circumstances which induce me to put up the treble, double or single. I rarely bother to take into account any other factor than that of making the fly fish in a manner which is correct to meet a given set of circumstances.

To sum up this chapter, I think that too much emphasis is placed upon pattern, and not enough on the amount of dressing a particular chosen pattern contains. We have examined the importance of fly size, but have come to realise that a lightly dressed No. 4 offers a similar illusion to that of a heavily dressed No. 6. We have seen that a heavily dressed fly on a treble or double hook might offer greater resistance to the water than a lightly dressed fly on a single hook; and therefore, in many circumstances, does not necessarily fish at a lower depth in the water. In fact, because of its bulk, it may well skate in strong, gliding water. There are, of course, a thousand and one permutations one can make in the construction of salmon flies. There is not a fly made that does not have a use at some stage of the game. The great problem is largely a matter of personal choice; and only experience will yield the secret of the tactics to adopt on a chosen piece of water, at the time of the year you fish it – coupled with the whims of the elements and of your chosen quarry, the salmon!

Many salmon anglers regard the taking of salmon on the floating-line fly as the epitome of their sport. I am not sure that I agree. Certainly I rate it very highly and enjoy it more than any other form of salmon fishing; but it is comparatively easy when compared with sunk-line fishing. The angler has less need to think of that third dimension, the depth of the water, which has such an important influence on sunk-line tactics. I suspect also that a fly on the floating line is more readily seen by the fish than a sunk fly might be, as it flutters in and out from behind the rocks and contours of the river bed. Thus the sub-surface fly searches more water, but the fish has to demonstrate its willingness to leave its lie and rise to intercept the fly. We have already examined some of the circumstances which may induce it to do this. Naturally the angler has either to know the water or have the services of a reliable gillie available. A good gillie can be a gem during a day's floating-line fishing, for he can position himself where he can watch the movement of the fly and note any reactions from the fish. On other, smaller, rivers, the angler may well be able to see these reactions for himself and my thoughts instantly go back to one of many tantalising visits to the Argyllshire Awe.

Fly-only was the rule; and I had access to a middle beat of the river during the early part of August. The best of fishing was over, and August is a notoriously difficult month in most places. The pools were full of fish but the river had an irritating habit of going up and down like a yo-yo as the hydro-electric administration, further upstream, diverted or halted the river flow. I was to have access to the beat for three alternate days during that week, and at 5.30 a.m. on the first day I was down at the top pool. I started off with a good old stand-by, a No. 6 Blue Charm, and had not been fishing for very long when I detected a salmon rising to it out of the depths of that gin-clear water. At the last moment it shied away and despite further casts showed no more interest. Following my basic tactics I changed to a heavier dressed No. 6, whereupon two salmon moved out of their lies but made no attempt to take. Further fishing seemed useless for the moment so I sat down to rest the pool for a brief spell. I really did not have a clue what to do next. Eventually I put on a No. 8 Blue Charm and cast again over the lie. A fish promptly came for it boldly; but I felt nothing more than the slightest touch as my fly swung free. After a further five minutes I tried again with a No. 10, but from then on no fish would look at anything I put over it. It was time to move to another pool.

Down at the next one I could again see the fish plainly in their lies; but although the No. 10 was cast most carefully over them I could get no response whatever. One of the fish was head-and-tailing very persistently, but it showed not the slightest response to my fly and despite further fly changes I could do nothing there. At the tail of the pool, though, the water

Summer on the Spey at Castle Grant.

looked quite interesting and, although I could not see any fish due to water turbulence, I reckoned it was worth a cast. By this time I was back with a lightly dressed No. 8, which I cast across the pool to cover the most likely looking water. The fly was halfway across when I felt a pull. The fly was left free. Then came another pull, but the fly was still swinging round. At the end of the swing, and just as I was about to retrieve, came the third pull. This time the fish was hooked. 'At last', I thought. 'I've got one.' It fought with all the dash and verve of a little game fish, leaping and twisting in the gin-clear water; and before thirty seconds had elapsed it threw the hook, leaving me to conduct a mental inquest into what had gone wrong. A little reflection convinced me that it was no use fishing that pool any more; so I went down to the next pool and had much the same result as I had achieved over the first.

By this time the sun was up, and it was not long before the best chance of the day had faded until the onset of dusk. In the three days I fished that water I rose or hooked thirty fish. I played one gallant creature, well over 20lbs, for more than twenty minutes before it gained its freedom. Another was tailed and on the bank before it slipped from my grasp and back into the water as the fly fell out of its mouth. Yet another ran me down two pools before it, too, regained its freedom; and one unlucky, solitary 7lb fish was the only one I knocked on the head to take home. Some of the fish merely boiled at my fly; others gave it a cheeky pull and some stayed on for varying periods. Doubtless the pundits would tell me that I should have fed line to the fish or, alternatively, that I should have been quicker on the strike. I don't *know* – and I suspect that they would not *know*, despite firm personal convictions! Some would tell me that the fly was the wrong pattern; or that my choice of size was all to blame. If this were so, then it is my greatest regret that they were not there at the time to show me how to do it . . .

During July 1969 I had an opportunity of a return visit to the Awe. The river was lower than I had ever seen it. I was informed that since the hydro-electric board had started regular operations, the river was now kept at a constant level. While it seemed to hold a good head of fish, they were all running grilse. The main salmon lies seemed untenanted and the only fish being caught were being taken from the tails of pools where they tarried awhile before continuing their upstream migration. It was difficult fishing during the heat of the day, so the bulk of sport was confined to the early mornings and late evenings.

Days with the floating-line fly are not always as tantalising as the ones I have described. Anyone fortunate enough to be on some of the middle beats of the Dee, Spey or Tweed during the month of May can make this style of fishing seem like child's play. At that time of year, and in good conditions, the fish are not greatly concerned whether the fly is a lightly dressed No. 6 or little more than a shaving brush. Fly selection factors are still important; but when fish are really 'on' the floating-line fly, the angler

Ed Zern, the Fishing Editor of American Field & Stream *magazine, with a salmon from the Upper Hendersyde water of the Tweed.*

who can make a reasonable selection, and can cast and cover the lies competently, is generally assured of some sport. We cannot, however, all be on such classic beats at the peak of the season. We have to make do with what is available. Many rivers during this peak floating-line month may still be waiting for their first runs of the season. Over on the Lune we had a theory that if the fish were not there in March, there would be little of consequence until the first floods of July; a time when the peak of the floating-line season has passed. Although May sees the prime time of the season for this method on the classic rivers, it does not mean that there will not be many other months when conditions will be good, even if only for short periods. September is frequently good, but is spoilt by the fact that most salmon are well past their best at this time of the year. They are full of eggs and milt, and colouring up considerably. Of course, there may well be some fresh fish entering the river all the time; and anyone who catches a fresh-run Tweed salmon at the back end of October or November will marvel at its lovely silver colouring.

As I have commented earlier, however, August is a notoriously difficult month, but is frequently a time when we get heavy rains and good runs of grilse and salmon into our rivers. Ideal floating-line conditions may only come for a precise and short period as the river fines off and before it gets too low – or, worse still, there is another rise in the water. An unsettled river is about the most difficult to fish. I have frequently timed a visit to the river to coincide with good floating-line conditions, only to find that overnight rain has thwarted me.

One such occasion which comes to mind was when I planned to take a guest over to the Newton water of the Lune. The river was enjoying one of its best seasons for many years. The pools were full of fish and a three-foot rise, two days previously, had brought the river into fine trim. 'With anything like luck', I told my friend, 'it should be right for tomorrow and you are certain to catch a fish'. During this particular season, catching fish had become the accepted rule. Back in the mid-sixties it was practically unheard of for my friends or myself to visit the river without catching something; and as I drove the winding miles to Lunesdale I was full of optimism. On arrival I was due for a shock. A thunderstorm had hit the valley the previous evening and the river was four feet above normal height, with most of the good lies unfishable. Conditions were such that, normally, I would not have bothered to put up a rod. But my guest, who had done only a little salmon fishing before, was anxious to make the best of a bad job. Who was I to dampen his spirits and tell him it was useless? So, suggesting that he spun with a large Toby spoon, I left him to his endeavours.

We fished all morning without an offer, slinging out our Toby spoons in the faint hope that something would hang on. By lunch-time I was despondent and decided to try for sea trout on a small fly and the floating line. When our water was slightly coloured, the sea trout would often take a fly during the daytime; and I felt that fishing the quiet tails and slack corners would offer the best chance. But, after an hour of abortive fishing, I was soon back to slinging the ironmongery around. Coming to the tail of a pool, I was startled to see a salmon do a head-and-tail rise within a few feet of the bank. Within seconds it rose again and I quickly dropped the bait rod and grabbed the sea trout rod. A short cast, and the small Invicta I had on for the sea trout was floating over it. Up from the depths it came, like a fat, chalk-stream trout rising to a lightly placed dun, with a perfect head-and-tail rise. Then followed the awful suspense until the pull; and suddenly it was on, fighting for its life in the turbulent water. By judicious walking up I managed to contain the fish within the pool. Any thoughts of beaching it, as I do with most of my fish nowadays, were out of the question since I was having a full-time job keeping it from going over the lip of the pool. With such slender tackle, I would probably have had to say goodbye to my quarry had it taken me downstream. Eventually it began to tire; and I was pleased to accept my friend's gaff so that in double-quick time there was a nice 10-pounder on the bank.

On reflection, that was one of the most satisfying fish I have ever caught. It was a triumph over adversity and it turned a depressing day into a victorious one. The main problem still remains unresolved, however. Why does a salmon rise to take a small fly? Why did *that* salmon take a small sea trout fly in flood conditions? Perhaps we shall never know the answer. Herein, for me, lies the challenge of salmon fishing.

There have been quite a few occasions when the use of the floating-line fly has, short of worming or prawning, brought me the only chance of fish. Its use on such days as the one above can be effective when conditions have appeared hopeless and, for want of something better to do, I have played about with a fly rod. There was such an occasion, many years ago, on the Association water at Grantown-on-Spey. It was during the month of May, but the water was so cold that all the locals were still spinning; and though dozens of anglers were fishing this water, there were days when no fish were being taken. When fishing a relatively strange piece of water, as that portion of the Spey was at the time, I am greatly influenced by what the locals are doing. They live on the water and know its every mood and whim: they know the lies for varying heights and the successes and failures they have had under diverse conditions throughout the years. For the first part of the week, therefore, I joined them in their spinning but met with no success.

On my last day there I pondered the problem of how I was to get a fish to take home. That there were a few in the beat was a certainty; but consistent spinning had failed to bring success. It occurred to me that it was just possible that the fish had seen too much of the spinner on that hard-fished water, and that they might respond to a change. That morning I put up a trusted cane rod, with a DT-9-F AirCel line (white this time), 10 feet of 11lb-test nylon as a leader, and a double-hooked No. 6 Thunder and Lightning. I had little confidence that this would work any miracle for me – but at least it would be a change! Had I been a resident of the area, I doubt if I would have fished at all. It was one of those days that did not inspire confidence; but I was prepared to fish for the simple reason that I had nothing better to do.

I dallied for quite some time. It was noon before I had donned my breast-waders and got up to my armpits in a favourite pool. I started casting, taking pains to present my fly neatly. Slowly, I became conscious of the fact that I was fishing with greater concentration. There was an air of expectation, even. I don't really believe in a sixth sense, but if there is such a thing I became conscious of it then. Suddenly there was a savage pull at the fly, and seconds later a salmon was thrashing on the surface of the water as my fly came back to me. When I examined it I found that the leader had fouled the fly between the double hooks while casting and, at the moment that the salmon had taken me, the fly must have been reversed. This was tragic when I had tried so hard all week for the chance of a fish. However, the salmon had meant to have that fly; and if one could take it so boldly why not another? I straightened my leader, re-tied the fly, and was soon back in the water again and covering the exact spot where the fish had taken me. I detected a lovely head-and-tail rise, with a firm pull coming a split-second later. There was no doubt about it this time. The salmon was firmly hooked and I bent the rod into it. The fish fought strongly in the rapid current; but before ten minutes had elapsed I led it down to a sandy bay and tailed it out. It was a fresh fish of 8lbs.

I sat down and gazed at my hard-earned prize. Was it the same fish that had taken the earlier fly? I shall never know. It was quite on the cards that there were other fish in the lie, so back I went and started casting again. I was getting towards the tail of the pool, and just beginning to think that I had fished the best, when I saw my line straighten and I was into another fish. It fought just as strongly as the earlier one and it took about the same time before I was able to lead my catch into the sandy bay and tail it out. It weighed 7½lbs, and a handsome brace they made. I was back at the hotel in time for lunch to learn that these were the only fish taken, so far, that day; and by the end of it they were still the only fish taken between the 50 and 80 rods fishing the water.

Many anglers claim to have a sixth sense when it comes to fishing. I don't accept this as such; but I do recall one instance when something on the verge of extra-sensory perception happened to me. I was once again on a favourite beat of the Lune and had a full quota of guests sharing the beat with me. My principal concern was to see that *they* caught fish; and I spent the bulk of my time gillieing for them and advising them how to fish the most likely places. By 4 p.m. we did not have a single fish to show for our efforts. I picked up my fly rod and started at the tail of the queue fishing down the main pool. We had done our best and all my guests were competent anglers. They had combed the water with spinners and flies.

What chance had I? I could not produce any magic; and I would be fishing over well-hammered water with little variation to offer the fish. I started casting. I don't even recall the fly I fished at the time; but it was obviously a standard pattern and may well have been one that the fish had seen on frequent occasions that day. As I came to a likely part of the pool I suddenly felt a most strange tension. It was a really uncanny experience, and the ensuing few seconds before I felt the pull of a fish cannot be described. Something had given me a prior warning of the encounter. The details of playing and landing a nice fish of 11lbs are immaterial: but, what on earth (or in heaven) gave me that brief warning that *something* was imminent? I had fished that same pool on hundreds of prior occasions without feeling the slightest expectancy. I had taken countless fish from the same lie without any evidence of fore-knowledge. It is doubtless true that one's concentration becomes more active at those 'known' taking places, but the feeling I got that afternoon was much more tense and strange than any I have ever experienced.

For the reverse of the coin, I have many times had my fly or bait taken when I was least expecting it to happen; and perhaps the most remarkable example of this was an incident when my wife took two fish under extremely difficult circumstances. At her request, we had gone over to the Lune for a couple of days to get away from things and not because conditions were promising. We arrived during the late afternoon to find the river running off a shade more quickly than I would have liked; but it was not so low that it would be impossible to fish the head of the streams. I was quick to take a fine fish of 13½lbs on the fly, while my wife was busy spinning; and at the end of the day this had been the only offer either of us had received. The following morning gave us a brilliant sun in a cloudless sky. By 10 a.m. the heat was of tropical quality. 'We haven't a hope of catching a fish today!' I groaned. 'But still, I expect you want to try?' 'Yes', my wife replied. 'I want to practise with your fly rod, so that I shall be able to cast with reasonable confidence.'

Up till then, my wife had few notches on her fishing rod, and the odd fish she had caught had been taken while spinning with a fixed-spool reel and a Toby spoon. She had yet to catch her first Lune salmon – and her first fish on fly. I made myself comfortable on the river bank and lay back in the sun in my shirt-sleeves. The curlews and oyster-catchers were circling and screeching high overhead. A flight of duck came our way and then banked quickly to the right to keep just out of shotgun range. A small dipper alighted on a rock and took in the pleasures of its environment; and just then a lazy old salmon jumped awkwardly in mid-stream.

My wife had received sufficient instruction to know the basic casting action with a fly rod and I left her to her own devices. She started at the head of the pool in her thigh waders, casting a short line with reasonable competence. I watched her fish the pool down until the water was lapping around the tops of her waders, which required her to cast that extra length of line to cover the pool properly. Women are nothing if not persistent, and for the next half-hour she almost lashed that pool into foam! Some casts went moderately well, while others fell in a heap. She stood in the same position for a further half-hour but her casting was improving slowly, even though all the salmon in that vicinity must have seen the fly for the past hour. By now, however, she was just content to cast. We both realised that there was little chance of taking a fish. The fly was prescribing the same arc for cast after cast. I was nearly asleep on the bank when I heard '*Help!*'. Thinking that my wife must have fallen in, I jumped up. Her rod tip was jerking, but I could only imagine that some small salmon parr or trout had seized the fly and given her a fright. Then the line screamed from the reel, and I was astounded to realise that she must be playing a salmon. Needless to say, I was quickly by her side and giving all the advice I could.

She played it cautiously and, despite all my entreaties to hurry things up a bit in case the fish got free, she took her own time. Some twenty to twenty-five minutes elapsed before I was able to tail it out for her – a slightly-coloured cock fish of 8lbs. She was delighted, and promptly grabbed the rod and went back to her casting over that well-hammered piece of water. Another half-hour went by then, suddenly, the same old cry, and I looked up to see the rod tip jerking again. Stupid woman! What on earth was she doing catching fish on such a hopeless day? Could she not realise that conditions were hopeless and that her constant casting should have been frightening all the fish? What right had the fish to defy the rules and take anyway? Didn't the fish realise that some clumsy woman was on the other end of the line and that it should have been sheltering from the hot sun, lying sullen and comatose behind a rock and gasping for breath?

My wife was much more confident with this second fish and played it with greater expertise. Barely ten minutes elapsed before she had it ready for tailing and I was then able to lift out another slightly-coloured fish of 10lbs. I had to eat humble-pie that day. For a long time, my wife was convinced that, despite my long experience to the contrary, such a day was ideal for taking salmon on the floating-line fly.

As if to add insult to injury, another day came when conditions were just as bad. I was sweltering in my office when the telephone rang.

'Can we go to the Lune this afternoon?' asked my wife. 'It's such a nice day.'

'Nice day for sunbathing!' I answered, but reluctantly agreed to go. On our arrival on the river, the sun was shimmering over the distant hills. I put up a fly-rod for my wife and despatched her across the river to do her best. There were a few salmon in the pools, I knew; but I felt no desire to fish in the circumstances so I just lolled around in the fishing hut. An hour elapsed before I began to feel as if I was being slightly unsociable. My wife, whom I could see in the distance, was having no joy. I had better put up another rod and go and join her. Because of the low water I put on a brown floating line; and for no reason at all, tied on a small Stoat's Tail tube-fly. Then I made my way across the narrow neck of water at the head of the pool. The river was much too low for fishing anywhere but the head of the stream where a few fish were jumping lazily and awkwardly. As an act of companionship, more than a desire to fish, I started fishing the pool down behind my wife. Barely five minutes had passed before I felt the slightest resistance to the fly; thinking that a floating leaf must have fouled it, I raised my rod point slowly to find that I was attached to a salmon. I was using only a very light leader of some 7lbs test, so I had to play that fish with kid gloves before I was able to lead it into the bank and tail it out. It weighed 12½lbs, and although slightly coloured it could not have been in the river for more than a few weeks.

In more recent years most of my fly fishing experience with a double-handed rod has been limited to the Castle Grant waters of the Spey below Grantown. I fish these waters regularly in the months of April, May and June. Occasionally, I am there in July and September as well. During the earlier months the bulk of my fishing is confined to the use of the double-handed rod, but in the later months, as we shall see, I get great delight in using a light single-handed carbon fly rod. As with all other salmon fisheries, the standard of sport at Castle Grant varies with the seasons:

Dick Wilkinson salmon fishing on the Spey at Castle Grant.

1976 was the year of the big drought, when fish were hard to come by, while 1978 was one of the greatest years we have known on that beat of the Spey. I was one of many who were able to take full advantage of large stocks of fish. Many memorable occasions come to mind, but there are two which are particularly noteworthy, because both occurred on days when I lacked some enthusiasm for fishing.

Much of my spring time on the Spey is devoted to instructing novices and others in casting and tactics. Friday is my free day when, if I so desire, I might have a cast or two. By lunchtime on the first day in question I had not bothered to wet a line. It was during a period of the season when both spinning and fly fishing are permitted, and the only fish taken from our beat that morning had fallen to one of the spinning fraternity. Frankly, I had little enthusiasm to fish, but our redoubtable gillie on No. 3 Castle Grant, George Smith, had reserved the right bank of the March pool for me, in case.

After lunch I rather reluctantly allowed George to persuade me to have a cast or two. I donned my breast-waders, collected my ever-faithful 15-foot 'Walker' fly rod, a box of flies and a spool of 13lbs test monofilament. In rather leisurely fashion I rowed the boat across the river and ambled down to the pool. To give George his due, the pool seemed at an ideal height. It was not long before I had waded in and was double-Spey-casting my line over the head of the run. I had on my usual long leader and heavily dressed No. 6 Monro Killer. Only slowly did I lengthen my casts and I was just about to leave the neck to circumnavigate a deep hole, when my line tightened and I was playing a fish. Wading out to the bank, I was just about to come to terms with my catch when it broke the surface, shook its head, and the fly came free. Nowadays, I accept such losses quite philosophically and I moved back into the stream to start casting again.

Within a few more minutes I was playing fish number two. This fought well in the strong water at the head of the pool and a few minutes went by before I could beach a nice, fresh fish of 8lbs. By this time I was beginning to get the bit between my teeth, and I was soon back in the water easing out another cast. Then, in the short period between 2.30 p.m. and 4 p.m. (a no-account time in some anglers' views) I was to land another three salmon, lose one more and have four pulls which failed to connect: ten offers to my fly in a stretch of water less than fifty yards long, and on an afternoon when I would not have rated my chances very highly. Who is there who will now tell me that, under such circumstances, the well-fished fly is not superior to spinning techniques?

A year later, on another spare Friday afternoon, I was on the No. 2 beat of the Castle Grant water where that expert Spey-caster, Eric Robb, is the gillie. Most of the best pools were occupied by guests, but Eric had kept the left bank of Polchrain free just in case I wanted to fish. With a reluctance similar to that of the previous occasion, I allowed myself to be persuaded to try. I motored down to Polchrain from the fishing hut and left my car at the head of the pool. My tackle was much the same as it always is during spring on the Spey and I had barely made my first cast before I was into a nice little fish. Once again I was fishing during that mid-afternoon period when some of my guests had retired for a nap. Of course, it has to be admitted that it is not always the best period of a May day, but I began to get hopeful and by the time I had reached the tail of the pool, at around 4.30 that afternoon, I had hooked and landed all four fish which had attacked my fly. Walking back upstream to my car with my burden of four fish, I was quickly accosted by a friend on the other bank with a shout of 'Why don't you go down it again?' Frankly, I could not think of an instant and adequate answer, but just replied, 'Surely four's enough?'!

These incidents, then, pose some of the mysteries of salmon fishing and to my mind they emphasise the fancy that, under the most difficult conditions, the small fly on a floating line will sometimes save an otherwise hopeless day – a day when other lures and baits might not stand much chance. The fly on the floating line is also one of the most pleasant ways of taking salmon and has earned for itself a prime place in our sport.

We have to thank North American anglers for the continued trend towards the use of short, single-handed rods for salmon fly fishing. Doubtless there is also the influence of the many reservoir anglers who take up salmon fishing. On many occasions now I take great delight in using a single-handed rod for salmon. My choice used to be governed entirely by the time of year, but nowadays I am influenced more by the height of the water. And, if there has been a poor snowfall on the Cairngorm mountains and little consequent rain to hold the river well up, then I might be using a single-handed rod on the Spey by mid-May.

The main drawback with this method is that it can involve tedious casting and limit the angler's potential 'water command'. But, with a sinking shooting-head and the same type of backing we examined in the chapter on double-handed sunk-line fishing, it is quite possible to make some lengthy casts with only a 10-foot or an 11-foot rod. The use of carbon as a rod-making material has not only revolutionised double-handed casting and fishing, it has brought great benefit to the single-handed fisherman. My choice of rods varies according to whim and fancy: most times I would opt for the 10½-foot salmon and sea trout carbon rod by Bruce and Walker Limited. Although this is a fairly powerful rod and may be found a little too strong for general use, it is ideal for fishing the sinking shooting-head. There may be some advantage in utilising the stillwater angler's technique of double-haul casting. When done competently, and particularly under exacting tournament conditions, it is possible to propel the fly to a distance of 50 yards or more. Most anglers would happily settle for 25 or 30 yards, which is well within the capability of this equipment. Of course, it is essential to be able to wade the stream and to use some ingenuity in collecting the hand-held coils of backing line so that they do not float off downstream when making a new cast. Although I have never tried a line tray, I have heard that they are very successful. I merely collect the backing line with my left hand in loose coils and then release them as I make the final fore-cast with my right hand. If the angler merely pulls the backing line on to the water, there will be severe limitations on the amount which may be shot. The adhesion of the water and the consequent downstream belly of the line will restrict its ultimate flow through the rod rings and is not advised.

Much the same tactics apply to single-handed fishing as they do to the use of the double-handed rod. Fly presentation requirements are exactly the same, and the choice of fly is decided by the same considerations as those we have examined in earlier chapters. In fact, apart from the extra joy I get from hooking a fish on a single-handed rod and then playing it and beaching it unaided, I would probably find the double-handed rod more appropriate.

Grace Oglesby fishes the fly single-handed on the River Lune at Newton, Lancashire.

Frankly, it is in the use of floating line with a light single-handed rod that I get most fishing pleasure. While the longer, double-handed rods give excellent water command, their use frequently involves necessarily thicker and heavier lines. In a normal water height in springtime I don't think that line size matters one jot to the fish – but I do feel that under low water conditions there may be something in the contention that a thick, heavy line can disturb the water. Even then, when used in competent hands and with a long leader, I am not sure that water disturbance is a meaningful threat. Of course, the use of strong tackle, such as a 15-foot rod and a No. 11 line does impose limitations on the strength and, therefore, the thickness of the leader you can use. On my double-handed rod I would not feel happy with much less than a 10lb-test leader, but would feel perfectly at home with only a 6lb-test leader on my single-handed rod. Although I have never been fully convinced of the importance of a fine leader for salmon fishing, it may be that, in very low water, a thick leader inhibits fish from taking.

My present fancy for a single-handed rod and floating line involves the use of the 10-foot 'Light Line' carbon rod by Bruce and Walker. I suspect that the manufacturers would be slightly horrified at my suggestion that this rod may be used for salmon fishing and I have to concede that it was not designed with this purpose in mind. Essentially, it is a delightful trout rod, but I have now caught too many salmon on it to discard it lightly as an excellent tool for that purpose. Frankly, until something new and brighter than white comes on the market, it would be the one rod I would choose to keep in the unlikely event that a one-rod restriction was imposed upon me. Naturally, I would not be able to do any great Spey casts with it, nor would I get the desirable degree of water command required at specific times. But I would be able to use it for all other floating-line situations and for the trout on my north-country streams.

My usual line for this rod is either a forward-taper No. 6 or No. 7. And, as I am not likely to be using very large flies, a leader of 6 or 7lbs test will do all that is required. Usually I make the leader quite a bit longer than the rod. Here it is important to attach the leader to the line with a nail knot or some other such junction which will enable the leader to be passed through the rod rings when beaching a fish. There must be no restriction by the knot or it may be that, at the very last moment of play, the fish will break the leader and gain its freedom.

Normal floating-line techniques are employed as they would be in double-handed fishing. The lower water will permit the angler to wade well out and, on all but the very big rivers, a cast may be made of adequate distance. It is not quite so easy to mend the line with a single-handed rod as it is with a double-hander, but I have noted few occasions when such tackle has proved hopelessly inadequate. With this technique I rarely use flies larger than size 8 and have come to discover that the use of 10s and 12s may sometimes hook fish which show little interest in larger flies. The main snag with small, single-hooked flies lies not in their inability to be of interest to the fish, but in the conclusion of a successful encounter, i.e. without the fish getting free. When the fish are taking properly the small fly will get as good a hook-hold as any other, but when they are merely 'nebbing' there is a grave danger that they can merely pull the fly without getting hooked. All too frequently I have heard of fish rising to flies smaller than size 12 – even to 16s – but when I have enquired how many of these fish were successfully brought to the bank, there has been a distinct reluctance to relate much more of the story. For really small flies the angler is well advised to use doubles or trebles.

Where the small fly does come into its own is under mid-summer conditions when the bulk of the anglers are giving the main pools a daily hammering and when the stock of fish have seen almost every fly in the catalogues. Thick lines and leaders sizzle out across the water and the now comparatively large No. 6 and No. 8 flies look exactly what they are – salmon flies. Fish become so disinterested that they will even jump over the angler's line and it becomes a nightmare task to know what to do to induce a take. As far as was possible I would seek to avoid the well-hammered water. I would opt for an unfished portion of water which might, at the most, hold only one or two fish. I would fish there with my single-handed rod and small flies in the hope that the salmon had been there for some time and had been completely unmolested by other anglers. I would wade with extreme caution. I would cast with the same delicacy I would use in dry-fly fishing for trout. I might take only one fish for a hard day's work; but it could be one more fish than the rest of the anglers would take between them!

Although I have commented on the question of feeding slack line to fish at the moment of the take and have stated my views that it is unnecessary, there are a lot of devotees of the slack-line technique. Every spring you see them with their double-handed rods and a large loop of line near the reel. At the moment of the take they let this line slide away, and possibly catch fish this way; but I have never seen a single-handed salmon fisherman or a spin fisherman adopt the same technique. I myself rely on the large amount of line sagging from the rod point to act as the main buffer. Couple this with the slender action of a light single-handed rod and you have an additional buffer to cushion the take in this style of fishing. Most times when I hook a salmon on a single-handed rod I am conscious of nothing more than the rod whipping into a tight bow as the fish hooks itself. For the life of me, I fail to see any reason for feeding slack line. Naturally, fish are lost on the single-handed rod just the same as they are with other types of tackle. But such losses are not adequately explained by failure to feed slack line at the moment of the take: or, for that matter, by any other apparent shortcomings.

I must emphasise, however, that to be at full potential with salmon fly fishing, the single-handed rod will never replace a stout double-hander which can cast a long line with ease. I shall have more comments to make about casting and carbon rods in a later chapter, but for now let us examine one or two occasions when I have had wonderful sport on the single-handed fly rod.

Some of my most memorable salmon catches with a single-handed rod have occurred when I have been wet-fly fishing for trout. On the Spey in April and May, with a full quota of guests on the water, there is often little room for me to fish. Sometimes, when fishing for salmon seems a fairly pointless exercise, I assemble my trout rod and go after some of the wonderful brown trout which are known to inhabit the river. Just occasionally, during late April and May, I may get a bonus sea trout, but now and again I also hook a salmon.

The most memorable occasion came during the spring of 1981. The river had been maintained very low by a lack of adequate snow in the Cairngorms and an almost complete absence of worthwhile rainfall. Salmon were scarce and I had a full complement of rods doing their best on the No.3 Castle Grant beat. Arriving at the beat one lunch-time, I was delighted to note that a big hatch of grannom was taking place and that the river was covered with rising trout. Quickly I assembled my 10-foot Light Line rod with a No.6 line and a 4½lb-test wet-fly leader. I tied on those three north-country favourite wet flies, Partridge and Orange, Waterhen

Sir William Gordon Cumming playing a salmon on Pollowick, on the River Spey at Castle Grant.

Bloa and Snipe and Purple. Frankly I cannot recall in which order they festooned my leader, but it was not long before I was essaying my first cast into the rough stream at the tail of Pollowick. Within minutes a trout was in play and was successfully brought to the bank. Minutes later number two was in play and landed; but my next cast produced a more solid tug and I began to realise that I might be attached to one of the best brown trout the Spey can produce. The minutes ticked by as my fish plunged into the strong current. My little rod bucked and heaved as the fly line disappeared and went on to the frail backing. Only very slowly did it occur to me that I might, after all, be playing a salmon – and it was not until it gave a resounding leap that I knew for certain that a salmon of about 7lbs was on the end of my line.

The contest continued for quite some time, with not a few hair-raising moments. Only slowly was I able to work the fish down into quieter water and only as slowly did my companion, Alastair Perry, realise that I might need some help. It was then that I began to ponder on the possibilities of which fly the fish had taken. If it was the tail fly then I might just succeed in getting the fish to the bank without the other two flies fouling up on some obstruction and causing a break. But, if it was one of the droppers, anything could happen.

By some miracle the fish stayed attached to the minute No.16 fly and when I finally got the fish to the side, where Alastair was able to tail it out, we were to note that the fish had, in fact, taken one of the droppers – but it was as firmly hooked as any salmon I have caught, and the tiny fly had to be prized out with pliers. There at my feet was a handsome fresh salmon of 7½lbs. The only other fish I heard of taken that day was a similar-sized one from the Association water. It had fallen for a 2½-inch Devon Minnow. So if there is a moral pointing towards correct lure selection in all this, it eludes me!

Although I have now caught scores of fish on a light single-handed rod, there is another occasion of note when the method finally won me over as a good fish-catching method in its own right. It was back in the mid-seventies and at a time when Bruce and Walker were making the early prototype carbon rods. They sent me a 10-foot single-handed sea trout rod for testing and, as I was just about to leave for a July week on the Spey, I offered to give it a good trial for sea trout. Most people know the Spey only as a prime salmon river, but it is also possibly the finest sea trout river in the kingdom. Much of my June and July time on the river is, in fact, spent seeking sea trout, and I reckoned that the new carbon prototype would prove an ideal tool to ensure their capture. Daytime fishing for salmon proved to be a none-too-profitable exercise, so on the first evening following my arrival I made ready with the new rod and a team of two sea trout flies.

Waiting for the sun to set, it was nearly 10.30 p.m. before I deemed it sufficiently dark to have a cast. I was fishing the tail of a pool known as

Dunbar and had not been casting for very many minutes when there was a heavy pull and my rod arched over into a tight bow. Almost instantly I knew that I had hooked a good salmon. It thrashed about in the tail of the pool and then with one headlong run set off for the March pool below. Stumbling around in the semi-darkness is not my idea of great sport, but I managed to follow the fish and after quite a time worked it into the bank and tailed it out: a fat fish of 14lbs. Slowly I trudged back to where I had started, but by the time I got fishing again the rise of sea trout had finished and that was that. This little incident might not have been noteworthy but for what followed. Every night throughout that week I was on parade at 10.30 p.m. to try to catch a sea trout on the prototype rod. And every night the first and only fish I caught was a salmon.

Normally during the summer months I fish with a salmon fly on the tail and a sea trout fly on the dropper. Frankly, I doubt if the fish are very concerned about my careful discrimination, for I have taken both salmon and sea trout on flies intended for the other species. One cast during a memorable evening in July got me a salmon on the tail fly and a sea trout on the dropper. In general such a situation would result in a break, but somehow I was lucky – and I remembered the cardinal rule of netting the tail fish first. On another occasion I got a salmon on the tail fly and a bat on the dropper. The salmon proved quite docile when I finally landed them both, but the bat bit me.

There have been other notable occasions when the single-handed rod has brought me good sport, but I must emphasise, yet again, that it can never replace the longer, double-handed rod for early season fly-fishing or fully compete with that type of rod's great capability in terms of water command.

Since writing the first edition of *Salmon* it has been my good fortune to fish on more of the classic beats of the Spey and it has become my favourite river. It was not until 1968 that I took over from the late Captain T. L. Edwards as chief instructor on the angling courses at Grantown. Following this, and through the courtesy of the Strathspey Estates, much of their water has occasionally been made available to myself and members of the courses. I have been able to fish these waters during the peak season in April and May and have also had opportunities of fishing there in June, July and September – so often a difficult time anywhere. The result is that I now spend nigh on three months of the year in Strathspey, and I am just beginning to learn the water.

On the question of spinning and fly fishing in marginal conditions I have had to modify my opinion somewhat. Most of our classic rivers are now subjected to higher fishing pressure than ever before. Even the best beats of the Spey are fished every day and every week, Sundays excepted. The fish get little respite from enthusiastic anglers, and as soon as one party are packing up after their week the new influx arrives full of their own brand of dedication. Beats are spun and fly-fished according to the preferences or competence of the anglers fishing them. But on the Castle Grant water at least there is now a fly-only rule which comes into effect on 1 May. Fish were caught by the other preference methods and, although it may sound slightly pompous, I suspect that more were caught by accident than design.

During May 1973 the Spey was maintained very low. Sharp snowstorms during the early part of the month caused a drop in water temperature and the bulk of the anglers were content to spin. At the end of a hard day instructing, I motored down to the No. 2 Castle Grant beat to see how the anglers were coping. The gillie on this beat is a talented young man by the name of Eric Robb. Not only is he a very competent and genial gillie, he is also one of the finest Spey-casters I have ever seen. Talking over the problems of the day with him, he complained bitterly that too many anglers were spinning – suggesting that if more anglers would fish a fly on the floating line, they would do better. Under the prevailing weather and water conditions at that time I found some difficulty in fully agreeing with him, and we continued to argue the point at some length. As an instance of his conviction, however, he suggested that if I got into my breast-waders and waded out into the tail of the Manse pool – which incidentally had not been fished that day – I would take a fish on the fly. I must confess that I did not share his optimism or enthusiasm, but suggested to him that he show me how to do it. Without a second bidding he donned his waders and got into the pool. His first casts took the fly over very sluggish water, but he continued to wade down quietly between each cast and was slowly

Beaching a salmon on the Spey at Castle Grant.

getting near to the tail of the pool where the current would give a slightly increased pace to the fly. He was throwing a very long line and his Spey casting was a delight to watch. At about his tenth cast, however, he made a comment that the pace of the fly was just about right and the words were barely out of his mouth before I saw the line tighten and he was fast into an 11lb fish which was eventually safely landed.

On the following afternoon I again went down to see how the anglers were doing. The weather was even colder and not a single fish had been taken that day. Eric was there, however, and in such a confident mood that I nearly had a five-pound bet with him that he could not repeat his performance of the previous day. Most certainly I had no inclination to fish myself and I urged him to have another try. A strong, cold wind hampered his casting, but it was not long before he had a good length of line out and was covering another likely lie in the main Manse pool.

The late Captain T. L. Edwards (seated) instructs a client at Grantown on Spey.

Within a few more minutes I saw his line tighten, but that was all – and when we examined the fly we saw the problem. The wind had caused the treble-hooked fly to loop over the end of the leader so that the fly was swimming in reverse; had he been more fortunate, he could, once again, have proved me quite wrong in my own assessment.

Talking the matter over at some length, I had the sense to realise that I was talking with a man who is not only a very competent angler, but one who has the distinct advantage of knowing almost every rock in his beat. He has that indefinable ability to assess all the factors and make an immediate tactical appreciation of the situation. He could, at any time during a day, take a client's rod to try and catch a fish for him, but he has that rare talent of knowing when it pays to fish hard and when it seems preferable to sit and watch the others. He is like many other expert gillies on the Spey, as far as practical fishing is concerned once April has passed:

as with the biblical lilies of the field – if you will forgive my pun – they toil not neither do they spin!

The general feeling among many Spey gillies is that once April is over, unless there is exceptional high water, fly fishing will not only offer the best chance of fish but it will also be less disturbing to the water. The fish are beginning to settle into lies following their long migration. In their book, the word 'spin' under these circumstances is classed with many other four-letter words: it is obscene. Spinning, they say, in comparatively low water, even though it may be cold, will not only put fish off the take, but it will also create upstream or downstream migrations of fish who seek little more than some respite from the ironmongery that flashes round them and intimidates them. If, therefore, the gillies can find a piece of water which has not been spun to a foam they feel very confident that, at a time of their own choosing, they will have every chance of taking fish on the fly.

I confess that in the light of this experience I have had some fresh thoughts on fly fishing and spinning. However, I am not going to give you the satisfaction of a complete contradiction of what I have said before, for I have successfully fly-fished in the wake of spin fishermen too many times not to see the full value of doing so. The technique can frequently be used to advantage on rivers that are not hard-fished. Conditions may be ideal for fly fishing, but a slight rise in the water brings anglers to the river when it may not have been fished at all for several days or weeks previously. The extra water may induce some anglers to start with a spinning rod, and it is then that I like to fish the fly behind them. If the fish are fresh-run, which well they may be after a slight rise, then the spinner may take a few, but it will not be long before the fly will be in with a better chance as water levels fall. Following that it may be that prolonged spinning will do more harm than good.

As a further example of the humiliation I suffered on the Spey during 1973, let me cite another instance when I was fishing with one of the world's most eminent anglers. It was mid-May, the scene was Pollowick, and my companion was none other than Al McClane. Now Pollowick is one of those classic Spey pools which not only holds a vast number of fish throughout the season, but has several good taking lies – two factors not always compatible. It joins with the Dunbar and March pools to form the bottom beat of the Castle Grant water. For many years this portion of the beat was retained by the late Countess of Seafield for her own private guests, but it is now let by the Strathspey Estates. If I had to choose one pool on the Spey as a favourite, I think it would be Pollowick, but it is not the most challenging I have ever fished and water temperatures have to reach a critical level before fish will take in the main stream.

To introduce Al McClane fully would require more words than I can muster. First as Fishing Editor and later as Executive Editor of top American magazine *Field and Stream*, he has become a legend in the US.

Not only has he fished his native country from coast to coast, but he has fished all over the world. Rumour has it that he accepted an invitation to fish in China as a guest of Mao Tse Tung – but I digress. He arrived at Pollowick one very cold May morning with nothing more than a single-handed rod and a pair of light thigh waders. Frankly I did not rate his chances too highly and was quick to tell him so, but I offered to lend him a spinning rod and a pair of breast waders so that he might shorten the odds. The spinning rod was refused with scorn and I was politely told that anyone who would spin would also steal. There was some temptation to take the waders, but eventually he settled for his own and made ready with his tackle. The rod was some $8\frac{1}{2}$ feet in length, carrying a No. 9 forward-taper line with a sinking tip, and his chosen fly was a No. 6 Jock Scott. Not knowing the pool at all and being confined to thigh waders, he was most insistent that I fish it down ahead of him so that he could see where I waded and thus follow as best he could. Grabbing my rod with a treble-hooked fly of my own tying, I quickly decided that the water was too cold for the head of the stream and I waded out into a portion of the pool known as Green Bank. Some long casts were required to cover the pool adequately, but I fished it down carefully, pausing frequently to see how Al was coping. His casting was impeccable, but was made tedious by the fact that he had to throw such a long line that the hand-lining of the backing took a long time. Several loops of hand-held backing had to be shot in the forward cast, some loops were held between his fingers and others between his teeth, but the final and important cast went out like a bullet.

As I came to the tail of the pool without so much as an offer, I glanced upstream again to watch Al's fly as it swung round to within a few yards of where I was deep-wading. Quite suddenly the water bulged and I saw Al's line and rod tighten at the same moment. The fish fought well on that short rod but it was not long before he hand-tailed a nice fish of 9lbs. I was really too delighted to be humiliated, but he had virtually taken that fish out of my pocket.

During the exceptionally low waters of 1972 and 1973 on the Spey, therefore, I added to my experience. I did catch my own share of fish, but the important thing was that I retained an open mind so that modified tactics could be absorbed and exploited.

We have seen that the fly, fished in its varying forms, is quite capable of taking fish throughout a season. We have examined the conditions for the big sunk-fly and the small, sparsely-dressed fly on the floating line. We have studied situations when a medium-sized fly may occasionally be fished to advantage on a floating line with a sinking tip: or even smaller or larger flies be fished on a sunk-line in the middle of the floating-line season. There is no end to the permutations in which the all-round fly-fisherman may indulge.

Over recent years, however, I have come to suspect that the number of times when conditions are *perfect* for floating-line fishing are not so frequent as some writers would have us believe. Disease in our rivers (commented on in a later chapter) affects taking habits. Land drainage and mild forms of pollution have combined to make some of our rivers less pleasant for the salmon to live in than in days gone by. Fish do not always respond in the same way as they did, even ten years ago. Doubtless, also, fish change their fickle habits slightly from season to season, and from river to river. I can recall seasons when specific lures were more productive than others. Current experience indicates, however, that there are few occasions when taking fish cannot be caught with some form of fly. But to work on the old contention that once the water temperature has reached 48 degrees the only satisfactory method is to use the traditional floating-line tactics might severely limit the angler's repertoire.

On the question of sub-surface activity from salmon, there are many anglers who think that the sight of a head-and-tail rise is sufficient inducement to persist with the floating-line fly. I refer, of course, to the lazy, rolling motion that a settled salmon sometimes makes, rather like an aldermanic trout sipping in a floating dun. I do not refer to the bold forward leap, so characteristic of a running fish; nor to the awkward, backward splash which is so typical of a resident fish that has been chivvied out of its lie; nor to the move of a kelt making its tedious way downstream. Surface-moving action of the salmon tells us something, if not very much; but the persistent head-and-tailer is worthy of attention, particularly if it moves in the same lie a number of times. Take care to

A salmon jumping at Sleights Weir on the Yorkshire Esk.

ensure that the fish has not been disturbed by your presence, since many a salmon that has been pushed out of its lie by the angler who has waded too deeply will head-and-tail its way down a pool; and so, at times, will a running salmon move in an upstream direction. Often, head-and-tailers at the top or bottom of a pool are also running fish. It is interesting, too, to note the behaviour of running fish at the foot of a weir. Invariably they do a head-and-tail rise before starting their leap, as though they are taking a sneaking look at the obstacle before tackling it in earnest.

As a general rule, then, I would prefer to see trifling surface activity by the fish rather than too much. Hectic leaping usually indicates a pool with too many fish in it for their individual comfort. In such conditions the salmon are often preoccupied with maintaining a comfortable lie, and constantly chivvy each other for the best position. Small wonder that they pay little attention to our offerings when they are so occupied. Under such conditions I have frequently watched them deliberately back away from an approaching fly or bait.

Perhaps the best information that may be gleaned from the regular head-and-tail riser is that it could be the sole resident of its current lie; and, as such, may well defend it against any and all intruders – even a small No. 10 fly or a thumping great spinning lure flashing past its nose. There can be no hard-and-fast rule; but tradition dies hard and, in general, the angler is better advised to follow basic rules and approach such a fish with the fly.

To sum up, therefore, we have examined the need for varying types of tackle for adequate cover during a season's fly-fishing. In the early, and often bitter, months of the season, a heavy fly rod is needed with a good sinking line and varying weights of flies in excess of 2 inches long. Colours may range from a garish yellow to subdued brown or black – depending on water height, temperature and clarity. The fly will be required to get down to the fish; certainly until the water warms to the mid-40s. Then will come a transition period; and then a time when, as the water temperature approaches 50 degrees, the floating line may be effective. This is a good time to experiment with fly sizes, for the fish are quite likely to show some indication of the wide range of sizes they are prepared to accept. By the time May comes, however, it may be safe to assume that a No. 6 fly will be the basic size with patterns such as Blue Charm, Thunder and Lightning, Logie and Stoat's Tail all worth trying.

Do not become wedded to this style of fishing for the remainder of the season; and be ever watchful for those marginal conditions when the use of a sinking-tip line, or a fully-sunk line, will save an otherwise blank day.

There is a common belief among many salmon anglers, particularly those who lean to the solunar theory – which relates to the moon's and sun's phases and the tides – that there are regular and predictable times when fish will take best. My good friend, Reg Righyni, speculated upon this topic in his book, *Salmon Taking Times*, when he claimed that there was some measure of predictability about that most unpredictable fish. The salmon, as we have noted, does not feed in fresh water, so Righyni had a doubly difficult task in attempting to equate his theories with any logical taking or feeding pattern. When we encounter fish which do feed it is a simpler task to examine their principal diet and establish the season or the times of day when they are likely to take food. Then at the appropriate moment we may sally forth, armed with the right bait or lure, with a modicum of confidence.

Some of my early knowledge of fish feeding habits was gleaned from the doubtful pastime of watching goldfish in a bowl. Of course, there are several factors which prevent satisfactory conclusions being drawn. Goldfish have their food delivered daily. The water temperature, and therefore their rate of digestion and metabolism, is usually much higher than that found outdoors in the natural state. And, if properly tended, they never get hungry. Wild birds which come to an outside feeding table give a slightly better clue to favourite feeding times, and it is interesting to watch cattle in a field. This, you may think, has little to do with fish behaviour. Also, as we do not live in an aquatic environment, we may find that full establishment of piscatorial activity is more difficult to ascertain than other natural phenomena. Fish can only feed when there is food available and there are quite a few occasions when they might be on short rations. Most times the habits of fish which feed are well known and documented. But the best angler is always the one who can tune in to nature and develop the stealth and cunning of the hunter.

Trout which rise to a natural fly are about the easiest of our fish with which we may come to terms. We see the flies hatch and we watch trout take them. We discover specific cycles of behaviour from both the trout and the flies on which they feed. This gives us a wealth of information which can be utilised to capture trout on an artificial fly. With a diminishing resource of natural fly the trout have become more catholic in their tastes. Now, it is probably more important to be able to cast with all the skill and dexterity one can muster and merely ally these skills with stealth, than it is to be able to identify the fly species on which the trout are feeding. To be able to do both is a great advantage and adds immense interest to the sport. In this type of fishing the magic moment may be quickly determined by the sight of a rising trout. With the right approach from the angler, it only needs one cast to catch it.

*Salmon fly fishing on the Manse Pool
of the River Spey at Castle Grant. Note
the salmon jumping.*

Left: *Arthur Oglesby's fishing school at Grantown on Spey, Scotland.*

Top right: *The complete salmon spinner. Mitchell 410 and Ambassadeur 6000C reels, shown with an assortment of spoons and baits as used by Arthur Oglesby.*

Bottom right: *Some spring salmon flies used by Arthur Oglesby on the Spey in April and May.*

Top left: *An assortment of fly lines. The dark green one is a sinking line and the others are floaters.*

Bottom left: *A diseased salmon taken from the River Lune in Lancashire. It is suffering from U.D.N. (Ulcerative Dermal Necrosis).*

Top right: *The Hon Mrs Peter Shand-Kydd fishing the River Spey at Castle Grant.*

Bottom right: *The late Captain T. L. Edwards, a champion tournament caster, demonstrates the roll cast at Grantown on Spey.*

*Arthur Oglesby playing a salmon on
Loch Voshimid, Outer Hebrides.*

*Hugh Falkus playing a salmon on the
River Spey at Castle Grant.*

*Late summer salmon fishing on
the Pollowick pool of the Spey at Castle Grant.
Note the salmon leaping under the rod point.*

*Odd Haraldsen playing a salmon of 33lb on
the River Vosso at Bolstadoyri, Norway.*

*Don Oliver of York handtailing a salmon
from the River Lune.*

With salmon and sea trout, fish which do not feed in fresh water, there is a vast amount of speculation involved as to what might induce a magic moment – a time when fish will snatch at anything to come their way. Certainly I have not been fishing for fifty years without forming some ideas of when it might pay dividends to fish hard and when it seems preferable to sit and watch or go home. But to suggest that I dare predict a taking time for migratory fish with any certainty is to endow myself with greater knowledge than a mere mortal can possess. The most certain statement one can make about migratory fish is that, following the first flush of fresh water, they do not take well on a rising river. Of course, there have been notable exceptions to this rule, but they are not sufficiently frequent to induce me to carry on fishing when the river starts to 'come away'. Also there is a vast difference in behaviour between those fish which are fresh run into a river and those which have been there for some time. There are considerations, as Righyni outlined, of relative water and air temperatures; barometric pressure; humidity; acid/alkali levels in the water; tidal influences; suspended matter and its influence on water clarity; and a host of other factors. The late J. Arthur Hutton in his book, *Rod Fishing for Salmon on the Wye*, stated that the height of the water 'is the most important factor in successful salmon fishing'. But I think that Hutton would have equated this factor with a lot of other considerations to make any real sense. I do know, from personal experience, that water height was of paramount importance in fishing one particular beat of the Lune, but there had to be other influences. Meanwhile, let us confine our thoughts to salmon. Sea trout present specific differences in the manner in which they sometimes take an angler's lure and, in many instances, they offer the best chance of sport when many of us are asleep in our beds.

The salmon's prime motive for returning to the fresh water in which it was born is to satisfy the basic requirements of species regeneration. Nature has ordained that they can only feed to full requirement in a saline environment; but nature is equally demanding that, in order to reproduce, the salmon must return to fresh water where the specific gravity does not cause the eggs to float away. From a feeding aspect, as we have seen, we must consider the salmon to be a saltwater fish, but from a natural standpoint it is very much a freshwater fish. Such fish are said to be anadromous.

When trying to understand salmon behaviour in fresh water, let us not forget that as young parr they fed avidly in it, that they are very much a predatory fish and that, although they do not now take food, they have not lost the instincts of self-preservation. Let us also remember our half-sleeping cat – ever the hunter – which occasionally chases blown leaves merely to demonstrate its basic predatory nature. With these instincts borne firmly in mind, let us move on to examine some possibilities concerning fresh-run salmon in the spring.

The best time to catch salmon, provided there are any in the river, is the spring. On our classic rivers the fresh fish come in from the sea at this time. Water temperatures have great influence on their speed of movement; but so long as the rivers maintain a good height we will be fishing for fish which are continually on the move upstream. No matter what our choice of lure, spinner, fly or natural bait, we will be fishing for 'gypsies' and itinerant commercial travellers – fish which are literally here today and gone tomorrow. We hope that there will never be a moment when our beat or chosen piece of water is without some stock, but few fish will be resident in a pool for very long. On many rivers this will not happen until late May, a time when a lack of rainfall or melting snow will cause many rivers to drop back towards summer level and fish to settle into lies which they might then occupy throughout the long summer, or at least until the next flood.

Whenever fresh fish are running there is little doubt that while some come singly there are others which come in a school or shoal. Periodically they take a rest. Usually this is done in the known lies where, presumably, the fish can tarry awhile with minimum exertion against the current. The salmon might stay for little more than a few minutes or several hours and there could be a thousand and one factors to influence their choice. Your guess on this matter will be as good as mine and the *fact* is that, other than the reproductive urge, no one really *knows* what influences them to move or to stay. It is my opinion that while fish are actually running they pay little heed to the angler's lure; but that when they settle for a rest – no matter how brief that rest may be – they could be in a mood to take a lure. Most times, therefore, we cannot fully predict the running and resting pattern. Under these circumstances the angler who fishes the hardest and in the most intelligent manner will often be the one to catch the most fish. Occasionally an angler will be lucky and fish down over a small school of salmon just at the magic moment when they are taking a brief rest. This could happen at any time during a spring day and the common belief that there is a specific and predictable taking time is knocked on the head by pure logic as a start. On any day one beat might report a good catch of fish and another nil.

I used to be convinced that morning and late afternoons or evenings were the best times for catching spring fish, and that the period immediately following lunch was a waste of time. Since then, as I have already recalled, I have enjoyed two of my best-ever, short sessions of fishing in an afternoon. The fact is that we do not *know* the time of the day when fish will pause and where exactly they will do it. A pool might be unoccupied one minute and then have several fish all waiting to be caught. If the angler is not there and set on a collision course with these fish, they might well pass on to another pool or beat and another set of circumstances. Sometimes the last hour of daylight will offer a good chance of sport. Here I liken the running salmon to the proverbial commercial traveller. He goes about his business for most of the day, but as the day wanes he seeks some hostelry or residence for the night and then becomes liable to succumb to any temptations which might be forthcoming!

As J. Arthur Hutton commented, water height does have great influence on fish response. It requires long experience of one piece of water to learn all the other considerations which must be brought into the equation before the best may be gained from a fishery. These days I spend nigh on three months of every year on or in one small section of the river Spey. I know almost its every mood and whim, but I am still learning how best to exploit its full angling potential. A lot of the theories of the pundits have frequently been knocked on the head and there is no formula for successful salmon fishing that I have not, at some time, seen firmly reversed. Many of my own long-held theories have also taken their share of punishment and may I remind you yet again that any commentator on salmon fishing must be ultra-careful not to use such words as *never* and *always*. Too many times I have suggested to friends that conditions were good or bad only to have them demonstrate the opposite. Too many times I have myself fished hard in anticipation and come home empty-handed. And, just occasionally, when I have been fishing without much enthusiasm, I have made a notable catch.

Throughout the months of March, April and part of May, when spring fish are running on the Spey, I am of the firm opinion that the angler who fishes hardest, in an intelligent and skilful manner, is the one who will catch the most fish. On occasions I might just guess when conditions will be better than others. There are also obvious bad times, such as when the air turns colder than the water, when brownish foam suggests a high level of acidity, or when a nor'-east wind scuds up the Spey valley and curls the water surface into waves. But even the worst day can have its moments. They may occur following a lull in the wind, a brief but bright appearance of warm sunshine during the late afternoon or that portion of the day, just before dusk, when fish might settle up for a night in their local 'tavern'. These same fish might still be resting when the first glimmer of dawn lightens the eastern horizon. The angler can never *know* the moment at this time of the year when a fish will take.

As a further example of this I need only cite one instance of a week's fishing my wife and I had on the Tweed in March 1970. By lunchtime on the first day I had six fish and she had two – a total of eight from the beat. Despite some concentrated hard work and prior knowledge of the beat, for the remainder of that week I did not catch another fish until I quickly got two when we were within an hour of our departure for home on the Saturday afternoon. We had caught the taking fish in the little school of salmon that had come into the beat shortly before our arrival, and there were no resident newcomers of consequence to rest in our beat – while we were fishing it – until we were leaving. These then are some of the factors with which to reckon in spring salmon fishing.

I have suggested that fresh-run spring fish are easier to catch when they are running from pool to pool and resting briefly and that if we can get on to a collision course while they rest we might take one or two. However, by the time mid-May has passed the rivers often begin to shrink – not necessarily to their bare bones, but sufficiently to induce salmon to settle into lies which they might then occupy for a considerable period. In conditions of very low water the fish will literally pack into every deep hole the river might offer them. In this situation they frequently become more preoccupied with keeping station with their neighbours than in taking an angler's lure. A pool that is heavily stocked with resident fish rarely produces as good catches as those pools which are lightly stocked, until there is a rise in the water and residential conditions for the fish become more tolerable. This then may be a time when salmon fishing sorts the men from the boys.

It is, of course, reassuring to know that the pool or beat we are about to fish is holding salmon. During the spring, when the river was much higher, there may have been little evidence to betray their presence. There might be the odd thrusting leap as the fish makes on upstream, or there could be a tell-tale head-and-tail rise when the fish rests briefly in a lie.

Two salmon from the Spey at Castle Grant. One weighs 19lb, the other 9½lb – exactly half the weight of the first. Clearly the larger fish is not typical of the Spey.

When fish become settled their leaps have a different style. They thrash more on the surface and frequently jump vertically and fall back in an uncoordinated manner which might indicate little else but sheer boredom. In the well-fished pools most of them will have seen every fly or spinner in the catalogue. Except for the odd, late-running newcomer they might prove difficult to catch. Under such circumstances I am of the opinion that it can pay dividends to show the fish something you think that they will not have seen for some time. As I have commented in earlier chapters, my first preference is for a very small fly on a floating line, with as fine a leader as I dare use in the circumstances. Sometimes, where deep wading is possible, I will use a single-handed rod as described elsewhere, and will try varying tactics to speed up or slow down the movement of the fly over the lies. Occasionally, if I suspect slight acidity in the water, I will resort to a sinking line and the same monstrous fly I might use in February or March. But I try not to become wedded to one style, for seeing too much of one thing could well cause the fish to lose interest.

You must bear in mind that I am only making vague suggestions for trial. Just when you think that you have established a taking time or pattern of behaviour the fish will quickly confound you. I recall a week spent on the Spey in June 1977. A high-pressure weather system dominated Strathspey, which gave high cloud in the mornings and brilliant sunshine almost promptly at noon. My immediate reaction was to make the best of the mornings and then give the afternoons a rest. To confound my best plans, I did not get a fish to look at my fly until the high cloud rolled away and the sun shone brightly. Most of my fish that week were taken when the rest of the party were sitting down to lunch – and all this in mid-June!

Every brief rise of water in late spring must be regarded with some optimism: but it can also bring a period of high acidity from peat in the hills. This may offer only a temporary setback, and when it clears there could well have been a big migration of fish from one pool to another – with some fresh fish straight in from the sea. Many salmon will now be in new lies and, during the time they are establishing themselves in their new but temporary homes, they might take well.

An ideal late spring and summer salmon pool is one with a good head of fast water at the neck followed by a long, deep dub in which the bulk of the fish will lie. The resident fish then make odd excursions into the fast water and it is here that they are more likely to be interested in the angler's lure. Such a one is the famous Pollowick pool on the Castle Grant water of the Spey, which I know well. Most times it is almost futile to cast a lure or fly into the deep dub where several salmon may be seen jumping. Instead, it pays to fish for occasional and very brief periods in the short run at the neck. Many anglers would flog such a pool into foam, but I am of the opinion that there is nothing more off-putting for salmon than to see flies continually sweeping across a piece of water. Occasionally, there might be

For the man who has everything. David Hield plays the pipes while Hugh Falkus fishes for salmon on the River Spey.

merit in the theory that, as with my sleepy cat, you can induce a fish into attacking your fly out of sheer anger or boredom. But generally I feel that there is more value in the old saw that familiarity breeds contempt. At the time of the year under examination I will spend a minimum of time actually fishing and a great deal of time just looking at the water.

Except on spate rivers, where the angler must be ever-ready to down tools at any time of the season to take advantage of a falling river, I am of the opinion that late evening provides the most interesting time in late May or June. On a river like the Spey there is also the bonus of ample opportunities with sea trout. Usually, as I have noted, I fish with a single-handed rod, a floating line and small flies. I do not know if I am going to catch a salmon or a sea trout and I am equally pleased with either. Sometimes I catch some of each and there really is something magical about playing a good fish on light tackle in the balmy twilight of a summer evening. This, for me, is the most exciting salmon fishing.

In concluding this chapter, I would like to emphasise that I have only briefly reflected upon a few aspects of salmon fishing. But it is a fascinating sport and it only needs access to a salmon river at the right time, competent casting, and applied and intelligent industry to get them on the hook and then on the bank!

In the first edition of my book, *Salmon*, there was no comment on loch fishing. The reason for the omission was quite simple: up until the 1970s I had not done any! Over the latter half of that decade, however, I was privileged to be invited annually to visit the Outer Hebrides, there to reside in the romantic Amhuinnsuidhe Castle and fish the lochs of the North Harris Estate. Stillwater fishing was never my favourite form of angling indulgence. Partly through ignorance of the differing tactics required and partly because of my great love of flowing water, I had not previously indulged in much worthwhile stillwater fishing. But my current love affair with the Hebrides has changed all that. Although my comments will refer to specific locations, I cannot imagine that salmon fishing on other still waters varies much in principle from the tactics adopted on the lochs of Harris.

The first sight which greets the angler on arrival at Amhuinnsuidhe in July is the little saltwater bay and the small stream which flows into it. Salmon and sea trout may be seen in vast numbers as they cruise around, sensing the fresh water, and leaping at the foot of the falls. Salmon intermingle with the sea trout and a big shoal, seen on a calm day, might well look like some gigantic Loch Ness monster as it weaves its black shadow along the coastline. The fish thrusting in the freshwater outlets at this stage seem interested only in playing. The serious task of running the short, but tough, obstacle course does not begin until the ever-present rain descends in quantity and the small burns increase their tempo. Those fish which have found their 'home' water will quickly run up into the nearby lochs. But there will be others who will cruise on, apparently aimlessly, until they find theirs. As we shall see in the next chapter, it is possible, occasionally, to catch salmon in salt water. But the bulk of the angler's interest is directed to the lochs. There may be a brief period when sport may be enjoyed in the short and narrow rivers connecting the lochs with the sea, but it is of little account when compared with what might be expected from the lochs once the fish have reached these in quantity.

It would seem that the first desirable quality of a good salmon loch – apart from a good stock of fish – is comparative shallowness. The three principal lochs of the North Harris Estate, Voshimid, Scourst and Ulladale, all measure up in this respect and they have little incoming water which might induce the fish to run further on upstream. Most lochs are fed by small mountain burns and it is only in the autumn of the year, when the fish are on the threshold of spawning, that they leave them and move into these smaller burns. Thus from early July through to the end of the season there are usually good stocks of fish to be found.

It has to be borne in mind from the start that the bulk of the Hebridean lochs under examination contain more sea trout than salmon. Catch figures indicate a ratio of about six to one. With that in mind there is little wonder that one's tactics are generally directed towards the sea trout, though this is not to imply that the salmon are caught merely by accident. For most of my Hebridean fishing I use the same 10-foot Light Line carbon rod which I use for a lot of my other single-handed fishing on rivers. Sometimes, as we shall see, distinct advantage is to be gained by using a longer rod; but I work on the theory that at least ninety per cent of my time will be spent casting and less than ten per cent playing a fish. I would rather have a pleasant casting tool than one which might better command a good fish, but which might break my back during a day's fishing. Longer rods do have other tactical advantages of course, so in the final analysis the angler must settle for a compromise.

The choice of line and leader is fairly simple. A No. 6 or No. 7 line will suffice and it is then quite easy to make up a 7lb-test leader so that it takes a dropper and a tail fly. Often I put a small sea trout fly on the dropper and a small salmon fly on the tail. It pleases me to do that, but I have grave doubts that the fish know the difference. Fly patterns vary with the whims and fancies of the anglers using them. I have great fondness for the Connemara Black, the Invicta, Heckham Peckham, Grouse and Claret and the Goat's Toe, but I really don't think that the fish give so much as a tinker's cuss what the fly is, so long as it is of modest size and dressing. Size 12s seem to be my most used patterns, but I often put a No. 10 on the point for salmon and have a few 14s handy for calmer water. I tend to make my leaders longer than the accepted norm and while this can have inhibiting qualities for salmon – as I shall show later – I am sure that it helps me to catch more and bigger sea trout from the lochs.

In an earlier chapter I referred to the vexed question of line colour. Most of my fishing in the Hebrides has, in fact, been done with a white line; but in 1980 I happened to find an old green line in my tackle bag. It was a No. 7 Teflon-coated one, so worn that some of the dressing on the front taper had frayed. Sadly, for this reason, these lines have been withdrawn from the market and I have not been able to replace it. During that year, however, I enjoyed more sport with salmon and sea trout than I have done at any other time. There were days when my catches were embarrassingly higher than my companions and at the end of my stay I deemed it prudent to leave the line with my host. Of course, my catch successes then may have been due to nothing more than good luck; but it might be significant that the most successful angler of our party in 1981 was using a green line.

Practically all the fishing we do in the Hebrides is done from a boat. Most times my wife and I share a boat with its appropriate boatman or gillie. Being the perfect gentleman, I generally urge my wife to take the broad end or stern while I go into the sharp end or bow. Most fishing tactics involve the gillie rowing the boat slowly across the wind. The flies are cast out and a slow or quick retrieve is begun. Depending on the severity of the wind the boat makes slow progress across the loch and it is

Grace Oglesby playing her first stillwater salmon on Loch Voshimid, Isle of Harris, Outer Hebrides.

usually my wife who contacts the first fish of the day. During our first year at Amhuinnsuidhe I was slightly perplexed, but highly delighted, that my wife caught more fish than I did. When it happened again the following year I became slightly suspicious and suggested that over one or two days we change places in the boat. Almost miraculously my catches began to exceed hers and I then realised that it was the position of the angler in the boat which had a pronounced influence on the catch potential.

In order to come to terms with this situation, and still occupy the bow position, I found that by casting a greater distance than my wife I was able, in some measure, to keep up with her catch figures. The accompanying diagram (Fig.5) will illustrate the tactical points I raise; by making longer casts, I was able to search more water before the boat drifted on. While my wife's casts were swinging in nicely behind the boat, I was compelled to make a fresh cast before she did. The adoption of this technique has prevented me from fishing a short line in the wave and there is little doubt that, on a rough day, this is a very effective way of taking salmon. A short leader also helps, as does a long rod, since this enables the angler to 'trip' his dropper fly over the wave. It is in this situation that the entire action of a salmon taking a fly may be seen within a few feet of the boat. On rough days the fish don't seem to be concerned with such close proximity. So long as I have to share a boat and take the bow, I do not see myself being able to exercise this tactic too frequently.

As an example of these points, let me cite an instance which occurred on Loch Ulladale in July 1981. At the start of the day the gillie navigated the boat to my advantage. Within minutes I was playing a fish, and by lunchtime I had five fish to my wife's one. Then during the afternoon, on the opposite side of the loch, he manoeuvred the boat to my wife's advantage, when she caught five to my one. I am not suggesting that the odds on the bow and the stern angler will always be five to one, but it does give some clue to the disparity created.

Although I have done very little dapping, there is some merit in dapping a large fly on a blowline. Again, a long rod is an advantage, but there is no casting involved and the angler merely seeks to keep his fly well-dressed

Fig. 5 The gillie rows the boat across or into the wind. Although the heading is maintained the track made good is strongly influenced by the wind. Notice how the angler at the rear of the boat has a more commanding position than the angler at bow.

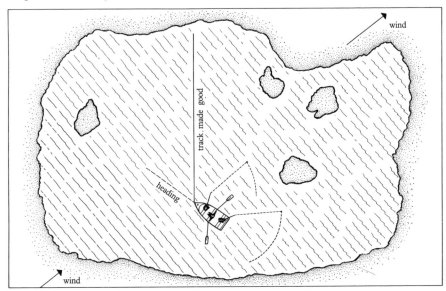

with floatant and just bobbing on the wave. In my experience there are more fish raised than hooked. Of those hooked, the bulk will turn out to be sea trout, but just occasionally a salmon will take boldly and it is very exciting to watch the slow-motion drama as the fish puts its head out of the water to take the fly. Various theories have been put forward as to how long the angler should delay before making the strike and I do not presume to know the answer.

Most of my stillwater salmon have been taken at times when I have not realised they were salmon until they were in the net. Frankly, in the circumstances under examination, I cannot differentiate between the take of a salmon and a good sea trout. A quick retrieve of the flies generally brings more response from sea trout, but I have known salmon to take when my flies have been trailing over the side while the boatman is rowing hard for a new drift. By far the bulk of my loch salmon, though, have come to flies cast quite close to the shoreline. Small islands are particularly helpful in this respect and the fish may be found in mere inches of water as they cruise round the circumference of the islands. I don't think that the pattern of the fly has much significance, but there are successful loch fishermen who swear by certain selections.

Perhaps Hebridean lochs lend themselves to this style of fishing more readily than others. Rain is plentiful throughout July and August and is usually accompanied by an appropriate wind. Only rarely are the lochs becalmed and fishing is possible throughout the summer on most days. A pneumatic cushion helps for a long day in a boat; but other than the need for some warm and very waterproof clothing it is an extremely civilised way of salmon fishing.

For those anglers who are content to sit in a boat and have the gillie row around all day, there may be some merit in trolling a lure or spinning bait. These methods are not permissible on the Hebridean lochs I have mentioned, but there are times of the season on lochs where such techniques are permitted, when a slowly trolled bait or fly might attract a dour fish. In order to fish like this with some chance of success, it is fairly important to know the likely places. Local knowledge is a great asset for there will be places which will prove more productive than others at specific times of the year. It is also important to have some knowledge of the type of lure to use and the speed and depth at which it should be fished. Frankly it is not a style of fishing which has any appeal for me. I have not indulged in it for well over twenty years and I feel that there is little point in enlarging upon the method here.

14   SALTWATER FISHING

Let me begin this short chapter with the admission that I have never caught a salmon in salt water. I have hooked one in a freshwater outlet and then played and landed it in the sea, but I have never hooked one in completely saline water. I don't believe that it is possible very often. Most times if a spinner or fly is cast towards a shoal of fish in the sea, the fish will give chase but will rarely take. Of course, it is possible for the poacher to foul-hook fish in this situation, and occasionally one becomes foul-hooked unintentionally. In my experience it is only when the fish start queueing up in a freshwater outlet that they might just succumb to a lure. Usually they are preoccupied with the prospect of negotiating the weir or fall which impedes their progress into the river or loch outfall. Doubtless there are also plentiful tidal influences, but I have not been able to establish a meaningful behaviour pattern.

While fish in close proximity to fresh water may prove difficult to catch, there is ample evidence that could we locate a feeding shoal out at sea, they would be just as easy to catch as mackerel. A friend of mine who has spent some time visiting salmon fish farms in the Norwegian fjords tells me that some of the largest salmon he has ever caught have been taken on a spinning lure when cast to a feeding shoal. A special dispensation from the hatchery owners permitted him to do this and he made the comment that it was impossible to throw a lure into a saltwater fjord where salmon were kept without hooking one. Some of the fish he encountered topped the 30lb mark and he claimed that such fish were identical to wild fish he had seen netted off Greenland by commercial fishermen.

One of the snags regarding true experimentation with fish in salt water near our shores is that they have already commenced their fast. They have lost their teeth and most of the voracious feeding instinct they had before their long migration back to the rivers of their birth. Additionally, when the water is calm and the angler can see where the fish are, there is little attractive movement from the flies that are cast to them. At other times, when a high wave action may impart some life or action to the fly, the angler cannot see the fish and does not know exactly where the shoal is moving or if, indeed, there is even one there. As with any other form of salmon fishing, it is important to know that your lures will cover fish, so it is possible to spend a lot of abortive time fishing in salt water without any successful conclusions being drawn. I have tried a wide variety of spinners, lures and flies in salt water; but, as I find the practice of foul-hooking contrary to my sporting instincts, I usually desist if I do so by accident.

To fish in a freshwater outlet to the sea requires a different set of circumstances. Here it is desirable to wait for the oncoming flood tide and to watch for fish moving into the stream. Many will jump playfully and charge around the edge of the current – alternating between the fresh water and the salt. Contrary to some opinions, I am quite sure that at this stage, fish can alter their body chemistry at will to suit abrupt changes in the salinity, or otherwise, of the water. A fish which is hooked in a freshwater outlet promptly tears off in one mad rush for the distant ocean. While out there it jumps like a miniature marlin and proves just as game right up to the moment of hand-tailing or netting.

Times to fish successfully in a freshwater outlet to the sea vary with the location; the obstacles facing the fish; the state of the tide and the amount of water coming down the river. No two locations could ever be the same in this respect and the angler must be ever-ready to adapt to circumstances. Even then his useful area for activity is strictly limited and such places are best left for the odd five minutes trial at different states of the tide. Sometimes there will be no response at all from the fish. Occasionally they will even roll over the line or leader, completely ignoring the best presented offering. But just once in a while they will go berserk to take, and if the angler is quick at getting them played out and landed he may be able to take quite a few in quick succession.

As soon as the rains come in quantity to swell the river, the angler is best advised just to sit down and watch. At a precise moment of their own choosing the fish will start to run. Now it is virtually impossible to catch them by fair means, but it is an exciting time just to watch and, perhaps, speculate on where they might be the next day – and where the angler would be best placed to intercept them higher up the river, or in one of the many lochs often associated with small river outlets. Spinning might be the order of the day on these short and often turbulent rivers and this is a branch of the sport which we shall now move on to examine.

A salmon swimming in a saltwater bay in the Outer Hebrides.

Let me begin this chapter by stating that up to the mid-sixties, by far the bulk of my salmon had been taken with a spinner. Of late years, however, I tend to favour fly fishing in all its forms and, consequently, do not spin as much as I used to in my fish-hungry days. Up to 1966, however, if anyone had imposed a severe restriction on the techniques I could use, but had left me to name the method (with the catching of fish as my prime objective), without question I should have selected a medium spinning rod, a fixed-spool reel and a 2-inch Black and Gold Devon Minnow. This combination undoubtedly accounted for the lion's share of the fish I caught up to that time. Although I do not now enjoy spinning very much and rarely indulge in it in this country, I can rightfully claim to know something about it and to know from considerable experience that it is not always as simple as is contended by those who scorn the method.

It is important that we deal with each of the varying aspects of the technique separately, since there is much more to successful spinning than the mere hurling of a bait into the water and winding it back for the next cast. The Americans draw a distinct line between what they call bait-casting and spinning. A bait-casting reel is what we would call a multiplier, while a spinning reel is generally referred to by us as a fixed-spool or thread-line reel. Both styles, as we shall see, have distinct advantages and disadvantages; but by being versatile with either, we are able to cope with all the different conditions to be encountered on a river throughout the season. It is generally accepted that spinning in the early spring and late autumn on fairly big rivers is best accomplished with a double-handed rod and a multiplier reel. Then for small stream, late spring and summer fishing, we turn to a single-handed rod and the fixed-spool reel. After taking my spinning very seriously for several years, however, I found that to be really versatile I required at least three spinning outfits to see me through a season.

My principal outfit for early season fishing in Britain or Norway consists of a 10-foot 'Multispin' carbon rod by Bruce and Walker, with a 6000C Ambassadeur reel and a line in excess of 15lbs test. There are those who argue that monofilament line is more liable to cause an overrun when casting, and thus prefer to use braided line. Some advantage may be gained from using oval section monofilament, but it is of little account which you choose. The braided line is more difficult to cast to the maximum potential distance, although it does minimise overruns. The above outfit will handle most of the heavier spoons and Devon Minnows, together with any additional lead weighting; but it is not the most suitable to use with terminal tackle weighing less than $\frac{5}{8}$oz.

For periods in between the seasons I like to have a slightly lighter double-handed rod (there are several made in carbon fibre and fibreglass between 8½ feet and 9½ feet) with a medium-sized fixed-spool reel. Those reels which find a place in my tackle bag include the Abu Cardinal and the Mitchell 410. The last named is particularly useful when rapid retrieve of the bait is required. A monofilament line of some 10–12lbs test completes the list; and such an outfit will handle a very wide range of weights. Indeed, if I were to be further limited to one specific spinning outfit throughout the year, this would be the one I would select.

For fishing in high summer or fishing a small river, my third outfit consists of an 8½-foot Carbon XP rod (single-handed) and the Mitchell 410 fixed-spool reel loaded with 8lbs test monofilament. The entire outfit is delightfully light and so easy to use. It has frequently shown successful handling of fish up to 20lbs in weight.

Before turning to spinning techniques, I would like to spend a little time outlining some of the advantages and disadvantages of the fixed-spool and the multiplying reels. For some strange reason the fixed-spool reel has, over the years, acquired a deal of adverse publicity. It is thought to be too easy to use, and it became 'not quite the done thing' to be seen using one. The label 'yo-yo' was applied and stuck. Die-hard salmon anglers turned their noses up at it and stayed with their old-fashioned centre-pin reels. Then the modern multiplier came on the scene and suddenly, almost overnight, acquired a status of respectability. Quite apart from its relative merits against the fixed-spool reel, the multiplier became the reel to use. Anglers with their early beats on Tweed, Spey, Tay and Dee took to it quickly; the multiplier became the tool of the angling aristocrats, and the fixed-spool that of the artisans. This, as I saw it at the time, was the only yardstick by which the merits of each reel were judged. It might be interesting, therefore, to investigate some of the known *facts* and thus assess the merits of each reel objectively.

Firstly, the multiplier has many commendable features: one, it carries a good length of strong line; two, it enables baits of terminal weights over ⅜oz to be cast further than with the same line on a fixed-spool reel; three, it does not put any kink into the line; and four, it is possibly more pleasant in operation when playing a fish – although this preference depends on the angler and is something I do not personally accept.

The multiplier does, conversely, have certain features which, in my opinion, outweigh many of the advantages: one, it has a tendency to overrun, particularly when loaded with monofilament line and when the angler is pushing for distance; two, there is a general necessity to use heavy baits, since few multipliers will handle small baits effectively; three, it encourages a tendency to use lead at a time when, for practical fishing reasons, lead may not be desirable; four, the multiplier usually necessitates use of a double-handed rod in order to achieve real casting distance; five, the multiplier often incorporates a level-wind device, which again restricts distance; and six, there is a serious risk of overrun when casting into a wind.

The curse of over-runs ever present for users of the multiplying reel.

Line bunching at the butt ring poses problems for users of the fixed-spool reel. It helps if the line is well loaded to the lip of the spool and if the rod has a big, wide butt ring.

Turning to the fixed-spool reel, its advantages are: one, overruns are impossible and casting into a wind is no real problem; two, it enables the angler to change his weight of bait at will, without severely restricting casting distance; three, it enables the angler to fish with or without lead, as fishing conditions dictate; four, it permits the use of a single-handed or double-handed rod, as preferred; five, it eliminates the need to change hands after the cast is made; and six, it has a quicker rate of retrieve than most multipliers.

To be fair, the fixed-spool reel has a few disadvantages too: one, its inability to carry heavy line without severely restricting casting distance, due to lip friction on the spool; two, it may, on occasion, put twist into the line when playing a fish, but only when the angler in his excitement is manipulating the reel while a fish is taking line; and three, there is a so-called 'awkward' feeling as the line is wound on to the fixed-spool reel at right-angles.

On balance, therefore, it would seem that the fixed-spool reel is the more versatile outfit, which I sincerely believe it to be; but if logic be applied to our fishing we quickly see that there is a strong case for equipping ourselves with both. The multiplier has merit for early spring fishing, when big baits are very much the order of the day; while the fixed-spool reel has merit for late spring fishing when the angler may be called upon to make drastic changes throughout a fishing day in the sizes and weights of bait he is likely to find effective.

It is fair to say that lines in excess of 12lbs test should not normally be used on the fixed-spool reel of average size. Unless one of the sea-type reels were used, a heavy thickness of line would severely limit the potential casting distance. On the other hand there are few rivers where lines in excess of this strength are necessary; but I do like a little more armour in early spring on Tweed, or the wild rivers of Norway. It is then that I go for lines of 15–20lbs test on the multiplier. If I had to restrict my fishing to one type of reel throughout the year, I should certainly be with the artisans and not with the aristocrats.

There are, perhaps, a few finer points of tactics to be examined. Most anglers are right-handed; and with the fixed-spool reel they can cast and begin the retrieve without changing hands. Much of my fishing is done from the left bank of a river (that is the side of the river looked at as one faces downstream) and thus, with a fixed-spool reel, I can hold my right hand well out over the river to help eliminate much of the line belly caused by the strong central current; whereas with a multiplier I should need to transfer the rod into my left hand before the retrieve started, and then have the slight disadvantage of facing partially upstream in order to have my left hand over the river. These may seem trivial points; but they matter to me and I suspect that they make a difference to the amount of fish I could catch during a spinning season. The angler who consistently fishes the right bank of a river, however, may well find that the multiplier has advantages for him.

The fact is that I have made a case for both reels; and the all-round spin fisherman would be well advised to equip himself with both, so that the variable equipment gives him the means of coping adequately with the problems faced in varying spinning conditions. Let us now examine, in detail, the various spinning techniques.

I have already outlined the details of the tackle I use for heavy spinning. There are occasions, notably in Norway (discussed in a later chapter), when a slightly stronger rod might be required. Bruce and Walker are now making a 10ft 8in 'Multispin' rod which is ideal for this purpose. I am never quite so concerned with rod action on a spinning rod as I am with my fly rods, but it is nice to have a rod with action through to the butt – particularly important when using a multiplying reel.

We have already seen that, in order to get the utmost advantage from our spinning rod and multiplying reel, baits weighing in excess of $\frac{5}{8}$oz are almost a 'must'. For general usage I would go even further and say that I feel in greater command of such an outfit when the terminal tackle weighs nearer 1oz (30gm). Throughout these chapters on spinning, you will detect a strong emphasis on the weight of the bait. It is a vital factor; the choice of tackle and weight of bait must invariably be dictated by size of river, height of water and strength of current.

Let us imagine a pool on the Tay or Tweed during the early months of the season. The river may well be running a few feet above normal summer level; the water temperature will doubtless be struggling to top the 40-degree mark; and the early run fish will be tending to hold up in the lower beats of the river. There will be little inclination on their part to take sub-surface lures or baits fished in mid-water. The angler will be obliged to get his bait well down so that it will swing into the lies at an acceptable level. A touch of frost at night will slow down any tendency the fish may

Gillie Eric Robb handtails a salmon for an angler on the Spey.

have to run at this time of the year; and, as I have already outlined in Chapter 3, spinning with a big bait is often a logical way of fishing, unless the big sunk fly is obligatory. Many of my comments concerning sunk-line fly fishing in the early spring, and the correct assessment of fly weight in that chapter, are equally applicable to spinner selection and tactics; and as such form a basis for all our thinking in the presentation of a lure, fly or bait to the salmon in cold water.

Having arrived at the water side, we are now posed with the problem of bait selection. We know that the bait has to get well down to the fish and that to use our multiplier to its best advantage the terminal weight should be in excess of $\frac{5}{8}$oz. We also know that early spring salmon like a good-sized bait; and that for clear water conditions there are few to beat a 2½-inch or 3-inch Black and Gold Devon Minnow or a Yellow Belly of the same size. The weight of these baits is very much a variable factor, depending on whether they have been constructed from wood, fibre-glass, plastic or metal. It is, therefore, quite possible to have a 3-inch Devon Minnow in varying weights, so that the correct weight of bait can be chosen to match river height and current strength. The use of additional lead weighting is something which I should like to examine at greater length later on; but as a general rule I am opposed to its use and feel that when extra weight is required it should be in the bait itself. It is, of course, essential to have an additional swivel (apart from the one on the bait) and this should be placed about eighteen inches or two feet from the bait.

We have already outlined the likely river conditions during the early weeks of the season, and it is then left to individual choice to make an assessment of the bait to use. Rarely would I bother with a bait of less than 2½ inches long at this time of year (January, February or early March); and, as we have seen, it is more than likely that a 2½-inch metal Devon would weigh as much, if not more, than a 3-inch plastic Devon. The weight, therefore, is the crucial factor. There may well be some need for practical trial and error – so that if I feel that my chosen bait is not fishing as near to the bottom as I would like, but am convinced that my size selection is just about right, then I shall seek out the same sized bait constructed from heavier material, or, as a final resort, use additional lead weighting. There are, of course, countless occasions at this time of year when rivers will be at near-flood level, and the clarity of the water may not be all that is desirable. At such a time I have found the range of Toby spoon baits to be most effective. These are available in various sizes and weights; and if the weight is stamped on the bait (as it should be in all commercially-sold spinning baits) it is an easy matter to decide which spinner to use in the circumstances. Choice of colour is, again, largely a matter of personal preference; but water colour and height are a great indication. Dirty water calls for a flashy, easily seen bait, whereas low, clear water may call for more subdued colouring. Don't be too concerned with colour or specific sizes in these early months but concentrate on getting the right weight, so

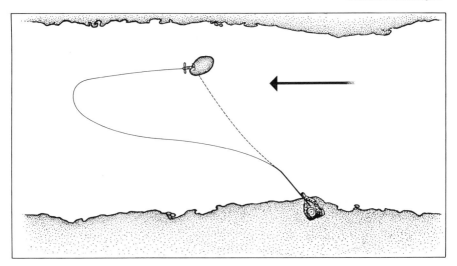

Fig 6 Dotted line indicates the path of the line when the bait becomes stuck in submerged rock. By releasing more line to form a downstream belly the angler may then strike sharply and release the bait.

that the bait will fish at the effective depth in the water. Of the baits I prefer for early fishing, the 2½-inch to 3-inch Black and Gold, or the Yellow Belly, are among my favourites; together with, in varying sizes, weights and colours, the Toby spoons. Natural baits are always worth a try, with golden and silver sprats heading the list; but due to their comparative lightness they generally require the use of additional lead. There are quite a few natural bait tackles marketed with built-in lead weighting, and at this time of year they are the best to use.

It is important to establish the likely lies of salmon on an early spring beat. In many instances the fish will take up different lies from those which they would take up in warmer water conditions. They will tend to lie in the deep and comparatively quiet water, or on the edges of the main runs. In order to induce them to take, the bait will invariably have to be spun slowly over the lies so that they can take it with little effort. The colder the water, the less the inclination of the fish to move a long way, or at any speed, to intercept the bait. Thus in all spring spinning the bait should be kept moving as slowly as possible, fluttering in the current, and as near to the bottom as is practically possible. Admittedly it is most infuriating to get hung up at every cast and, with a varying depth of river bed, some compromise has to be reached. Frankly, it is a source of great amazement to me the lengths to which anglers will go to retrieve a stuck bait. They pull and tug in all directions and may eventually resort to the use of an 'otter' device to release it. This might have the desired effect or it might not; but it does disturb the water and may well frighten the fish the angler is hoping to catch. I have seen anglers despatch their wives and their gillies to the other side of the river to cast over the offending line in attempts to release it. Quite apart from the water disturbance this creates just think of the sheer waste of good angling time. If an angler can afford to fish for salmon, he should be able to afford a few baits to be left in the bed of the river. Most times, however, there is no need for the bait to get so rigidly stuck. As soon as the angler is aware that his bait has fouled the bottom and that it is not a fish, he should refrain from pulling hard which will merely drive the bait further into the obstruction. Instead, he should open his reel and let a bundle of line float off downstream. Eventually a belly of line (as in Fig.6) will be formed downstream of the stuck bait. If the angler then closes his reel and initiates a sharp strike, the initial pull against the bait will come from a downstream direction. In many instances this technique is all that is required to release it.

When spinning for early salmon, my aim is to select a weight of bait that, when cast out to the required point, will swing round at the right depth without any turning of the reel handle. Turning the reel handle speeds up the passage of the bait through the water; and, as we have already seen, the great object is to keep the bait moving at its slowest possible pace. There are those, I know, who cry, 'If I don't wind the reel handle, I get hung up on the bottom'. There are also those who, in order to simplify their casting (particularly with a multiplier), add additional lead weight where tactically none is required, and have to wind in order to keep the bait from fouling the bottom. All these things militate against the successful presentation of a salmon bait. Sometimes, in really slack water, some winding does become necessary. But such conditions are rare on

Adding lead wire to a Devon Minnow flight is better than using a spiral. If the spiral must be used, it pays to bend it to prevent line kink.

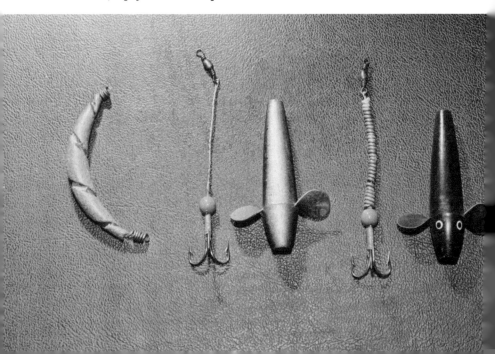

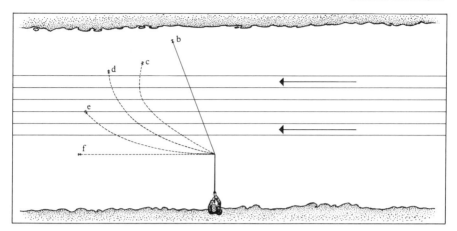

Fig. 7a When cast across a strong, central current the line forms a downstream belly. This is tactically bad technique as the bait moves too fast and too high in the water.

most spring rivers; and I feel fairly safe in commenting that a weight of spinner should be selected so that it will revolve slowly in the current without any assistance by winding the reel. The only occasion when I like to use an additional spiral lead is when I am fishing comparatively shallow rivers with a wooden Devon Minnow. The lead acts as a keel and prevents the Devon from floating. It is also the lead which encounters the bottom – rather than the bait – if the angler is using a spiral lead which is too heavy for the circumstances.

The casual observer of spinning may regard it as about the simplest possible form of angling. It seems that the angler merely throws out the spinner and retrieves it slowly, then, taking a pace downstream, repeats the process until a salmon takes hold. For many novices their spinning *is* just as simple as that; and the fact that they occasionally catch fish leads them to believe that spinning is easy. The plain fact is that to be really successful at spinning a great deal more skill is required than is immediately apparent; and it is only when the basic elements of spinning have been mastered that more success will come the way of the angler.

If we imagine ourselves to be on the left bank of a river (there is always some confusion as to which is the right and which the left bank, but this is quickly assessed by looking downstream), the approximate point to which we shall make our initial cast will be between half-past ten and eleven o'clock (see Fig.4 in Chapter 6).

Although it seems perfectly elementary, it must be realised that the spinner we throw across the river will be greatly influenced in its behaviour by the line connecting it to rod and reel. As soon as the cast is made, the bait slowly sinks; but, unless you do something about it, the line, now extended across the river, will be subjected to a heavy pull by the central current across which it lies. It stands to reason, therefore, that whether you turn the reel handle or not, with a downstream belly in the line, the bait will travel the first part of its journey with its head pointing slightly downstream (Fig.7a). More important, it will also travel faster than is desirable in order to have the best chance of taking a fish – certainly in the early spring months. I am frequently amazed at the number of anglers who, after casting their baits in the manner described, suddenly start to wind the reel handle as well. If only they stopped to think, they would realise that such tactics are not going to permit the bait to get down anywhere near the fish; and, what is more, it will be moving so fast through the water that none but the most foolhardy salmon would condescend to take it. Here again, if you dare challenge them, the general retort would be, 'Well, if I don't wind it, the bait will get stuck in the bottom'.

Few of these anglers would dream of doing a partial retrieve of their lure when they are fly fishing. They would cast their fly out and let it prescribe its full arc before starting a retrieve and casting again. Give that same angler a spinning outfit, however, and he seems to come under some strange compulsion to wind the reel handle while his bait is 'fishing' round. Had he taken the trouble to note the performance of his bait, he would quickly see that, when merely dangled in the river current, the bait will revolve without additional influences – and it does not need to be revolving very quickly to be of interest to the fish.

We have examined, briefly, the use of additional lead weight. There are many anglers, I know, who advocate the use of extra lead. They say it makes the bait swim better and on an even keel. This is certainly a factor in their favour. But how do these same anglers explain the fact that they would not dream of putting the same hunk of lead on their fly cast to make the *fly* swim on an even keel? I know of occasions when I have done it; but it is the very devil to cast. So I only use additional weighting, as I have said,

Fig. 7b After the bait has been cast it is sometimes possible to induce a slight upstream 'mend' in the line. This is a sound tactic as it slows down the movement of the bait and enables it to fish lower in the water.

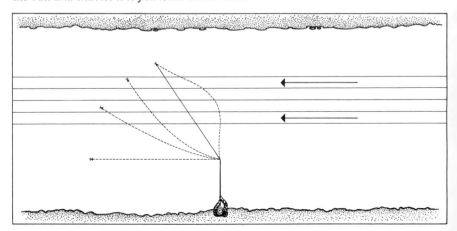

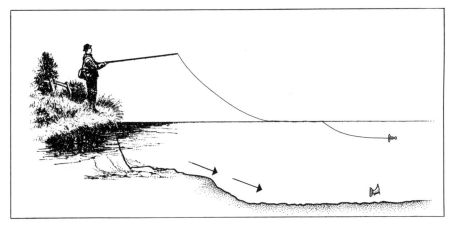

Fig. 8a If the angler does not mend his line or hold the rod point well up the central current will have too much influence and the bait will move too quickly and too high in the water for the fish to be interested.

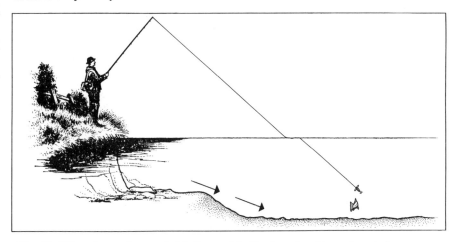

Fig. 8b When the angler mends his line and holds the rod well up, there is less influence from the central current. The bait then sinks deep enough to move slowly over the fish, which is clearly more likely to take.

when spinning with a light, wooden Devon Minnow. Despite the insistence that, without lead, the bait tends to swim nose-high, I feel that it does not make a ha'porth of difference. The basic requirement is to select the weight of bait carefully, as best suited to river conditions, so that it will fish just clear of the river bed without the necessity to wind the reel handle at all until the bait has come round into slack water immediately downstream of your position.

One most useful method of altering the weight of a Devon Minnow – provided that it has a sufficiently wide sleeve for the trace – is to wind fine lead wire round the trace before it is slotted through the bore hole of the Devon. Varying amounts of wire may be added to a variety of traces and it is then a simple matter to choose the one most likely to be effective.

Having selected a suitable bait, it is cast across the stream. Immediately it strikes the water every effort should be made to mend the line upstream (Fig. 7b). I know that this is not easy, particularly with a downstream wind, but every attempt should be made to stop the central current from causing too much belly in the line. The point of the rod should be held high and in line with the bait, and should not be brought round until the bait is ready for the retrieve. It is very important to hold the rod well up. The higher the rod is held, the lower the bait will fish in the water. This is simply due, of course, to the amount of line being subjected to water drag. The longer the sunk-line, the greater its tendency to raise the level of the bait in the water (Fig. 8).

In actual fact, it often pays to keep the rod point at right-angles to the surface of the river. This eliminates about a rod length of extra line belly, due to the central current; and thus makes the bait fish at the lowest possible depth and speed. If, however, you are compelled to wind the reel handle in order to keep the bait from snagging on the river bed, it is advisable to change to a lighter one; and I mean a lighter one, not necessarily a smaller one.

On this basis it is quite understandable that a heavier bait will be required for the head of the stream, whereas towards the tail of the pool the current may only carry a lighter one. There is, I know, a tendency to put on a piece of lead for the first part of the stream, and then take it off halfway down the pool. In my lazier moments I have done this myself; but I am firmly convinced that, except when using wooden Devons, a bait unfettered by additional lead, and just of the right weight for the current in which it is fishing, is more successful in the long run. Certainly such baits are easier to cast since, with additional lead, the two separate weights at the end of the line tend to compete with each other during the cast, and this can kill a good deal of your potential distance.

There are those who argue that distance casting is not important in salmon spinning. They say that, often, the fish are lying near the angler's own bank; and that long casting only serves to cover a lot of dead water. There are some occasions, of course, when this may well be true; but it is almost impossible to make a short cast and still have the bait fishing at reasonable depth and speed. So, while I do not advocate casting into the next county, the cast should be long enough to cover the water adequately; to present the bait at the right depth; and to cause the bait to move at the right speed across the fish lies.

A great friend of mine, and quite a successful salmon fisherman, having fished down a pool and drawn blank, will often make the remark, 'They are just not taking today'. At which my prompt retort is usually, 'Well let's set about making them take!'; and in spinning for fresh-run fish in the early spring, this philosophy is not as stupid as it may sound. We have already discovered in Chapter 3 that if a heavy fly is scraping the bottom and down among the fish, a salmon is quite likely to take it in sheer self-defence. It is true that there are many times when the salmon will not take; but there are quite a few occasions when this is a faulty conclusion to draw and by further effort a fish may be induced to take. Sometimes a change of tactics might yield a fish. If there is reason to believe that the bait is not covering the lies properly, try a heavier or a lighter bait. You may even make a slight change in size, but in the early spring we have seen that this is often less important than weight. Whatever else you do, keep persisting. You may never know the moment when, due to some subtle and undetected change in atmospheric or water conditions, the fish will suddenly come into taking mood. Then, at the umpteenth cast, you will suddenly feel an electrifying tug on the line – and a spring salmon is on!

I have mentioned nothing of fishing with plug baits for the simple reason that I have never used them. That they are very effective on some waters I have no doubt, and I believe they are very popular on the Hampshire Avon. Indeed, they may well be worth a try on other rivers of similar character. Anyone interested in plug fishing should read *Hampshire Avon Salmon* by Lieutenant-Colonel S. H. Crow.

For a general summary, early spring fishing on big rivers usually requires long casting, and careful fishing through all the likely water; correct selection of the right weight of bait in order to spin the water at the slowest possible speed; and also spinning at the lowest depth without continually feeling the bait touching the bottom. You should be able to make a reasonable assessment of the appropriate size and colour of the bait; and, above all, you must have the persistence to fish hard through all the hours of daylight that come your way during these early months. The fish, in the main, will all be fresh-run, and thus that bit easier to tempt. They do, however, require the angler to 'get down' to them; and this factor alone can make all the difference between success and failure.

Thus far I have made no mention of harling, a technique which involves the gillie or boatman rowing back and forth across the river in 'criss-cross' fashion while the angler sits in the stern with a rod (or rods) trailing behind in the current. It is a method much practised on the Tay and it may entice a dour fish with minimum effort from the angler. I have tried it on occasions in Norway, at the end of a dour day. Just occasionally I have caught fish with the method; but there are no words of mine which will express the sheer, dull tedium which is involved. If much of my salmon fishing had to be done like this it would not be very long before I reverted to delinquency. Sadly, I can offer no meaningful philosophy to help the novice in this technique.

The season for the multiplying reel is generally short-lived in Britain. Those anglers who persist with them throughout the year, either for reasons of snobbery or because of a general preference, are usually imposing limitations on their full angling potential. There may be a case for the multiplier's continued use on Tweed or Tay when bait sizes and weights never seem to get too small; but as a general rule, as late spring approaches, the currents of the majority of rivers get too slack to warrant the use of big, heavy baits. We have already seen that the multiplier will not handle small baits effectively without the undesirable use of additional lead weighting; and thus, on lower water, it is necessary to wind the reel handle. The most obvious course then is to revert to the fixed-spool reel.

The fixed-spool reel is a very versatile piece of equipment. It has been much maligned in the past, but it still emerges as the most popular reel in general use throughout the entire angling world. It is said to be too easy to use – but the antics of some anglers when using one show that there are few who are really competent in exploiting it fully. The simple act of casting, whether it be with fly, bait or lure, is a subject I shall touch upon in another chapter; but general standards are deplorably low and, as we shall see later, this factor alone is often largely responsible for indifferent results in any type of fishing.

For general spinning, I load my fixed-spool reel with monofilament line between 10 and 12lbs test, perhaps the near-maximum line strength to be recommended for standard size fixed-spool reels. For those who prefer a fixed-spool reel for all their fishing, larger models are available (designed mainly for sea fishing) which are constructed to carry lines in excess of 20lbs test. Such a reel, however, will not handle a small bait adequately, and may be likened to the multiplier in that respect. Loaded with such heavy lines they are not capable of casting the distances that may be achieved with a multiplier with the same strength of line and terminal weights of around only 1oz. This clearly indicates a case for having both types of reel.

The standard size fixed-spool reel is more than adequate for normal spinning, provided that the line is loaded to the lip of the spool (a very important factor in gaining the full potential casting distance). Take care, though, not to overload the spool as this will have an equally restricting effect by line bunching at the butt ring when casting. The reel will hold more line than is ever likely to be required with the most playful fish. For the transition period, between early spring fishing and the delicate days of upstream spinning in low water, I prefer a double-handed rod of some 8½ to 9½ feet in length. I am not greatly concerned if the rod has tippy action or is not the most pleasant tool I can find: in other words, in this instance, rod action is not of paramount importance and many of the tippy, fibre-

Group Captain George Westlake plays a salmon of 20lb on the Tweed at Upper Hendersyde.

glass rods now on sale should prove adequate.

Although the use of a swivel is important when using any type of spinning tackle, it is even more important to use one with a fixed-spool reel in order to avoid serious line kink or twist. The swivel should be mounted not less than 18 inches from the terminal bait; but if a long overhang is to be avoided, it should not be a great deal more than this. Additional lead is again something which I deplore for general circumstances and the same factors would govern its use as in heavy spinning with a multiplier.

Perhaps the prime feature of this lighter type of spinning is the greater degree of accuracy that may be obtained in casting. With a little bit of practice it will soon be possible, literally, to hit a dustbin lid at 15 yards. Thus the angler is able to place his bait in all the likely-looking places without the necessity of changing hands. He is then in immediate control of the bait the instant it touches the water, sometimes a very important factor.

The same basic rules for bait selection as those we examined in Chapter 16 will still apply; but the angler is now able to use a wider range of bait weights without seriously limiting his potential casting distance. Obviously, a 1oz Toby spoon may be thrown much further than a 1½-inch plastic Devon Minnow; but the latter may still be cast a worthwhile distance, and certainly further and more comfortably than would be possible with the average multiplier tackle used in the early spring. A good spinning day, with such tackle as I have described, may well come after a rise in the water and may happen at any time during a salmon season. Perhaps the angler has doubts about the relative merits of fly on a sinking line; or that there is any merit in using a medium-sized spinner on this occasion. So we presume that he has made up his mind to spin and, with water temperatures approaching 50 degrees, that he has selected a 1½- or 2-inch Devon Minnow of the correct weight to suit the prevailing water conditions. The technique of fishing will be virtually identical with that outlined in Chapter 16. At this stage there is little point in trying out low-water spinning tactics, so the basic technique is just the same as for heavy spinning. The bait should be selected on a weight basis and still made to fish fairly deep in the water; but there is not quite the same necessity to scrape the bottom as in early spring fishing.

Fish will be prepared to move a little more freely for the bait and will often accept it in mid-water, or even near the surface sometimes. But the movement of the bait through the water should not be speeded up – here again, movement of the bait without winding the reel handle is the target at which to aim. Doubtless there will now be many more occasions when some winding of the reel becomes necessary; and it may be advisable to wind slowly when the river is coming down to a good fly height. Choice of size and colour of the spinner at such a time is largely dictated by the clarity of the water; and there are many days, following a dirty flood, when it pays to resort to the same flashy Toby spoon that you may have used back in February. My own favourite bait for a clearing water in late spring is a 2-inch Black and Gold Devon Minnow made in plastic. I have taken too many fish on this bait to discard it lightly and a stock used to accompany me on any salmon fishing expedition. Under such water conditions as I have described, however, the ideal time for spinning does not last for very long. The angler must always be watchful for a fall in the water level when fish will shy off the spinner and seek a more elusive lure – such as the floating-line fly or a fly on a light sinking line, as suggested in Chapter 11. The reason is that the salmon may soon see the bait too readily, and perhaps for what it is. If the angler persists too long with the spinner he might only succeed in frightening the fish, and thus spoil his chances with the fly. It is at this period when I take a secret delight in fly-fishing behind a good spin-fisherman. The fish may be just about to go off the spinner and may give me the sport for which he was hoping!

As late spring moves on to summer, and conditions still dictate the use of the spinner, it may well pay dividends to vary one's tactics a bit. The fish should now be in a much more playful mood. They may well be prepared to come out of their lies more readily to intercept a bait. Size, weight and colour of bait will still be determined by water conditions; but the angler may well find that there is less need to restrict his tactics to fishing the bait as slowly as possible.

It always pays, I think, to start in the traditional manner; but if success is not quickly forthcoming, it is sometimes worth speeding up the passage of the bait or even casting it upstream and winding back quickly. I well recall one such occasion on the Lune when both fly and traditional spinning had failed to produce an offer. I knew that there were plenty of fish in the beat, but was at a loss to know just how to get them to take. The same 2-inch Black and Gold Devon Minnow, which had been on my rod all morning, was still on; but I was on the wrong side of the river to fish it properly in the traditional manner. So, casting upstream into well-known lies, I reeled the bait back as fast as I could. In the short space of an hour I hooked five fish – but have to confess that not a single one of them was landed. Man-made groynes, with steel mesh gabions, saw my downfall, since every fish hooked ran me under these, and I was powerless to avoid a break. One of the fish literally took the bait at my feet just as I was about to withdraw it from the water. He was a good fish for the water and I was just as open-mouthed as he was at the instant he took the bait. I reckoned that he was all of 30lbs.

In the past two chapters we have examined the basic requirements of early and mid-season spinning. Under suitable conditions, of course, it is possible to fish throughout a season with a medium spinning outfit. Inevitably, however, there comes a time when waters are low and the current is reduced to a mere trickle. At such a time it may be that the current becomes so slow that it makes any form of fly fishing a great trial. Then, unless the angler wishes to resort to prawn, worm or shrimp, he has only his spinning rod on which to rely. Following the first floods of summer, some of our smaller rivers receive their first runs of fish. Sometimes, within a matter of hours, the fish are lying in waters at summer level; and the angler is confronted with the problem of how to catch them. In this brief chapter I will suggest one or two tactics for trial.

Deep holding pools may be almost stagnant at this time of the year. In such conditions they obviously lend themselves to prawn or worm fishing, but it is now that a small spinner, on light tackle, may produce results. Spinning baits should be little more than one inch long, so a small quill minnow may come into its own. Now, there will of course be an urgent need to wind the reel handle continuously, and in the slack water it will matter little whether the bait is cast upstream or down. The thing to do is to try all ways; that is, to alternate the speed of the bait, and to make it move at different levels in the water. In such conditions, with plenty of fish in the water, there may be a danger of foul-hooking them; but if the bait is getting down to where the fish are lying there is also every opportunity for it to be taken properly. There are no rules for this type of fishing; and I know of many instances when the most remarkable things have happened. Fish have taken the bait while it was dancing on the surface of the water during a quick retrieve for a new cast. They have made passes at it while it dangled in the water prior to the next cast. I even recall one instance of this nature when a friend was worm fishing for salmon. The worm flew off the hook as he was casting, but a salmon seized the bare hook as it was being retrieved for re-baiting, and was duly landed. Such incidents, while not commonplace, do occur at times and may have induced the late A. H. E. Wood to try a hook with a painted shank in lieu of a fully-dressed fly. The smaller the bait, sometimes, the more intriguing it seems for the salmon; and in order to cast these minute baits, short rods and lines not exceeding 8lbs test are very necessary. It can be a fascinating form of fishing; and, moreover, if the water is reasonably clear, the angler is often able to witness the entire action of the fish as it takes the bait. Concealment thus plays a very important role and in this respect it can resemble chalk-stream fishing for trout.

Apart from the quill minnows I have mentioned, several other baits are worth a trial: the Mepp range of spoon baits in sizes 1 and 2, for instance, while small Devon Minnows, barely ¾ of an inch long and of the heavyweight type, have taken fish for me on many occasions. Sometimes the most effective tactic is to make the bait spin through the water at maximum speed. If it is spun too slowly, there is a chance that the fish might see it for what it is, whereas if it seems a fleeting thing the fish may take it before their suspicions are raised.

There are, of course, many occasions, other than those I have described, when the use of ultra-light tackle has a definite advantage. I well recall an incident when I was fishing the Lune in the company of a former editor of *Trout and Salmon*, the late Ian Wood. Both of us had achieved limited success with the fly; but the water was on the low side, and quite a few fish were concentrated in the rough, streamy shallow water at the head of a narrow run. We had tried our flies over them without success. I had even failed to get an offer with either traditional or upstream spinning tactics and was sitting on the bank at the head of the run wondering what on earth to do. As I sat there, I picked up the small spinning rod and dangled the tiny quill minnow in the water. The current was sufficiently strong to make the bait revolve, and I slowly let it drop downstream by paying line off the reel. Such tactics had occasionally worked successfully with the fly; why not with a spinner? Suddenly I was into a fish. I hustled it quickly downstream and out of the way of the other fish. After successfully playing it out I went back and repeated the process. Within a few more minutes I was fast into another fish and then took a third before the rest of the shoal became aware of the tumult, and moved out of the stream. Later that night in the pitch darkness I even took a salmon of 10lbs while fishing for sea trout with a small fly. That was an unexpected ending to an unusual day.

Light spinning has brought me plenty of fun and little formula. In its strange way I used to find it as fascinating as fly fishing. The angler makes up his own rules as he goes along; and the best of long-held theories have been shattered time and time again. Nowadays, however, I tend to spend the bulk of my time with a fly. In terms of fish to be caught I think that I am imposing too many unnecessary limitations upon myself: but I have to ask myself whether it is the method, or whether it is the fish on the bank that matters most. I think I know the answer, but so long as any form of fishing remains a challenge, I suspect that I might just indulge in it from time to time.

Much of my early spinning for salmon was done on such rivers as the Eden, Tweed, Spey and Yorkshire Esk. During later years I also did some on the Lune; and, in terms of fish caught, I had some very successful times. Some of the most memorable days, however, were those when it was a struggle to get even a single fish; days when fly, prawn, worm and shrimp had all failed – or because I was out of baits for the last three. Sometimes it was only persistent spinning that saved a blank day, or even a blank week. In those early days I had much more confidence in my ability with a spinner than with a fly, so consequently I tended to resort to the spinner more frequently when the going was tough.

During the early sixties I became an angling reporter for Granada Television and then followed this with a two-year period of similar activity for Tyne-Tees Television. There was never much coverage of angling on television and, even to this day, despite the fact that angling enjoys higher participation by the public than any other sport in the country, it gets scant television time. There are several reasons for this, not least of which is the great difficulty in getting cooperation from the fish when a camera crew lurks on the river bank; or making a film with sufficient interest to hold a general audience. In the end I resorted to making the films myself and giving commentaries on them from the studio. The method worked. I could go unobtrusively along the waterside and film my friends as they caught fish. But there were many blank days and there were occasions when I had to do the fishing and then hand the rod over to some chum while I made ready with the camera. At the end of every month, however, I had somehow obtained a small item and we never had to resort to any form of faking in order to show a live fish being caught.

One of my early salmon fishing features depicted activities on the river Tweed. There were to be two of us fishing, Ken Morritt and myself. Since Ken was no mean performer with a cine-camera it was agreed that whoever hooked a fish, the other would run up and take over the camera. Day after day we tried to hook a salmon; but it was not until the latter part of the week that we detected a fresh run of salmon going through. Surely on that day we should get some fish? We fished hard and all thoughts of the camera were put to one side. At the end of the day Ken had hooked and lost no less than seven salmon while I had one little salmon to show for my efforts. Tomorrow, I thought, I will concentrate on the camera!

The following day we made an early start and I fished close to Ken, with the camera at the ready. We were spinning with Black and Gold Devon Minnows (it was March) and these baits, we reckoned, would offer us the best chance of sport. It was not long before Ken hooked a fish. I gave my rod to the gillie and dashed up with the camera. Just as Ken was bringing his fish ashore, the gillie hooked one and I was thus able to film continuously and come back with some good footage of two fish being caught and landed. No more fish came our way for the rest of the week – but I had got my film.

Other memories of days with a spinning rod and a camera bring to mind some of the very pleasant times I spent in the company of the late Oliver Kite. Oliver was one of the most delightful people I have met in the angling world and his untimely death in 1968 robbed the angling fraternity of a truly wonderful character. In the early days of our friendship we fished together for trout. Salmon were things of which he was just a little scornful and he frequently pulled my leg about being just another trout fisherman who had gone to the dogs. In the end, however, Reg Righyni and I persuaded him to come north to the Lune, where he was to catch the first two salmon he had ever landed. I never did make a real salmon angler out of him; but in later years he became more tolerant of me – and of salmon!

On many occasions when he came north, he was accompanied by Southern TV cameraman Ted Channell, constantly on the look-out for material for his programme, *Kite's Country*. Oliver would rove the banks in search of elusive bird-life or some aspect of nature not commonly found in his native Wessex. There was one notable occasion when Righyni and I were to try and catch a salmon for the camera to record. As luck would have it we both hooked fish at the same time and the camera was able to pan from Reg to myself to witness us doing battle. My fish turned the scale at 19lbs and I quickly hooked another one which made the 11lb mark. Doubtless Southern TV viewers would get the impression that salmon fishing was easy; but things did not always work out that way.

Another experience, when I was glad of a spinner and another angler, came in the autumn of 1969. We were just finishing one of the worst Lune seasons in history, with a grand total for the season of ten fish for the three-rod beat. Of these ten, my wife and I had accounted for four apiece. Mine had been taken on fly, and hers with a spinner. Her best made only 10½lbs, whereas my smallest went to 12½lbs. This made her very keen to win on sheer numbers of fish caught; and we agreed to have a final outing on the last day of the season.

The day before that, however, I received a call from the BBC. Could they come and film me catching salmon? At least they could come and try, I said, but with a forecast of south-westerly gales it would be a near-miracle if anything was caught. We assembled in the bar of the Royal Hotel in Kirkby Lonsdale. Soon we were on the river bank and I was being fitted up with a microphone to link me to camera. With only a short lead connecting me to the sound recordist and a further one connecting me to the director, we were a pretty formidable team as we bulldozed our way along the river bank. For my first attempts I tried the fly, but it was a back-breaking business trying to make the fly act effectively as the wind kept whipping it upstream. Eventually I changed to a spinner; and it was well

Playing a salmon on the River Spey at Castle Grant.

turned 1 p.m. before we were successful in getting the introductory shots in the can.

As far as serious fishing was concerned, I had not yet done any. My wife was still casting away at the water further downstream and out of camera range, and was still fishless. I felt obliged to tell the director to uncouple me from the sound recordist and let me spend some time on my own, in order to have a better chance. If I was successful there would be ample time to re-connect the mike and let me describe the action. It was an anxious hour I spent in search of a taking fish. The day was deteriorating rapidly and I felt sure that my chances were getting slimmer by the minute.

There were a few fish in the beat; but by their skittering leaps I recognised that they were in the early stages of the disease UDN. I roved up and down the best pool on the beat, but all was to no avail. Two companions were also on the river; but by 2.30 p.m. none of us had anything to show for our efforts. Throughout the day I had warned the film director of some of the pitfalls of making angling films, and of the unlikelihood of my catching a fish when restricted by the requirements of the camera crew. 'My wife', I said, 'has a better chance of catching fish than I have'. We were just about to call it a day when a shout from my wife indicated only too clearly that the miracle had happened. She had hooked a fish. The four of us thundered down the river bank and I quickly waded out and grabbed the rod. As I came quickly ashore the mike was again plugged in and I opened my commentary with: 'The miracle has happened – I'm into a fish!' What I do for Art's sake. With camera whirring, the fish was quickly played out and brought ashore. It was a small cock salmon of 8lbs and was triumphantly held up in front of the camera. My wife looked on with quiet satisfaction. Not for her the glory of the silver screen, but perhaps the far greater satisfaction that she had not only wiped my eye, but had brought me down to size in the most unassuming way possible. How could I be anything but grateful to her? As for myself, I felt a bit of a fraud. The film looked good and was quite convincing; but I have to record the whole story. She beat me!

Since those far-off days I have frequently been thankful to the spinner for saving an otherwise tough situation. Involved as I am in the photography and filming of angling scenes and subjects, it is advisable to have a few aces around in case of non-cooperation from the fish. The trouble is that the fish never see the script and are completely unaware of the starring role demanded of them. Even then there might be other complications from camera gremlins, so it is not always the fault of the fish. One notable occasion which comes to mind was when a producer from Tyne-Tees Television hired me to spend two days on the Tweed. He was in the middle of a production entitled *To Catch a King* and was short of good footage of fish being played. On arrival at the river I was appalled that we had such an inadequate piece of water available for location purposes. After some initial trial I made a phone call to see what chance there would be of getting on my regular beat. Fortunately I found I had friends fishing there and a place was quickly found for me. By the time I got there with the camera crew they were a little exhausted from their long walk, but leaving them to set out their stall, I was quickly equipped with a radio microphone and into action. Within five minutes I was playing a salmon.

Announcing the news over the radio microphone, I was urged to wait. In their consternation at the move the camera crew had forgotten to change to a new magazine of film. Slowly, I worked the fish down to where the camera was located but it seemed like an age before the director shouted 'running'. I let the requisite few seconds pass before opening my commentary. The fish, despite the fact that it was now quite tired, rallied a little and gave a nice display. My commentary sounded slightly pompous, I thought, but it was all going too easily. I was just about to lean down and tail my fish out when I thought I had better make the comment that 'it is not always as easy as this and sometimes the fish gets free'. The words were barely out of my mouth before the spinner flew out and my fish swam away to freedom. The sequence was used in the film, but instead of making a grand finale I appeared just before the 'natural break' for advertisements!

On yet another occasion involving a cameraman and a salmon, I had just hooked a fish when the cameraman announced that he had only $2\frac{1}{2}$ minutes of running time left. I don't think that poor fish realised our problem, but with a 'sink-or-swim' attitude I quickly horsed-in a fresh-run Tweed fish of 7lbs in two minutes flat. Of course, I don't recommend such tactics and I was indeed lucky to be able to land it safely in that time.

These incidents give some indication of how a spinner has saved my professional 'bacon'. There were times, in the past, when I was also glad to have those other three aces up my sleeve – worms, prawns and shrimps. Let us move on to examine some tactics with those baits.

It was a hot June morning, back in the early sixties, when Ken Morritt and I met at breakfast. We were staying at a small hotel on Deeside and for the past few days had been fishing the famed Dinnet water for salmon. Throughout the week we had limited ourselves to flies and spinners and by concentrated fishing had each managed to average a fish or two a day. This, however, was to be our last day. I perhaps had a slight edge on Ken in terms of the number of fish caught, so we agreed to take the gloves off and fish with any legitimate style we happened to fancy. We even made a little bet that the one with the lowest catch would pay for champagne that evening. I should have known before I started that I was doomed to lose.

Our gillies arrived and we went our separate ways. I was to take the topmost pool (Pol Slache) for the first part of the day. Knowing this to be a good holding pool, I thought that the sensible thing to do would be to try the worm. The gillie seemed reluctant to agree until I explained the bet, and as we both felt that under the conditions we only needed one fish to win the day, on went the worm.

I cannot pretend any great expertise with a worm; but it was not long before I felt a few light touches, and in due course the fish moved away with the bait and was firmly hooked. Shortly afterwards we tailed out a nice little fish of 8lbs, and duly knocked it on the head. 'That', I thought secretly, 'should win me the day'. I then removed my worm tackle and went back to fly and spinner with not so much as a further offer all day.

A day's catch from the River Dee in the good old days.

Back at the hotel that evening I was quick to tell Ken of my success. 'You've been very lucky', he said, as he opened the boot of his car. And there before my very eyes were eight prime salmon. 'All on the worm', he said, with a twinkle in his eye. 'I expect that you got yours on fly?' It was then that I had to tell him that I, too, had taken my fish on worm; but not realising that he was an expert in this method, had thought that I should win the day with my one fish. We did drink a little champagne that evening; but I only paid for one bottle.

Worming is, at certain times and seasons, a very effective method of taking salmon. It is regarded by many as not quite the done thing; and comes in for a deal of criticism from those who, I suspect, are not very competent in fishing it correctly. Quite apart from any ethical considerations, I should say that on fast-flowing rivers its effective use requires as much skill as any other type of salmon fishing. But, having said that, I must confess that it is not a method which has great appeal for me. If all my salmon fishing was to be limited to the use of worm bait, then I would sell my tackle and resort to playing marbles. I am no longer the fish-hungry youngster I was in the early days of my salmon fishing; and if it is necessary to fish the worm in order to catch fish nowadays, then as far as I am concerned the fish go uncaught. I would rather sit on the bank and drink the wine of Scotland, or watch the birds, or take photographs – or anything.

This chapter, though, is meant to analyse – however briefly – some of the tactics to be used in fishing the worm. As I say, I claim no great expertise with this bait; but in my early days of salmon fishing I did catch quite a few fish with the method on waters which lent themselves to its use, and where worming was permitted. There are some rivers where it is less likely to do harm than indiscriminate prawn fishing; and we have already seen how it can sometimes turn an apparently hopeless day into quite a bonanza.

There are some rivers where, at certain times of the year, in order to be in with a chance of fish it is advisable to be able to use the worm. Small spate rivers such as the Yorkshire Esk, many of the Welsh rivers and those in the Isle of Man, all lend themselves to worming. The Esk is a river I used to know very well indeed; and in the late fifties and early sixties I fished it frequently. The river often fished well following a dirty spate, but the bulk of salmon taken at that time fell to the worm fishers. By the time the water had cleared for successful fly fishing, the river was invariably too low for preference and the current insufficient to carry a fly properly. The spinner could be used as the spate was clearing but usually it gave more success with the large sea trout which run that river. There was a time when all the migratory fish in it were lumped under the heading of *salmon*; and there still remains a tendency to refer to them all as *fish*. One had then to enquire if the fish caught were in fact salmon or sea trout. The inevitable answer was that those taken on the worm, prawn or shrimp were salmon; and those on the spinner . . . sea trout. This is not to imply that salmon were never taken on the spinner, since a good number were actually taken this way. But this was at times when the river had fined down somewhat, and then the prawn, worm and shrimp were still likely to be more effective. Many of the pools had a sluggish current. The old hands at worming used to sit on a box, put their rod in a rest and wait for the rod tip to start shaking. Such tactics with the worm require no greater experience than knowledge of where the salmon were likely to lie and I do not propose to elaborate any further on that particular style.

On many of our classic rivers, however, there comes a time, however brief, when salmon become almost uncatchable on flies and spinners. There are various reasons for this; and the period of inactivity may vary from the odd day to several weeks. Exceptionally low water conditions, with fish in the pools but insufficient current to make effective the use of fly or spinner, may dictate the use of a worm. A dirty spate followed by a period of turbid water often puts fish off the general take; and the same might apply to a period following good sport on fly or spinner when stocks have not been replenished by a fresh run of fish, and the uncaught fish are tending to get stale and potted. The shrimp and prawn can be effective on these occasions but to dedicated worm fishers not quite the same skill is required.

As a general rule, although not vital for success, the water temperature should have reached at least 50 degrees before worming is contemplated. Another important factor, often overlooked, is that all the main lies are known to be tenanted with fish and that they have consistently refused all

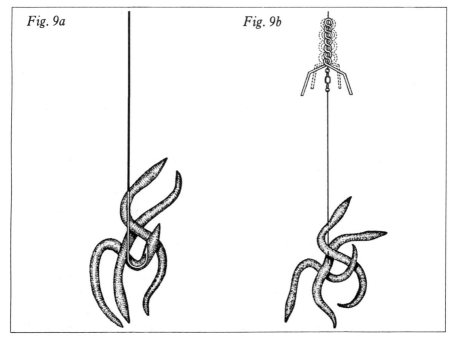

Fig. 9a   Fig. 9b

efforts with fly or spinner. If, for your own reasons, you decide to fish the worm, the weight factor we have examined throughout earlier chapters will be paramount in its influence in making the worm fish in the most effective manner. Ideally the worm or worms (Fig. 9a) roll along the bottom of the river without getting hung up in rocks and snags. In practice, the angler often selects too light or too heavy a weight, with the result that the worms either fail to reach the bottom or get hung up at every cast. The weight of lead to be used, therefore, requires some careful study; and for the angler trying out worming for the first time, inevitably a great deal of trial and error is necessary before correct weight selection is mastered. Even then the angler must be prepared to change the weight as he fishes down a pool, since pools vary in depth and strength of current. Watching an expert with the worm is to realise the close attention he pays to weight selection before making a cast.

There is no doubt that for many forms of salmon fishing a thorough grounding in all the methods used by coarse fishermen is a great advantage. Many of the best salmon fishermen I have met served their early apprenticeship with a float or a ledger; and thus have a decided advantage when it comes to thinking in that third dimension, the depth of the water and the strength of the current.

Choice of leads is largely a matter of opinion; and even among the experts there is little conformity. Some go for a spiral of lead wire wound around the line and so placed that it cannot get within two feet of the hook. If a salmon mouths the worm the line will run freely through the lead spiral and no resistance will be felt by the fish. Then, when the angler is satisfied that the worm has been taken, he can make a firm strike to set the unusually large hook generally required for worming. A running lead, therefore, is almost a must. Leads which are fixed to the line tend to get caught in rocks; and resistance is then felt if the salmon mouths the bait. With all types of lead, there is always a danger that it will get wedged in the bottom and it is advisable for the angler to devise some breakaway system that will spare the hook and worm should this happen. One of the great advantages of a spiral of lead wire is that the angler may continually add weight, or take it off, as the strength of the current dictates. Ken Morritt even evolved a method of leaving the spiral ends free, claiming too that he got caught up less (Fig 9b). Running bullets are sometimes used, but the angler has partially to dismantle his tackle in order to add or take off weight. And, as we have already seen, it is vital to judge our weight of lead very critically, so this can become tedious.

Of course, above all you must have a good stock of lobworms. There are quite a few commercial wormeries, but if you have a reasonable-sized garden it is an easy matter to extract and maintain a stock which will be ready when required. Lobworm hunting is quite a sport on its own and I recall many dark nights, following a shower of rain, when I have gone out on my lawn with a torch to grab a few by the head. Even by torchlight they are very shy and the angler must tread warily on the moist grass if he is not to send them scurrying back into their holes. A firm grip is required and care must be taken not to pull until the worm is losing its hold. Pulling too harshly will sometimes cause them to break in two – but once they slip out of your fingers they are down like a flash. If a worm collector averages fifty per cent success he is doing well.

Once collected, the worms should be kept in a cool, dark place. Damp moss is one of the finest things to keep them in for reasonable periods, but damp, shredded newspaper is just as effective, and much easier to come by. If the worms are to be of the best angling quality they require several hours in the moss in order to scour themselves, and thus become tougher. Freshly caught worms are full of earth and quickly fall off the hook when subjected to the rough treatment they are likely to receive. The greatest care must also be taken to keep the worms cool; anyone who has left a tin of them in the boot of a car under a hot sun will have experienced the wonderful aroma they produce . . . ! Preferences for hook sizes vary; but I usually select about a No. 1 or No. 2. All hooks for worm fishing when purchased should be tied to a short piece of strong nylon line of approximately 12 inches in length. This may be looped or attached directly to a swivel and then to the main reel line. Hooks with eyes are not recommended, since the worms should be threaded on the hook and well up the shank. Normally about three lobworms are threaded this way. Once the angler has made a correct assessment of the type and weight of lead to use, he is ready to begin fishing.

My idea of the best type of tackle to use is a medium-sized spinning rod such as we examined in Chapter 17, together with a fixed spool reel. Initially a cast should be made slightly upstream, then the rod point held well up as the angler feels the bait rolling along the bottom. As the bait trundles down, the angler can let more line slip off the reel by keeping the bale arm open. Eventually the worm will come to rest downstream of the angler, at the edge of the current. It is now that the angler should wait patiently in the hope that a salmon has followed the worm round and is prepared to show some interest. Occasionally salmon will intercept a rolling worm; but they are perhaps more likely to follow it out of their lies, and may then be prepared to pay it some attention when it has come to rest. There will be many casts when, apart from frequent hang-ups, nothing happens; but the angler should always leave the bait in the resting position for a little while until he is satisfied that no salmon has followed it round. The reel should still be able to give immediate slack line and the angler must be prepared to make many casts before the tell-tale twitching of the rod suggests that a salmon is interested. Of course, it may well be a trout, or worse still, an eel that is mouthing the bait; but whatever happens, no attempt to strike should be made at this stage. Every time there is a good pull at the worm a little line should be slipped off the reel. Only when the angler is confident that a salmon has picked up the bait, and is firmly taking it back to its lie, should the reel be re-engaged and a firm strike made. The greatest mistake possible at this stage is to strike too early, and I have known many occasions when a full five minutes of twitches have had to be tolerated patiently before the fish made off with a solid hold. Some anglers are prepared to wait interminable periods; and invariably, when the fish is landed, the hook is found a long way down the gullet. Short of a break, the fish would have little chance of escape.

As a method of taking difficult fish, therefore, worm fishing has much to offer the unfortunate fisherman who cannot combine a visit to the river with ideal conditions. Competent worming for salmon requires a type of skill, and a persistence, not very often found in the general run of salmon anglers. For me, it is tedious; but I admit to a certain feeling of excitement once the tedium is over and there is a salmon twitching at the line. Will it take – or won't it? The seconds seem to tick by very slowly, full of suspense. Perhaps this is the greatest excitement that worm fishing has to offer.

Just how a salmon can differentiate between a shrimp and a prawn remains a mystery to me. But I have plenty of evidence which indicates that they can, in fact, do so and that the manner of taking each bait is different. Both can be effective baits for salmon; but it is not always right to think that a big prawn will be effective in a big water and a small shrimp in a shrunken stream. This may well be the answer in some circumstances; but for those who enjoy these methods of fishing, there is much to be said for an intelligent selection based on angling conditions.

Prawns come in various sizes. The best to purchase are those commercially packed in a good preservative. If they are too soft or too brittle, they will not stand the sustained punishment of continued casting. They should retain a good salty tang; and those with a cluster of spawn between their legs, known as berried prawns, are reputed to be the best. Dyes may be added to give them a rich red colouring. Although most natural prawns are not seen in these vivid colours, there are several crustaceans that do bear a rich red coat in their natural habitat, the depths of the ocean.

I have little doubt that on occasions the prawn scares a lot of fish in a pool; whereas the shrimp rarely seems to do so. Widely different views are held on this topic, and I know of at least one eminent angler who refutes my suggestion. I do think that a great deal hinges on the length of stay the fish have had in the pool being fished. I have little doubt that fresh fish are not so easily intimidated; but the behaviour from stale fish, which have been in residence for a long time and who may have had unscrupulous anglers casting over them and snatching, is not so easy to predict. There are times when salmon will take the prawn with such ferocity that the angler is inclined to think that it is the only bait worth using. There are other times, however, when, upon its first entry into the water, the fish go berserk in their attempts to flee from it.

The prawn may be fished in several styles and is, generally, another good ace for the salmon angler to have up his sleeve. But there are some waters and conditions of water where its continued use might only make the salmon uncatchable. The prawn must be used with a little forethought, and not fished persistently if there is any indication that it will scare the fish. On many Norwegian rivers the prawn is used continually; and, although it seems to account for many big fish, I have never been fully convinced that it does not sometimes have a detrimental effect – despite the fact that given the choice many Norwegian gillies will fish a prawn right through the season.

As with worm fishing, the bulk of my prawn fishing has been enjoyed on the little Yorkshire Esk. I have taken my quota of fish with it on occasion; but have also seen a whole pool of salmon go completely wild shortly after my prawn entered the water. The fish leapt and skittered all over the pool and there were some that charged off downstream and dived headlong over the sill of a small weir. Something certainly gave them a shock and I was forced to the only reasonable conclusion that it was my prawn. I don't imagine that a seal or an otter in the pool could have caused more panic. This, however, was in a small stretch of water where salmon reaction was easy to see. How many times might there be on a big river when the prawn has the same effect, but the effect goes unnoticed by the angler? My old Tweed boatman would not permit the use of the prawn during a normal season; and if he heard that rods fishing lower downstream were using it, he was fully confident that we would have some fresh fish in our beat before twenty-four hours had passed.

Continual prawning, therefore, may do more harm than good. Initial catches may be very encouraging, but the fish may then slowly shy off the bait and become uncatchable by any legitimate means, including fly fishing, as long as they remain in that location. A further rise in the water, to lift the old stock upstream and bring a new batch in, will then have to occur before prawning is again likely to result in any success. At best the prawn is a method of getting the odd fish in an otherwise difficult period: at worst, it will spoil fishing with any other type of lure and will make an angler very unpopular among those following on behind, or fishing the beat later during the week.

Conditions under which to try the prawn vary a great deal; but they are generally much the same as those appropriate to the worm. The general conditions suggested are crisp early mornings, with a touch of moisture on the banks; days when, due to condensation, you would get your boots thoroughly wet while walking through the long grass to the riverside; days following overnight rain or frost; and at times when the salmon have had a good look at other lures, and have refused all efforts to tempt them.

One of my favourite methods of fishing a prawn is the sink-and-draw technique. The prawn, suitably weighted to match the current strength, is cast out with a normal spinning rod and reel suited to the water. The prawn is allowed to sink, and is then slowly retrieved with a sink-and-draw motion by winding a little line back on to the reel between each jerk of the rod. The bait eventually swings out of the current and may then be retrieved for the next cast. There may be many casts when the prawn will sink on to the bottom and get hung up, but every bit of resistance should be treated as a take and a strike made. The actual take is usually firm and decisive, but if there is a vast array of hooks on the tackle there should be little delay in responding with a hard strike.

There are many ways of mounting a prawn but in all cases it should be mounted with its head and whiskers at the bottom. The choice of tackle is left to individual preference, or the fashion for the water. On the Esk I used to favour a normal triangle of hooks about size 6. The prawn was straightened with a baiting needle and the line threaded through and tied on to the triangle. A straightened paper clip was then placed through the middle of the prawn along the same path taken through the body with the needle and line, in order to keep it straight. For extra weighting a piece of fine lead wire, wound around the shank of the triangle, was generally sufficient for a sluggish current. On faster rivers, of course, the shank may not be long enough to carry the required weight; and the lead is then placed above the swivel and some eighteen inches from the prawn. Care must be taken to ensure that the prawn does not rotate when a sink-and-draw motion is applied to it. For this reason it is better to snip off the two small pieces of prawn tail, to prevent any likelihood of their acting as a propeller. A larger, single, worm-sized hook may well be used as an alternative to the triangle, but it might not give such good hooking potential (Fig. 10). There are many commercial prawn tackles on the market, with a built-in straightening device. They have some advantages; but the prawn has to be tied down with red elastic thread to prevent it from

Fig. 10

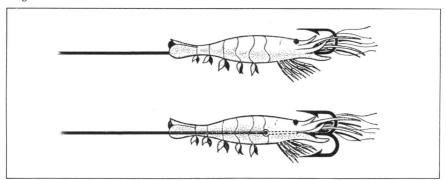

falling off. The latter method is much used in Norway and has the great advantage that several tackles can be assembled before starting a day's fishing. The array of hooks on these tackles usually ensures a good hook-hold and the elastic thread binding protects the prawn from encounters with the river bottom.

As with all the other methods of salmon fishing we have examined, the selection of the correct weight of lead to suit the current is equally important in fishing the prawn. Tactics in Norway, where a great deal of lead is used, will be commented upon in a later chapter. For most British rivers, it is very important to find the right balance of weight to keep the bait off the bottom, but not too high in the water. The sink-and-draw action should not be done too quickly and a slack line avoided by slow lowering of the rod during the period when the prawn sinks. If the line is allowed to go slack it is possible for the bait to be taken without the angler feeling the tell-tale pull; and as a salmon can eject a prawn very quickly this lack of feel of the take must be avoided at all costs.

In very sluggish water salmon will sometimes nip at the prawn; but oddly enough they are more likely to do this with a shrimp, as we shall see in the next chapter. Sink-and-draw is not the only method by which a prawn may be fished. The spinning prawn is often very effective, with the prawn mounted on a spinning flight, and fished in a similar manner to a Devon Minnow. Sometimes it might pay to 'trot' the spinning prawn down a fast run, letting it drop down with only the current to make it revolve, in a series of jerky actions. But the bulk of my success has been with the sink-and-draw method and I have little experience of successful prawn spinning.

On some rivers it is possible to fish a prawn from a fly rod. The prawn is simply lobbed out and allowed to swing round slowly in the current. This method lends itself to some sluggish waters; but not to most of the classic, fast rivers of Scotland.

To sum up, therefore, the prawn should always be used as a last resort. It is a method of getting a few fish when all else has failed. Its use should not be prolonged, though, since there is a serious danger of making the resident fish almost uncatchable by you or the angler following – particularly if the fishing has been indiscriminate and a few fish have been 'stroked' by the prawn. On many Association waters the use of the prawn is rightly banned; but it has saved many a blank day for me and in Norway the method provided me with the second largest salmon I have ever caught.

In the last chapter we examined how salmon seem to be able to differentiate between a prawn and a shrimp. We have seen how a prawn will sometimes frighten the fish, but on occasions will also serve as a very killing bait. It has been my experience that the shrimp rarely has this frightening effect; and in the early days when I did a lot of bait fishing I eventually came to have a distinct preference for it as against either worm or prawn. It may be fished delicately and is perhaps one of the most killing baits for salmon that an angler can find.

Shrimps, of course, are smaller than prawns; but the same rules should be observed in their selection and preservation and they may also be dyed in various colours to suit individual preferences. I have never been fully convinced that colour matters a great deal and have caught the bulk of my fish on those of natural colouring, or those dyed a dark scarlet. They may be mounted in a similar fashion to a prawn; but because of their smaller size do not show to their best advantage if mounted on prawn tackles. I frequently used the single-hook method, with a piece of paper clip, as described in the previous chapter, and only used the triangle with extra-large shrimps. The bait may be fished sink-and-draw or, for that matter, in all the styles I have described for prawn fishing, although one of the most effective ways I know is fishing the shrimp with a float. For this it is important to know exactly where the salmon are lying. The float is then adjusted so that the shrimp will 'trot' just above the river bed, and the cast is made to a precise spot so that the shrimp will pass within inches of the nose of the salmon. Fairly quiet water is essential, and great care must be taken to ensure that the fish do not see you before they see the bait. Deep holes and backwaters make ideal spots and in clear water conditions individual fish may be stalked and cast over so that the shrimp approaches the angler's selected fish. In many deep holes, however, it may be impossible to see the fish you hope are there. Small air bubbles floating to the surface may sometimes betray the presence of salmon in very calm and sluggish water, but often you just have to guess. The first indication of fish interest you are likely to get is a slight tremor of the float. A shrimp take is usually very timid, and a slow dip of the float often indicates that the fish has taken the shrimp quietly into its mouth. Anything more than a slight tremor should therefore be treated as a take, and a prompt strike made. The bulk of fish hooked in this manner will generally be found to have the hook in the roof of their mouths, which rarely allows them to get free.

Smaller rivers seem to offer more opportunities for float-fishing with a shrimp. It is fairly essential, I think, not to have too much line out. Again, the shrimp should be so weighted that it will not only keep the float fishing in an upright position but also so that it enables the bait to get down to the right place. Old wine bottle corks make ideal floats and champagne corks seem about the best of all. In general, little weight is required, since it is not practicable to fish in this style in very fast water; and the method only lends itself to quiet pools and backwaters. Care must be taken when assessing the depth of the water and the float should be adjusted so that the shrimp will move slowly over the bed of the river. To have it scraping the bottom would give too many false alarms on the float; while to have it fishing too high in the water would cause it to pass over the heads of the fish. It is when the fish get an 'eyeball to eyeball' confrontation with the shrimp that they respond best.

Times to try this method may be difficult to determine if the angler is not fully conversant with the water. I recall days on the Esk when the shrimp sent me home with fish that seemed uncatchable by any other method. On one occasion I had a guest accompanying me. The river, we knew, held a good stock of fish; but our continuous spinning up to 4 p.m. had not even produced an offer. 'Come on' I said to my guest. 'We'll go up to the dam and try the shrimp.' He looked on in amazement as I put on a float and a small shrimp mounted on a single hook. I adjusted the height of the float carefully to match the depth of the water, and quietly walked to the edge; there I let the tackle swim slowly down in the deep water beneath my feet. The bait had travelled barely six yards before the float slowly submerged. I struck hard and handed him my rod. 'My God' said he, as he felt the tug of a fighting salmon, 'I would not have believed it possible!' As soon as it was played out, the fish was quickly brought ashore and knocked on the head. A fresh shrimp was mounted and it was not long before he was playing number two. A third was finally brought to the bank before I called a halt. It would have been more than likely that we could have gone on catching fish for a further period by that method; but there were other anglers waiting to fish the water and the taking of three prime fish ranging from 11 to 15lbs was more than satisfactory under the circumstances.

On another occasion I was on the river, barely an hour's drive from my home, by 5 a.m. The river was too low for the best spinning and, as this was in my fish-hungry days, I was quick to try a shrimp. It was destined to be one of those scorching-hot late summer days and I had planned to be back in my office for 11 a.m. A two-mile walk got me down to some likely water and in the next two hours I took four prime fish on the float-fished shrimp, totalling about 57lbs in weight. The two-mile struggle back in the hot sun took the sharp edge off some of my enjoyment, but I was back in the office at the appointed time, where my colleagues were quite confident that I must have got the salmon from the local fishmonger.

During those far-off fish-hungry days, it was inevitable that I enjoyed some unpopularity on that hard-fished Association water. In the end I got to the point where I concealed my catch so that fellow members would not know how many I had caught. I then sneaked them away to the boot of my car, and quietly went on my way. On arriving at the river very early one morning, I passed the time of day with a fellow angler. He was obviously

Arthur Oglesby shrimp fishing for salmon early in the morning on the Yorkshire Esk.

a member of the same Association, but evidently did not know me nor I him. We did not trouble to introduce ourselves, but just made brief enquiry from each other where we intended to fish. Upon telling him that I had thought of going downstream to a favourite place, he retorted: 'I wouldn't go down there, if I were you. They tell me that that bugger Oglesby is going to be down there today . . . ' I did not enlighten him about my identity, but merely said that I would go and join that very fine angler! I never did divulge the best day's catch I took from that water on the float-fished shrimp and nothing will induce me to do it even now. It is something, in retrospect, of which I am not very proud.

Sometimes it may pay the angler to remove the float and just let the shrimp rove around in the water. It may be cast out and retrieved as slowly as possible. For this method, the shrimp should be practically weightless. And, if the angler positions himself behind a tree, it is possible to drop the shrimp among the semi-comatose salmon lying in a quiet backwater. Sometimes the shrimp is taken eagerly; but at other times the fish will only mouth the bait, without taking hold of it properly. I have even watched salmon playing with a slowly-retrieved shrimp; they have come up and taken it in their mouths, but before the pull has been transmitted up the line and to the rod, they have quickly blown it out again. Sometimes a salmon will attack the shrimp five or six times in this way before taking it firmly or rejecting it altogether.

Fishing with the shrimp is a fascinating form of the sport in low water, and enables the angler who has carefully stalked to the pool and remained quiet to see a deal of salmon reaction to the bait. Of all the forms of natural-bait fishing, it was always the one that I found the most interesting.

You may think that being a conservative-minded Britisher, I would hold dear many of the theories put forward by earlier British writers on the question of salmon fishing. On the contrary, I think that one of the best works on Atlantic salmon, from a fly fishing point of view, was presented to the angler in 1958 by Lee Wulff, with his book, *The Atlantic Salmon*. Although Wulff fished briefly in the British Isles, he spent the bulk of his time with the same breed of salmon which run the rivers of the north-east coast of Canada. Essentially he is a fly fisherman, and has achieved some eminence for his development of ultra-light tackle for salmon fly fishing. With certain of his doctrines on casting I am not in full agreement, but I found myself endorsing almost his every word concerning tactics. Any reader interested in the finer points of fly fishing for salmon would do well to read him; but, in a work which aims to be a broad-based textbook on British methods, I cannot afford to be so specific.

We have already examined most, if not all, of the legitimate methods utilised for the capture of salmon in Britain. Some, as we shall see later, are also applicable to Norwegian salmon. But there will be many known and unknown influences which will affect our sport, and it is now my aim to explore some of the known ones and speculate on the unknown. The successful salmon angler may be said to be the one who is fully versed in all legitimate methods of fishing for them. He will know his floating line techniques; will have mastered spinning under all conditions; and, if he is not content to go home fishless on occasions, he will have those three aces up his sleeve in the form of worming, prawning, and shrimping.

The experienced salmon angler will have extensive knowledge of the signs and seasons when a certain method is likely to bring him the best chance of sport; but if, like many salmon anglers, he has to book a beat in advance and travel some hundreds of miles for the fishing, he might never find ideal conditions for the particular stretch of water he is to fish. Right at the start of our chapter, therefore, we have established the number one factor which influences our sport: the remote chance that it can be anything other than mediocre for the one week out of fifty-two which we have chosen to be on the river. We increase our chances slightly if we opt for a two-week period during what is established as the best of the season. But the only real way to take advantage of a piece of water is to live on it and have access to it throughout a full season. This may involve not only owning that piece of water, but the elimination of other guests or tenants who might just monopolise it when we want to fish. That, dear reader, is the only way you might exploit a piece of water to its full potential. The rest is little more than pot-luck, and we can only examine the specific times of the year and deduce which methods might suit us best. For example, if the early months of February are the angler's chosen time then, as we have seen, it is a fairly safe bet that the spinning bait, fished slow and deep, will be the wisest choice. Alternatively, a classic beat in May could well maintain nearly ideal conditions for the small fly on the floating line. But, even though fish may be caught, there will never be any certainty that sport is likely to be at its best.

From all this it may easily be seen that the nomadic salmon angler, while being able to experience the great variations of different rivers, will never have the intimate knowledge necessary to judge correctly a most important issue: the height of water most likely to ensure successful salmon fishing. The angler who is fortunate enough not only to live on the banks of a salmon river, but to have access to the fishing, has advantages far outweighing any other consideration. After the continual fishing of one stretch of water over the years, he will know (perhaps quite subconsciously) when it will be worth putting a line in the water and when it will be more comfortable to stay at home. The casual visitor has no such luck. He can only fish diligently during his chosen time – in the *hope* of sport. This very fact may well account for the reputed dourness of many Scottish gillies when they are lured to the river by enthusiastic tenants, in the full knowledge that if they (the gillies) could fish the river themselves at that time, they would stay away. For this reason the finest angler in the land would be hard put to compete with a local expert on his own stretch of water. The native would know the precise height when certain pools would fish best; he would also know the alternate lies under varying heights of water; and the precise method most likely to achieve success.

For the non-resident angler, who consistently takes a beat at the same time every season, the odds do narrow down. He might well spend the first two years serving an apprenticeship to the water; but if he persists, he will begin to acquire some of the knowledge of the native and will ultimately be in a position to exploit favourable conditions. There will be occasions when he is likely to find the river either dead low or in a roaring flood; but he will be able to draw on his experience to know whether fishing is worthwhile or not at any given height. Although it may seem desirable, therefore, to fish a great variety of rivers, the angler who persists with one specific beat will be able to fish with greater potential than the roving one.

In his excellent little book, *Rod Fishing for Salmon on the Wye*, J. Arthur Hutton states, quite categorically, that the height of the water is, in his opinion, the most important factor in successful salmon fishing. I endorse this comment; but feel that temperature, overhead conditions and humidity must also be taken into consideration to make the best assessment. With all the signs of the zodiac in their correct orbit and fish in the pools, the choice of a particular fly or bait is comparatively simple. The late A. H. E. Wood was, perhaps, the best example of 'one man – one beat' for season after season, when he fished the Cairnton beat of the Dee. Wood no doubt knew, by a casual glance at the river, whether it was worth fishing or not. With an annual catch to his own rod of something like three hundred fish, I suspect that he would not bother too much with the doubtful days. Richard Waddington did not to my knowledge live on a river; but, like myself, he had sufficient access to well-known beats of the Spey to know the water in all its moods, and how best to take advantage of prevailing conditions.

Some of my earliest salmon fishing was done on the Argyllshire Awe; yet I fished that river for three seasons before I caught my first Awe salmon. Of late years I have tended to concentrate my salmon fishing on the Tweed, Lune, Spey and Vosso. I used to take the Upper Hendersyde water of the Tweed for two weeks in February and a further two weeks at the end of November. I could not possibly know that beat as well as the local gillie, but I got to know it pretty well and from sheer experience I knew its varying moods at different heights of the water. During the last two years (1980 and 1981) I have been most fortunate in securing an early November tenancy on the cream of Tweed fishing at Upper Floors. Due to excessive high water over both my visits I have yet to see the beat at low water, but so long as His Grace The Duke of Roxburghe will have me as a tenant, I shall stay with it. Maybe then I shall eventually get to know it and be able to exploit its vast potential.

Although I have little involvement with the Lune these days, during the sixties and early seventies the Newton water was available to me throughout the season; and if ever there was a stretch of water which was more influenced by its height, I have yet to see it. Unfortunately we had no measuring gauge on the river; but I had one small rock which, when it was just showing above the water surface, told me that the river was at near-perfect height. For me, it was as good as a micrometer, since the water level assessment it gave usually informed me whether I could expect the sport to be good or indifferent.

A typical occasion which comes to mind was when I was to visit the river for a period of three days with another well-known angler as my guest. We arrived one Thursday evening in late July 1966. I had heard that the river was in fine trim with plenty of fish about; but on arrival I was greatly dismayed to learn that there had been further rain and that my tell-tale rock was submerged and not to be seen. My companion, who had rarely fished the river before, thought it looked perfect. He quickly tackled up and was away before I had time to unload the car. For my part I was in no hurry. We were to spend a few nights living rough in the fishing hut, and I spent the evening preparing camp beds and generally making the hut tidy. When this was completed I relaxed lazily in a deckchair and watched the sun set over a comforting glass of Scotch. Darkness had fallen before my companion returned. He had seen several fish but had not touched one; nor had the sea trout obliged in the failing light. Over a few more drams we discussed the prospects for the morning before turning into our sleeping bags for some quiet, peaceful sleep.

At 6 a.m. my companion was up and about, clambering into waders and generally disturbing the entire household. With one sleepy eye open I raised my head off the pillow to look out of the hut window and examine the water level as shown by my tell-tale rock. The top of the rock was still below the surface, although a faint wave line could now be detected from the water disturbance it caused. I slumped back on to my pillow and wished my companion the very best of British luck, 'tight lines' and all that. By 10 a.m. he was back again, fishless, but hungry and keen to get at the bacon and eggs I was frying over the cooker. This time he had seen even more fish and was completely mystified why at least one of them had not taken his bait. Fully refreshed he was soon back on the water, while I contented myself taking photographs and generally relaxing. By nightfall on that Friday evening he was still fishless; and seemed to be coming rapidly to the conclusion that the fish were uncatchable. Before I turned in, however, I had a last look at my rock and noticed that the tip was now showing slightly. With no more rain, I thought, the river would be at a perfect height for the morning.

At 6 a.m. it was I who was up and about, creating a commotion; and it was my friend who, between intermittent snores, risked one sleepy eye at me with the news that he would have breakfast ready by 8 a.m. Back at 8 a.m. I was too, with three prime salmon, all covered in sea lice and all in the 'teens of pounds. This was too much for him: what had I got them on? A 2-inch Black and Gold Devon Minnow, I replied. With that he was off, Devon Minnows coming out of his ears, while I completed my breakfast.

By 10 a.m. my rock was showing a little more; so I put the spinning rod to one side, and got my fly tackle ready. A No. 6 Blue Charm seemed about right for the conditions. I waded across the river to join my friend to find him still fishless. By midday I had a further two fish on the fly; and it was not until 1 p.m. that my companion finally got one to take his spinner. By 2 p.m. we had to be on our way to join a friend on another river; but I had mixed feelings about the move. It was my impression that if I had been able to fish that day out, I could have broken the record for the beat.

The height of the water can therefore be the paramount factor as a guide to a successful day. But other factors must be combined with it to give the perfect day. It is only by intimate knowledge of one piece of water that this initial guide, the near-perfect height, can be estimated accurately, and thereby a correct assessment made of the most effective method to be used.

It would not do to think that the height of the water will be the only factor to affect things as dramatically as I have illustrated. Water chemistry has great influence, as do relative air and water temperatures; acid/alkali levels; biochemical oxygen demand (B. O. D.); barometric pressure and a host of other known factors as well as those which remain unknown. Acid rain, the sulphur dioxide fall-out from fossil fuel combustion in our factories, is an ever-increasing threat to stable and acceptable water chemistry. It is proving a dire threat in some Norwegian and Canadian rivers and there is ample evidence that it has already demonstrated its effect on specific British rivers. Not only may it put fish off the take, but it might well cause mortality to an entire run of fish. Certain Canadian and Norwegian rivers have ceased to provide a suitable environment for the maintenance of life for *salmonid* species. The ever-increasing growth of weed on such rivers as the Tweed and Spey all demonstrate that, over the years, water chemistry is in a state of change. Anglers argue that the weed must have been transplanted from other sources; but there is evidence to suggest that the seed has been lying dormant for thousands of years and that it is only a change in basic water chemistry, due to fertilisers, which has released the correct catalyst to encourage growth. Some years ago a downpour of rain in America's perennial desert area of Death Valley created pools of water. Suddenly there were fish in the water, from eggs that had lain dormant and dehydrated for longer than man thought possible.

These days, more than at any other time in history, the angler has to share his playground with other water-associated sports. The passage of canoes and other river traffic has a disturbing influence on salmon. Many fish lying in shallow water will flee, upstream or down, to seek shelter from the threatening shadows. From experience of watching fish in this situation I know that it might be nigh on an hour before the fish creep back to their original lies. The passage of traffic on high water has less influence than on the low water of summer; but it is a factor with which to be reckoned. Such a disturbance could arouse the fish into taking mood when they re-occupy their lies; but the general effects of river traffic can be upsetting to the angler. Where canoeists use a specific salmon pool as a marshalling or training area the effects may be more far-reaching. Indeed, I have known a pool to be vacated by the salmon and not re-occupied until a rise of water brought in some fresh fish from the lower beats.

Disease in our rivers has also been a great influence on fish-taking habits. The angler who casually accepts a beat on a one-week-a-year basis is never likely to know many of the factors affecting his sport. I now spend nigh on three months of my year in Strathspey, but I cannot claim to have full knowledge of the water which I should like to have. Also there are unknown factors concerning our choice of lure: we still don't know why salmon take them, and can only speculate on their full effect.

The multitude of spinning baits, lures and flies now on sale to the bewildered angling public – aided by the general gullibility of salmon anglers in these matters as they religiously keep changing their lures – is very confusing. Some are claimed by the makers to have 'sonic' qualities: others to have vibrating qualities. Doubtless by shaking their sensual hips and emitting high frequency vibrations they lure the unsuspecting fish into trouble.

My own, and indeed general, experience has proved that there is no such simple formula for the wholesale capture of salmon. As I have grave

Colonel Eric Stevens (in the high seat) studies the reaction of salmon to canoes passing over a well-known lie on the River Spey.

doubts about both sonic and vibrating qualities, I feel that the main line of thought and experiment should be along the lines of the visual image that persuades a salmon to take a bait, spinner, or lure of any type, including the so-called 'salmon fly'.

We must presume that when a salmon takes a lure in fresh water, we have awoken the urge to prey. It has been argued that the salmon takes a lure out of anger or sheer boredom. The fact remains that in the case of the worm (a natural bait) the fish will often swallow it; though whether it can subsequently digest it is highly doubtful. It may thus be reasonable to suppose that if a salmon found a Black and Gold Devon Minnow to be soft, appetising and unarrayed with hooks when taken in its mouth, it would do precisely the same thing – that is, it would swallow it. I have seen salmon pick up a bunch of lobworms and appear to chew them for some considerable time before spitting them out. This is an exception to the rule. Many salmon anglers who are experts at worming will often confirm that if the strike is delayed too long, the bait and hook are frequently found in the stomach of the fish.

In my opinion, it is the appearance and movement of the lure which persuades the salmon that here is something that is alive. Whether it seizes upon such a lure out of hunger or under the influence of some other motive is not important. The fish is more likely, perhaps, to attack something which, at some time, has represented food. But it may well attack an enemy or merely be influenced by reflex action as with our example of the playful cat and the blown leaves.

I have commented upon the action of the lure: I think that this is important. Modern salmon-fly dressing trends indicate that a fly should give a greater semblance of life when fished in an average stream. The old inanimate and over-dressed patterns are fast dying out; and in their place we get the more logical designs, such as the Waddington range, constructed with long, flowing hackles, usually of black heron fibres. Buck-tail is also becoming a popular material; and hair-wing flies are rapidly gaining prestige.

Some years ago I had an opportunity to film various types of flies moving in a current of water. A glass-sided tank was used, to which was attached an ordinary hosepipe. The flies were then submerged and left to flit and dance in the current, in much the same manner as they do in a river when attached to the end of a line or leader. The cine-camera seemed the ideal instrument to record their behaviour, since it conveys their true appearance as seen when moving. Such flies as the Waddington series showed an exceptional resemblance to a living creature. Experiments with the more conventional salmon flies showed less action, in the sense that they looked like – conventional salmon flies!

My next problem was to convey, by means of a still picture, the life-like quality of certain flies. For ordinary work my cine-camera is operated at 24 frames per second. In other words, the illusion of movement is created by projecting 24 progressive still pictures every second. The persistence of vision of the human eye, however, is capable of overcoming 'flicker' at 16 frames per second, or even slightly less. As projector speed moves below this, our eye tends to see a series of well-defined still pictures again and the persistence of vision is lost.

In order to take a moving picture, a cine-camera must move the film forward a frame before exposing it. Normally, for half the time of the operation, the shutter is closed and the camera mechanism is transporting the film. During the other half, the film is stationary; and with the shutter open, exposure takes place. (I apologise to cine-enthusiasts for being so elementary: I merely wish to explain why, when operating at 16 frames per second, the camera gives an effective shutter exposure of half this speed – that is 1/32 of a second.)

If we assume that the salmon has the same persistence of vision as our own – and it is only an assumption – it is reasonable to suppose that, in order to capture a still picture depicting a bait or a fly as the salmon momentarily sees it, we should utilise a shutter speed of 1/32 of a second or longer on the still camera. As a keen photographer, I have always aimed at having a sharp, well-defined print. These can easily be obtained, of course, by using still cameras with high shutter speeds or in conjunction with electronic flash. In such an operation, the fly or bait is completely 'frozen' into a well-defined photographic reproduction. But this is well within our persistence of vision limitations, and could not possibly convey the slow moment when a salmon sees a bait or fly.

Initial experiments were then tried using lower shutter speeds, in the order of 1/30th second to 1/15th second. Blurred, uninspiring photographs were the result. It could be argued, nevertheless, that they do represent the illusion which the salmon sees. What was very noticeable, in the case of a series of Devon spinners filmed in colour, was their overall similarity in tone. Various colour combinations were tried, such as Black and Gold, Yellow Belly and Blue and Silver. When seen on the screen, it was difficult to determine which spinner was which. In fact, when spinning at critical revolutions, certain colour combinations blended to form a tone on the 'grey scale'. Combinations which lacked a full range of colours took on much more delicate shades than the basic static colours.

I think that it is quite a true statement that more fishermen are caught with the multi-coloured baits which now litter the tackle shops than fish. The problem, therefore, reverts once again to reactions from the salmon; and we shall never know their views on the matter. The significant factor is that, for some reason, a salmon may be induced to take a bait or a fly. I really think that the type of lure matters less than we imagine; provided, of course, that we make our choice of size and colour to conform with basic rules concerning colour and temperature of the water. Until we learn differently, it would seem that the old rules of 'bright for a bright or cold day', and 'dull for a dull or warm day', are fairly safe guidelines. It would also seem reasonable to match the colour of the water with the colour of the bait; but if we must keep changing our lures at the end of every quarter-hour of fruitless fishing, I suggest that that change should be a bold one from the colour standpoint.

The increasing use of spoon baits for salmon in coloured water is interesting. I have had marked success with the French-made Mepps and with the Toby spoon. When conditions are such that the angler would not normally consider fishing with a fly, these lures have consistently taken good bags of salmon and sea trout. On one occasion, fishing a coloured spate stream with these baits, I caught no less than seven fish one day and five on the next.

I feel that it is very important, in view of these findings, to weigh up the water conditions, and to present to the salmon something which can readily be seen in turbid water (though less readily seen in clear water) in a manner that looks reasonable and natural to the fish. The rest depends on fish mood and all the other factors and influences we have examined. And, if it is inclined to take, all is well. If not, well, hundreds of thousands of words have been written on this subject by more erudite persons than myself. The main point is that, for our good fortune, salmon continue to run our rivers and occasionally they take our flies and baits. This ensures, as Pritt wrote, 'this endless field for argument, speculation and experiment'.

It is my view that no salmon angler can consider his education complete until he has fished in all the Atlantic salmon-producing countries in the world. If this is the case, I still have some little way to go. I have not yet fished the famous rivers of the eastern sea-boards of Canada or Newfoundland, nor the rock-girt rivers of Iceland. But I keep hoping to do so one day.

A hundred and fifty years ago salmon were commonplace in the rivers of Britain. Over the years the number of rivers suited to maintaining salmon stocks has declined; and today, England can barely claim even double-figure numbers of worthwhile salmon rivers. Scotland, Ireland and Wales still have their classic salmon waters, as yet only marginally spoilt by the march of progress; but beats on the Spey, Dee, Tweed and Tay are expensive and hard to come by, and the fifty-pounders of bygone days are rare.

Before the turn of the century, British salmon anglers were the first to realise the vast potential of Norwegian fishing. Names like Laerdal, Namsen, Alta, Mals, Aarø and Vosso gradually became the hallmark of all the best in salmon fishing; and certainly all the rivers that held the biggest salmon. Perhaps the Aarø gained the most exotic reputation of all. It is a short and turbulent river and was said to yield more fifty-pounders than any other Atlantic salmon river in the world. The late L.R. Hardy fished there and was filmed catching monster fish. Richard Waddington achieved a lifetime ambition there by beaching unaided a fish of 51lbs, caught on a fly of his own tying. Charles Ritz in *A Fly Fisher's Life* referred to it as 'The Aarø – The Terrific!'; and mentions a fish of 76lbs apart from twenty other fish of over 50lbs. Thus to the British salmon angler the Aarø became the pinnacle, the ultimate of salmon rivers in the world. Alas, it is not the same today!

Almost from childhood days the lure of Norway has drawn me. By the spring of 1961 I could no longer resist the great temptation, and I planned a family holiday to that country in the company of Ken Morritt and his family. We were to go there during August of that year, a time, I was to learn, when the bulk of the best fishing was over. It was not, however, to be essentially a fishing holiday. Most of our time was to be spent in sightseeing and amusing the children. Our chosen hotel was on the higher reaches of the Vosso river at Bulken, and within easy access of the town of Voss. The hotel had fishing rights on some of the upper Vosso water and it was on this water that I first wet a line in the quest for the Norwegian salmon. To say the least, the hotel water looked magnificent; and a photograph of a visitor to that water, taken in June of that year and showing him holding a brace of fish weighing 64lbs and 55lbs respectively, did much to keep us on the ball. We fished in vain for most of the first week, but towards the end of our stay we got access to some water lower downstream at Geitle. There I managed to catch the largest and smallest salmon I had ever taken until then; a lovely fish of 27lbs and a mere tiddler of 4lbs. On our last day we arranged a further visit to a beat of the river at Bolstadøyri; and on that beat although I drew blank, Ken Morritt wiped my eye with a fish of 28lbs. I had no idea then that the Bolstad beat of the Vosso was to see a great deal more of me in the years that lay ahead; and that it would produce for me a few salmon of large enough dimensions to fulfil my wildest dreams.

On my immediate return home, I must confess to a little disappointment. Where were all the fish? Why was such a magnificent river apparently so desperately short of salmon? Doubtless, the many nets and traps I had seen throughout the river were taking more than their fair share and the angler was left with the oddments which remained. Anyway, I had been to Norway and I had caught a fish. There was no longer the same urgency to try conclusions with their salmon. Instead I renewed my efforts on the more prolific rivers of Britain. If they could not offer the monsters of Norway, they were at least full of smaller fish.

During the years which followed, tales of monster fish from Norway occasionally drifted across the North Sea. I still had a nattering desire to go back there again and to fish in what were, perhaps, more famed waters. The Norwegian bug started to bite me again. By the end of 1965 I still had caught nothing bigger than my fish of 27lbs in 1961. Let's face it, there are not a great number of salmon anglers – even very competent ones – who have caught fish of over 30lbs, and the size bug was biting me hard. When was I going to get a fish of 30 or 40lbs, or even more? That great salmon angler, the late Captain T.L. Edwards, in all his wide experience of salmon fishing had never taken a fish of 40lbs; admittedly, he had taken two of 39½lbs, but anything bigger eluded him to his dying day.

While at home I had been able to do more research on many Norwegian rivers, particularly the Vosso. There was Fraser Sandeman's *Angling Travels in Norway* to enlighten the Vosso fisherman, but I was more grateful to Mr Jack Chance for some of the facts regarding the Bolstad beat between the wars. It transpired that a Mr Cyril Mowbray Wells, a housemaster at Eton, had been a tenant of the Bolstad beat of the Vosso from 1920 to 1939 and from 1946 to 1950. During that time Wells caught every pound weight of fish between 20lbs and 58lbs, excepting one of 55lbs. He did not classify his fish below 20lbs, but on his eightieth birthday in July 1950 he caught his eightieth fish of 40lbs or over. Although Wells never caught a 60-pounder, his guests caught quite a few over this weight – the biggest going to some 65lbs. In those periods Wells caught no less than 848 salmon to his own rod, with an average weight of 27½lbs. Jack Chance also drew my attention to the fact that the only larger fish of which he had records were two taken by Nicholas Denissoff on the Aarø, in 1923 and 1927, of 68lbs and 72½lbs.

It was in the early spring of 1966 that I received the first intimation that I might be going back to Norway. It may be interesting to relate how my next visit there, in June 1966, became possible. A letter from one of our leading angling journals indicated that a Norwegian travel agent was keen to have a party of British anglers over in Norway to sample some of their fishing. A list of six anglers was to be submitted to him, from which he would choose two to go to Norway as his guests. His objective was to show them the full potential of Norwegian fishing, so that on their return to Britain they could write of their experiences for the national angling press. Naturally I was keen to have my name on the list. Being a Yorkshireman, with some Scottish connections, I am always interested in cutting down on non-essential spending. My name was duly put down along with those of other salmon anglers with names more widely known. Frankly, I did not think that I stood a chance; and, except for sheer coincidence, I doubt whether I would have been considered.

However, there was on that list the name of one angler who was a friend of mine. I refer, of course, to the late Eric Horsfall Turner. In those days Eric was the town clerk of Scarborough! He had fished before in Norway, but as luck would have it, he had to go over to that country on official duties during the early part of that year. While in Oslo, he enquired whether there was any trout fishing available locally; whereupon he was told to call on a Mr Odd Haraldsen who was a travel agent in Oslo and had access to some fishing. During Eric's discussion with Odd, it transpired that he (Odd Haraldsen) was the self-same travel agent who had approached the British angling press for a party of anglers. Eric was requested to give details of those nominated, all of whom he knew. The list was read through, and answered with factual brevity. Finally, the names of Oglesby and Horsfall Turner were mentioned for comments. 'Oglesby', he said, 'is a good friend of mine and is a competent salmon angler, and also knows his angling photography'. 'What about Horsfall Turner?' The angler in question rose and bowed, with a broad grin! So Odd Haraldsen put forward two invitations as a start; one to an angler he had just met personally, and the other to an angler given a good recommendation.

In the weeks that followed I received full details of the tour that was to be arranged. We were to fish the river Jolstra and, once again, the Bolstad beat of the Vosso. Inquiries from friends who had fished the Jolstra revealed that it was a very fine river, with plenty of big fish. So on 15 June 1966 Eric and I took flight for Bergen accompanied by a press photographer and budding film cameraman, Keith Massey. I was quite determined to enjoy myself, whatever sneaking suspicions I had that the Vosso fishing might be past its best and that the fishing would be mediocre.

Norway in June! The magnificence of it! I am quite lost for all the necessary superlatives: mountains, lakes and fjords; tall pines and the

Odd Haraldsen prepares to gaff a 23lb fish from the Vosso in August 1967.

foaming torrents that rush, barely slowing, until they tumble into the sea. The impressive Jolstra river flowed past outside my hotel room. Behind us was a two-hour flight from Newcastle to Bergen; then the overnight steamer trip from there and a fifty-mile car drive from Florø to Forde. The Forde Hotel proved to be very comfortable indeed and was within a few minutes drive of the Bruland beat we were to fish. Despite a sleepless night on board the steamer and an 8 a.m. arrival at the hotel, we could hardly wait for the arrival of our gillies at 9 a.m. so that we could start fishing. The Jolstra river is perhaps not very well known to British salmon anglers but I had heard such glowing tales of its big fish that I was impatient to try conclusions with them.

The sun was already high in the heavens. At this time of the year, in these latitudes, it just does not get dark. The shade temperature was in the region of 80 degrees and the melting snows maintained the river at a good level. In such bright overhead conditions, our chances did not appear good but the melting snow kept the water temperature at a mercifully low level; and being only a few miles from the salt-water fjord, we reasoned that there should be fresh-run fish with an inclination to take, to ease our chances of a catch.

Shooting the rapids in a small boat is a bit alarming at first; but after the first four pools I soon became accustomed to the hectic ride through the foaming torrents from pool to pool. Kjell Bruland, the gillie, advised me to use a large spoon bait, since the water was a little too cold and heavy for the fly. At about the fifth pool down our beat, he put me ashore on a small island and indicated the best salmon lies. At about my third cast my bait stopped abruptly and on raising the rod point I thrilled to the tug of a good fish. As the fish began taking line, Kjell pointed to the clutch mechanism of the reel and shouted in broken English, 'More tight, more tight!' I tightened as he suggested, but still the fish took line. Again came the command 'More tight – or it will go down the rapids'. So, straining line and rod to a point where I felt the tackle might break, I heaved all I dared. Slowly and log-like, the fish moved upstream inch by inch, away from the lip of the pool. The crisis, for the time being, was over. Occasionally, as I worked the fish back towards me, both Kjell and I caught a glimpse of it in the gin-clear water. 'Big fisshe – 15 kilos!' he shouted. Quickly translating this into something in excess of 30lbs, I knew that I had within my grasp a salmon larger than any other I had caught up to that time. The fish was one of the fittest I have ever played; and although I had put on a 17lb-test line instead of the normal 12 or 15lbs test I use at home, I had to continue straining the tackle near to its limits. Every time I tried to get the fish into the slack water it used its brute strength and weight to get back into the current; after fifteen minutes of this I began to despair of ever getting it within gaffing distance. I had reckoned without Kjell. As the fish came round yet another time, the gaff went out like a scimitar flashing in the sunlight and my fish was suddenly on the bank: a beautiful fish of 31lbs, gleaming like a bar of silver, with the sea lice still on it. That was to be my only fish that day, despite continual flogging of the water. But my enjoyment was complete. Not only had I caught my largest-ever salmon, but photographer Keith Massey had faithfully recorded the entire action on both still and movie film. If it was to be the only fish of my visit, it had been worth coming for!

Telephone calls that evening indicated that the Vosso was having a tremendous run of very big fish; fish that made my 31-pounder seem commonplace. Could it be that the Vosso I knew had been metamorphosed – or that something exceptional had taken place?

The following day we were on our travels once again. The steamer took us back to Bergen and then an hour's train ride got us to Bolstadøyri on the banks of the lower Vosso. At last I should meet the man with whom I have since developed a firm friendship – my host, Odd Haraldsen. We arrived at 11.30 p.m. in the twilight of a Norwegian midsummer evening. Odd commanded us to get quickly into the car as one of his other guests was playing a large fish down on the fjord. We arrived just as it was being brought ashore – a magnificent fish of 37lbs, dripping sea-lice and as fresh as they come. It had been hooked in the river, but had fought so valiantly that the angler had been forced to follow it to the fjord in order to have a chance of landing it. All the excitement over, we retired to the superb Oddsbu Fishing Lodge. There we learned that a fish of 37lbs was nothing extraordinary. The records for the Bolstad beat from 24 May to 20 June that year showed that no less than eighty-seven salmon had been caught. Thirty-nine of these had been over 30lbs; eighteen over 40lbs; eight over 50lbs; and one over 60lbs. I hardly believed it possible. Where else, in the entire world, was there such fishing for Atlantic salmon? Could my dream river, the Aarø, even compete with such a record? My 31lb fish caught only the previous day paled into insignificance. I could not sleep a wink that night. I could not even imagine that this was the same river I had fished only five years previously. Yet the Vosso it was; and there we were – with an odds-on chance of getting a fish that would qualify for headline status back in Britain. I felt that the Almighty had indeed been very kind to me: not only was the fishing almost unique, but the hospitality and friendliness of everyone left me deeply impressed.

The next day Nils, my gillie, arrived at 9 a.m. It was even hotter than it had been on the Jolstra, with the mercury just short of the 90-degree mark. Fishing in breast-waders, even in shirt-sleeves, is no easy task under such tropical conditions. During that morning I sweated and slaved, only to lose a good fish after playing it for a few minutes on a heavy Devon Minnow. The hook-hold just gave way and I have no way of knowing if it was a monster or not. With the heat of the afternoon fishing became impossible. I lay on my bed restlessly, waiting for the sun to lose some of its power.

By 8 p.m. we were back on the river, still in shirt-sleeves, but with most of the shocking heat now dissipated. Nils commanded, 'Now we try the prawn'. Having indulged in a certain amount of prawn fishing some years earlier, I had more or less reserved its use for poor conditions; but if it meant the possibility of getting one of those Norwegian monsters, who was I to stick to loosely-held principles? On went the prawn. I was soon to learn that the sink-and-draw methods used on these very powerful rivers were more difficult than they had been at home; and to manipulate the prawn correctly required some knowledge and skill. Eventually I got the hang of it again; and as Nils boated down the Upper Bolstad pool, things happened. The bait stopped. As I raised the rod and felt the heavy movement I leaned over to Nils and said 'Fish!' At first I wondered if I had not in fact stuck on the bottom. Nothing moved. Then I felt the solid weight of a heavy fish. For ten minutes I just heaved, trying to get the fish out of the strong current. The heaving seemed to have no effect. The fish stayed where it was, apparently oblivious of the fact that it was hooked. Doubtless the prawn and hooks in its mouth were little more than an annoyance. After a further ten minutes of this tug-of-war game I asked Nils to boat me down into a position where I could impose some side-strain on the fish. Nils was very reluctant to do this, since it meant taking the boat dangerously near a point where he would be unable to row it back upstream again. He kept repeating, 'Verra bigg fisshe – maybe 23 kilos!' Realising that he meant something in the region of 50lbs, I paled at the prospect of ever getting a sight of it – let alone getting it ashore.

Eventually, however, I persuaded Nils to move down a little. The side-strain I was now able to impose on the fish began to have an effect. Slowly it moved, but used its stupendous strength to fight upstream into the really heavy water of the main current. After five minutes of this gruelling encounter it turned tail in a flash and rushed downstream. As my reel began to empty with an ever-increasing scream, Nils shouted, 'It's going to the fjord!' He then rowed the boat into the main draw of the current and we set off in pursuit. The great fish continued its headlong flight downstream. As we came to the rapids, with practically all my line gone, the fish moved violently into them. Down we plunged, fish and boat together. Foaming water splashed over the gunwales of the boat as it bobbed up and down like a cork in a storm. Within a very brief period all was quiet as we smoothed out on the placid waters of the fjord. Where was the fish? Winding the reel handle as fast as my hands would go, I took back the slack line; and to my great delight it was still on. Now in the quieter waters, I could at least get on better terms with it, terms that would perhaps be in my favour. By this time the entire village, it seemed, was on hand to watch – and offer advice! My cameraman had taken a hurried bike-ride down the river to film the vital action. Then, at the end of a

The author with a salmon of 46lb he caught on 18 June, 1966 from the Vosso.

gruelling forty minutes, as the sun set behind the beautiful backdrop of mountains, Nils' gaff went home and out came my new record salmon of 46½lbs. It was covered in sea-lice – and, to me, the most beautiful creature in the world.

After that, the rest of the trip was a bit of an anti-climax. I had caught my big fish; possibly, I thought at the time, the biggest fish I might ever catch. We continued fishing and I hooked and played another monster for over an hour, without even seeing it. Eventually the tackle was strained almost to breaking point, and somehow I felt that it was not to be mine. I gave the rod to the gillie and took the line in my hand. Very slowly, the fish moved and we won some line back on to the reel; then, suddenly, with a mighty rush it roared downstream, and as it turned the bait came out of its mouth. It was all over. I shall never know its weight, but to expect fate to give me another of similar size to the one I had already caught would have been asking too much. Quite apart from the excitement of the fish, I again had the unique satisfaction of the entire action being recorded on film. This was subsequently shown on Tyne-Tees Television and one of the American networks, and I religiously guard the master negative. Although taken in his neophyte days as a cameraman, the film was to prove a good entree for Keith Massey into the world of television and he is now one of the BBC's top north-country cameramen/directors.

It would seem that as far as the Vosso was concerned, the prophecy of Odd Haraldsen was slowly coming true. This fishing is already commanding fees that keep it in the millionaire class. Odd Haraldsen has done much to improve the river and its amenities.

The next year, 1967, I was to strike up an increasing friendship with Odd Haraldsen. Eric Horsfall Turner and I were once again on our travels to Norway. This time we were to fish some new rivers, and in the space of two weeks were to take in the Vefsna, Forra, Tengs, Aurland and Sand, not to mention a further brief visit to the Vosso – where I incurred my host's wrath by taking a mere tiddler of 10lbs on the fly, thus helping to lower the 28lbs *average weight* of fish for his beat! All in all, I have now fished a total of ten Norwegian rivers, including the following year a visit which covered the Laerdal, Namsen and Bindal rivers.

The Vefsna is reached by a six-hour train journey from Trondheim. The river empties its waters into the North Sea near Mosjoen. It is still a little south of the Arctic Circle, but enjoys a great reputation for big fish. Leering down at us from the walls of the lodge at Laksfors were woodcuts of Vefsna monsters of the past, the most notable one topping the 65lb mark. Like many other Norwegian rivers, the Vefsna suffers from inadequate fish passes – it would produce some really fantastic fishing if adequate passes were installed. In the short time I was there I took a lovely fish of 17lbs on the fly, and a small grilse of 4lbs.

The Forra is small and, as a tributary of the larger Stjordal river, is situated quite close to Trondheim airport. I barely had more than a few hours to fish this pleasant little river, but did succeed in landing two very fine sea trout up to 4lbs.

The Namsen is truly a mighty river; undoubtedly the largest salmon river I have seen. Methods to fish it consist mainly of harling from a boat. It is, therefore, dull to fish; but does provide some very fine salmon specimens. In the short time I was there one fish hooked itself on my trolling rod, but only made the 5lb mark. Another notable salmon river is the Sand; but I had barely one day on this river, and this at a time when it was running a good ten feet above normal height. I should dearly love to go back and fish the Sand when it is at more normal height. The Tengs, like the Sand, is in the vicinity of Stavanger. It is a small river, but gets very good runs of grilse and small salmon. Some of the fishing on both these rivers may be leased from the Atlantic Hotel in Stavanger.

The Bindal river, also known as the Å-Elv, is one of the most inaccessible, and a float-plane is a decided asset. It is a most attractive river, and in addition to having good runs of salmon, it is noted for sea trout. Much the same applies to the Aurland river in Songefjord. At the time of my visits to both these rivers they were either too high or too low. Perhaps the classic river for fly-fishermen is the Laerdal. Again, I spent little more than a day plying a fly over its crystal-clear waters, and all I got for my efforts was a lovely rise at my fly. I witnessed the entire incident, from the fish leaving its lie to the time when it returned there without my

A salmon leaping on the Tengs river.

fly in its mouth. It is a truly lovely river, and is yet another ear-marked for a return visit.

As a guest of Odd Haraldsen, I saw much of Norway's wonderland as we winged our way in small float-planes over that magnificent country. For me, however, the Vosso remains supreme as the real sportsman's river. On many of the rivers I failed to catch salmon – in fact the only ones where I have met with any success have been the Jolstra, Namsen, Vefsna and Vosso. But fish taken on most other rivers have failed to match the magnificence of those Vosso fish.

Since 1966, it has been my good fortune to be invited back to Norway every year. Over those years some notable notches have been etched on my fishing rods, and as far back as 1968 I caught my first salmon on fly to top the 30lb mark. It was, of course, once again taken from the Vosso, but this time in August – a time when all the best fish are reckoned to have moved on upstream and the small summer fish are all that are likely to be encountered. Late July and August are ideal for the fly on this water, but the flies used tend to be about two sizes larger than would normally be used at home under the same conditions. It had been a delightful day with brilliant sunshine. Daytime fishing had proved most difficult, and as my gillie and I pondered on the chances of sport for the evening we waited patiently for the sun to sink behind the lofty mountains which surround the Bolstad valley. I had selected a $13\frac{1}{2}$-foot rod with a forward-taper No. 10 floating line and had put up a No. 4 Silver Wilkinson tied on a gilt hook. As the first shadows cast themselves on the water we started our operation. I had barely extended my casts so that they would cover the pool before I detected a lovely head-and-tail rise at the fly. My line slid away slowly; but as I raised the rod point I knew that I had hold of a good fish.

It fought hard in the powerful water. At the end of one valiant run it came crashing out of the water and we were able to get a rough idea of its dimensions. 'Nice fisshe', said the gillie. 'Nearly 15 kilos.' I was quick to realise that I was playing possibly the largest salmon I had ever hooked on a fly and that the battle was not yet won. I fought it as hard as I dared and within fifteen minutes I had it laid on its side and ready for the gaff. I even had a notion to tail it out, as I do with the bulk of my fish nowadays, but a glance at the fly in its jaw galvanised my gillie into instant action. The fish was still attached to my fly, but held by a mere thread of flesh. It was indeed a very unfortunate fish; for had the battle been sustained a moment or two longer it would have gained its freedom. Back at the lodge my catch weighed just a fraction over 30lbs, and it is still my largest fly-caught salmon.

The salmon rivers of Norway enjoy a short season. Many rivers do not now open until 1 June and the bulk are ready to close by the end of August. The first breath of spring comes in the month of May. Quickly, it seems, the sun moves into the northern hemisphere and slowly wins over the Arctic ice. As the snows melt, so the rivers rise until, by the end of the month, they are roaring down in full spring-time spate. The first fish to run the rivers seem to be the big ones, and it is not normally until the end of June that the bulk of the snows get melted. Even then, much snow remains; and the hotter the weather, the higher the rivers. As early as February Odd Haraldsen can often make a good prediction of the season's sport, his assessment being based on nothing more than the amount of snow – the more snow there is to melt the better the chances.

It is a pretty awesome sight which greets the angler who visits a river such as the Vosso after a heavy winter of snow. The river may well be six to ten feet above normal summer level, and any notions of traditional casting of fly or bait are soon put to one side. Heavy baits are required to get down to the fish and the rods and tackle normally used at home have to be replaced with stouter equipment. Prawn fishing is very popular at this time of the season and it may well require a good six ounces of lead to ensure the bouncing of the prawn on, or near, the bed of the river. Alternatively, a big spoon bait up to six inches long – with additional lead weighting – will often be successful. It is not until the bulk of the snows have melted that the tackle we would normally use for early spring fishing in Britain comes into its own in Norway. Usually, however, by the middle of July and into August, it is possible to use traditional floating-line methods. There is not the quantity of big fish coming into the river at this time; but as the *average* weight for the river is maintained at around 28lbs for the season, it is not uncommon for the angler to encounter several fish in the 30lb bracket. In all my visits to the river I have caught more fish over the average weight of 28lbs than I have under it. It is truly a 'trophy' river in every respect, perhaps only marred by the fact that the monsters of May and June may not successfully be fished for with a fly and floating line. Apart from excessive water height at this time, one of the greatest factors inhibiting this is the low water temperature. Freshly melted snow takes quite some time to be influenced by the sun to raise the water temperature. I have known days when air temperatures have hovered around the high 80s, yet the water had to struggle to make the low 40s.

Techniques for prawn fishing, because of the torrential current, are slightly different from those used at home. It is still essential to find a suitable weight to get the bait down, and the lead is mounted in ball form,

Fig. 11

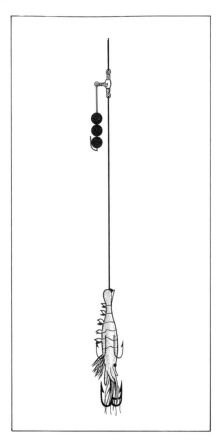

with the number of balls dictated by the force of water. (See Fig.11) Great skill is required in keeping the lead weights banging on the bottom, without getting hung up, as the angler makes a slow sink-and-draw motion. A rod with a strong tip is required; and the strong carbon fibre rods now being marketed by Bruce and Walker for this purpose fill the bill admirably.

During June 1969 I was once again on my travels to the Vosso. This time, too, I had television cameraman Keith Massey with me, and we were hopeful of making a feature-length film of monster fish being caught – with the added pleasure of Odd Haraldsen's company. The third fishing member of our party was the late T. B. 'Happy' Fraser of the Atlantic Salmon Association of Canada. Happy Fraser had done much to highlight the grave dangers of salmon netting on the high seas and he proved a very interesting companion. There were many evenings when, with a bottle of Scotch on the table, we would talk into the small hours. We were all a bit despondent. Odd Haraldsen had particularly reserved the middle week of June for us as being the most likely to produce bumper bags, but the fish had not come in any great quantity and we guessed that it would need some very hard work to make a showing for the cameraman.

On the first morning it was agreed that the cameraman should go with Odd who, with the pools he was going to fish, seemed to have the best chance. I was to take my favourite pool, the one in which I had taken my big fish in 1966; and which would form the backdrop, in future years, for many more monsters on my rod. I had not been fishing for more than ten minutes when, in the identical spot where I had hooked my monster, another fish took my bait. I fought it hard in that strong water and within eight minutes – tough ones that they were – I had it ready for the gaff. Out it came, dripping sea-lice and topping the scale at 30lbs. Later that evening one of the gillies caught a fish of identical weight, but, alas, the cameraman had not been around to film either of them.

The following day it was decided that the cameraman should come with me. We might have known that it would now be someone else's turn to catch a fish. At lunchtime that day Happy Fraser came in with one of exactly 30lbs. By now, of course, Keith Massey was tearing his hair; but it took him to our final day to admit defeat. He was spending the last day with me, while higher upstream Odd Haraldsen was about to do battle with the best fish of the week – a magnificent fish of 42lbs. Such, then, were the frustrations of making an angling film. With the advent of CB radio communication it may just be different in the future. But that was the best we could do in 1969 and it was a sad farewell to Happy Fraser, whom I was not to see again. Following a long illness he died in 1972.

Through the years, and right up to the moment of writing (1982) it has been my continued good fortune to visit the Vosso at Bolstadøyri for a week during the prime month of June. Most years it is the third week of that month and it is possible to leave my home shortly after breakfast on a Monday morning, catch the Danair flight from Newcastle to Bergen and be fishing at Bolstadøyri late that same afternoon. Some years, as recalled, have proved more memorable than others. And, as I commented in the previous chapter, my host, Odd Haraldsen, is in some measure able to predict our chances merely by an assessment of the amount of snow on the surrounding mountains. A good flow of water in the river will diminish the netting potential in the fjords and will afford good access to the migrating fish. Additionally, the colder and heavier the water, the greater will be the inclination of the fish to stay in the lower beats. During years of poor snowfall and consequent higher water temperatures, the fish make upstream with all haste. It is during such years that the early season catches at Bolstadøyri are reduced. For instance, over the years of 1970, 1971 and 1972 the Norwegian winters were comparatively mild with only modest amounts of snow. Fishing there during June 1971 was hard work and I had to be content with one fish for my week. It was, however, a most unlucky fish and it might be interesting to recount how I came to catch it.

I had been fishing for four days without so much as an offer. No fish had been seen and general enthusiasm was waning rapidly. On the evening of the fifth – and another blank – day I was ready to throw in the towel and admit defeat. As I retrieved my bait for another cast I leaned over to the gillie and told him that I was about to make my last cast of the day. I cast out and the bait swung round nicely. Quite suddenly it stopped and I felt convinced that, once again, I had got hung up on a rock. I tugged and heaved impatiently, then all of a sudden the 'bottom' started to move and I realised that the miracle had happened and that I was into a fish. The salmon made a spirited run upstream and then it jumped. It did not take us long to realise that it was a good fish – probably in excess of 30lbs – as it continued with its headlong plunge against the strong current. Slowly the gillie moved the boat towards the shore where he landed me. The fish seemed to be well-hooked, but quite suddenly I felt something give and all went slack. I was just cursing my luck when I became conscious that the tension had been renewed. With that the fish turned and fled downstream and we had no alternative but to jump back into the boat and follow as best we could. My reel was emptying at a high-pitched scream as I urged the gillie to make the boat go faster down the torrent of water. Out of the pool, headlong we went, down through the next pool and thence into fierce rapids at the neck of the third pool. Under normal circumstances I would have feared for our safety: but I had a fish on, and a good one at that, so we threw caution to the winds and headed for the maelstrom.

By yet another miracle, when I wound in the slack line my fish was still on and had taken up station in a quiet backwater beside the roaring torrent. We moved the boat quickly ashore and then I got my first good glimpse of the fish. It was certainly not as big as my monster of 1966, but it was by no means a tiddler. As I worked the fish closer inshore my gillie began to get anxious, suspicious of the hook-hold. 'I think we lose it if not very lucky', he said. I must confess that I too had detected two bare hooks hanging from the mouth. However, the fish was still firmly hooked somewhere and I proceeded to haul it to within gaffing distance. Both the gillie and I breathed huge sighs of relief as the gaff went home and the fish landed on the bank. It was a fine fresh-run fish with the sea-lice still on it. By some strange quirk of fate, the mouth hook-hold had broken from the trace, but the remaining hooks were firmly embedded in the muscle of the pectoral fin. Little wonder that my fish had taken off when the jaw-hold had broken. But for the gillie, the boat, and the blessing of the Almighty, that fish would still be in the river. Though short and deep, I doubted if my catch would make the 30lb mark. Back at the lodge all estimates put it in excess of that and I was surprised and delighted when the scale swung down to 33½lbs. For the remainder of that week I fished with renewed interest, but it was to no avail. Another year would have to elapse before I would get a further chance at that elusive 50-pounder.

In June 1972 I was once again on the Vosso, but apart from enjoying Odd's company and the delightful scenery of the Bolstad valley, I need not have bothered. I fished all week for nothing – not even a good pull – and came home reflecting slightly on my sanity. What was wrong with the Norwegian fishing? The river had been maintained at a good height, but the fish were just not there in quantity. Back home the situation was little better. The Lune sweltered low and clear under a hot sun and I caught my last salmon of the season during the first week of August.

During the first few months of 1973, however, heavy snow was being reported in Norway. A letter from Odd Haraldsen virtually promised that this time we would hit the river right and that the fishing would be good. Like many other salmon anglers of long experience I am highly suspicious of such promises, but the visit to Norway is always a highlight of my angling year.

On arrival in mid-June it was raining heavily and the river was higher than I had ever seen it before. Catches prior to my arrival could only be described as modest. But I was to have my choice of pool for the first evening and I elected to try one of the top pools where I had hooked the fish of 33½lbs back in 1971. On my second cast in this pool, the bait – a big Norwegian klepper spoon – stopped abruptly, and it was not long before I

Photograph overleaf: A catch of salmon (best 46lb) from the River Vosso at Bolstadoyri.

was contesting the odds with a strong fish. It fought well, but without any spectacular developments, and it was not long before my gillie gaffed out a lovely fresh-run fish of 25lbs. Moving down to the next pool, my very first cast produced another solid pull and after another ten minutes of tough fighting I was able to lead ashore another beauty of 22lbs. 'Not bad for my first evening out', I thought, but the rain continued to pour down and I needed little encouragement to call it a night and take some light refreshment in the lodge.

The following morning the river was a good two feet higher and still rising, and only an odd fish was caught by one of the gillies. By the third day it was up to the six-foot mark, but I did take a fish of 26lbs by deep spinning in the slack corners near the bank. That evening the river started to fall and we retired to our beds hoping that there would be no more rain.

On the morning of 17 June, 1973, the Vosso was fining down into good fishing ply. The day was soft with a suggestion of humidity, but it was not actually raining. Odd Haraldsen and I both commented on the fact that it seemed a good fishing day. I was to spend the morning in the Upper Bolstad pool – the pool where I had taken the fish of 46½lbs back on 18 June, 1966. The river was still fractionally too high for perfection, but I elected to begin my operations fishing from the bank with a heavy Bruce and Walker spinning rod and an Ambassadeur 7000 bait-casting reel. My terminal tackle was the same big Norwegian klepper spoon I had used for most of the week, but I added a spiral lead to assist in getting the bait down to a reasonable depth.

Beginning at the head of the pool, I fished down to the tail without so much as an offer. My last cast had to be a long one so that it would get well across to the other side of the river and then swing into the exact lie where I had taken the 46½-pounder. The cast was a good one, but the reel overran slightly and I paid out the extra few loops of line before closing the reel. The bait seemed to be swinging out of the main current very nicely and I was just about to start the retrieve when the rod was nearly pulled out of my hand. I was into a fish! Thinking that it might be another fish in the 25 to 30lbs bracket I tried to walk it upstream, but it seemed very reluctant to move. Fortunately I had Einar, a very experienced Vosso gillie, with me and he urged me to get into the waiting boat in case we had problems. I did as I was bid and Einar then tried to row the boat upstream to give me some room for manoeuvre. The fish was still most reluctant to leave its lie and many minutes passed as it lay there, log-like, without any apparent movement. The thought occurred to me that it might have got off and left me hooked into the bottom, but Einar knew better. 'I think this a verra big fisshe', he quietly observed.

After a few more minutes the fish started to get annoyed and it cruised about in its lie with vicious shakes of the head and tail. Slowly, Einar let the boat drop down towards it and then, quite suddenly, it took off in a mad downstream dash with my reel emptying as though I were attached to an atomic submarine. We set off in hot pursuit as Einar swung his boat into the main current to assist his rapid rowing – it was like 1966 all over again. Within seconds my reel was empty and I was just bracing myself for the inevitable 'twang', when, as it reached the tail of the next pool below us, the fish turned and started swimming back upstream. My next problem was to make the line knot 'bite' at the reel spindle to get some line back. For a few nerve-wracking seconds I wound the reel and nothing happened; but by hand-lining some line back through the rings I got sufficient slack line to make the knot bite on the spindle. Moving down quickly, I soon got the bulk of my line back on the reel; the fish was seemingly content to take a rest in the quieter water near the bank. Soon, however, it was off again as it pulled into the main draw of the current. Now it had become obvious that it would go down through the rapids and into the nearby fjord. We had no alternative but to follow as best we could. The ride down those rapids can only be described as hair-raising. Frankly, I doubt if I would have had the nerve to do it if I had not had the challenge of a fighting salmon at the end of my line. Halfway down the rapids everything went slack and I feared the worst. But our boat was merely gaining on the plunging fish and by winding the reel handle as rapidly as I could we eventually regained contact. Then it was not long before we smoothed out on the placid waters of the fjord.

Although the worst seemed over, my fish was still far from being fully tired. For one horrifying moment I thought it was going to try and head back upstream through the rapids. During this time Einar was slowly making for the shore where he eventually landed me. By now I had a large audience who were just as aware as I was that this was no ordinary fish. We got occasional glimpses of it as it tried desperately to shake the hook. I say hook (singular) because it had become painfully apparent that there was only one hook of the triangle in its mouth. Slowly and quietly I led the fish to the shore. The first gaffing stroke missed and there were further moments of tense anxiety; but the next time the great fish came in, the gaff went home and out it came. All immediate assessments indicated that I had, at last, got my coveted 50-pounder, but when the fish was hung on two different scales it was just a few ounces short of that magical mark. It was, however, the biggest fish from the Bolstad beat of the Vosso for the past three years and at the end of the 1973 season it was also the biggest for that year.

On my last day on the Vosso that year I was accompanied by a French photo-journalist who wanted some good action shots. I am always reluctant to try to catch fish to order, but after I had tried the spoon to no avail, I decided to have a try with the prawn. This usually means fishing from a boat and, as explained in earlier chapters, using heavy lead weights banging on the bottom. It can be a very efficient way of taking dour fish and I had not been casting for very long when I got another heavy tug and a fish was on. Thinking that it might be another monster I was careful at

Jim Deterding with a Vosso monster of 38lb.

first, but the fish played with more dash and sparkle and when it jumped we saw it was of more modest proportions. As I brought it in, the hooks fell out just as the gaff went home. Suddenly it fell off the gaff and there was an anxious gillie bundling it into his arms to get it ashore! He just made it and at our feet lay another gleaming fish, of 25lbs.

Of the 24 fish we got for that week all had carried sea-lice and some even still had their teeth. Not only had I caught the biggest and my personal best, I had also caught the smallest (22lbs) and the most. My own catch averaged out at 29lbs per fish and I cannot think of another river in the world where this might be possible.

When all the Norwegian rivers closed for 1973 I got an overall report on some of the more notable rivers. Some, indeed, had suffered from too much winter snow, but in the main they all reported exceptional sport. In a letter from Laerdal, Mr R.J. Brooks wrote: 'There is no doubt that in 1973 all Norwegian rivers have seen one of the biggest runs of salmon for many years. The Laerdal, although the water was high, was never out of order and the lowest beats had phenomenal catches with the best fish weighing 54lbs and with over 300 salmon from one pool. I have personally landed 93 salmon averaging slightly over 18lbs – ninety per cent of which were taken on fly. I am sure that a good angler, fishing full time, could have multiplied this take by five times.'

From the information I received and my own limited experience, it would seem that in 1973 the Norwegian salmon made a dramatic comeback. Only history will prove if it is to be sustained, but there seems an increased awareness on the part of fishery owners, management and authority of the vast potential of the sporting resource. In more recent years there is evidence that certain commercial activity is being curtailed and that the future emphasis will be placed on the sport potential. There is still no sign of disease in Norway and, apart from some fall-out of acid rain, there is little pollution or abstraction of these virgin rivers; but rents are now high and going higher. In the meantime, there is little doubt that Norway could still be the great Mecca for the salmon angler.

In the years that followed my great success of 1973 there was rarely a year when I failed to catch the odd fish near to the average weight for the river (28lbs). Most years gave three or four fish for my week and it was not until 1978 that I again fished all week for nothing. This was a strange occurrence following the best spring season I had ever enjoyed on the Spey; but these are the ways of salmon. It was not until 1979 that I again got among some notable fish and my week on the Vosso was made more memorable by the fact that three of the fish I caught then were taken on the fly.

It has to be admitted that the month of June is not an ideal time to catch Vosso fish on the fly. Most certainly the river is too high and too cold to expect sport on the floating line. Instead, I compromised. If my baits and prawns could catch fish, why should it not be possible to catch them on a

Odd Haraldsen with three fish, weighing 45lb, 37lb and 28lb respectively, taken from the Vosso in 1975.

heavy sinking line and one of the large tube flies I might use in February on Tweed? Over the first three days of my Vosso visit I had taken three fish up to 25lbs on an assortment of baits. On the Thursday morning I made ready with my 17½-foot 'Walker' carbon fly rod; a lead-cored shooting head line; a 25lb-test leader and a large Yellow Dog tube fly tied on to a brass tube. Frankly it was not the most pleasant line I might have chosen; but a little bit of practice with it gave me every confidence that my 'fly' would get down to the fish. I started operations on the Upper Bolstad pool, the same pool which had seen memorable encounters with big fish. I had barely worked the line out to its full casting distance when down from the depths came a hefty tug. My gillie was some distance from me and seemed highly sceptical of my claim that I was into a fish. Eventually he saw my long rod bow into a broad hoop and I was quickly urged to get into the waiting boat, in case the fish took off. My battle with that fish was quite prolonged. Eventually we had the, by now, usual ride down the rapids to the fjord below where my gillie was able to gaff a beautiful fish of 29lbs for me. On the day following, in the identical place, I hooked another fish on the fly. It too indulged in similar tactics and the same ritual had to be observed before a fish of 26½lbs came to the gaff. The best fish of my week, one that I took on the 10-foot Multispin rod, Ambassadeur 7000 reel and a prawn bait, made the 36½lb mark, but it was to prove the easiest fish of the week from the playing point of view.

During 1980 the river was again exceptionally low. Within ten minutes of starting to fish on the Monday evening I was playing a fish. Within a few seconds it threw the hook and that was to be the only offer I had all week. During June 1981, however, things were vastly different. A phone call from Oslo on 4 June gave the exciting news that over the first three days of the season my host, Odd Haraldsen, had taken seventeen salmon to his own rod. The best fish had swung the scale down to the 55lb mark and there were two more just topping 40lbs. Additionally, his total catch had made a remarkable average of just over 30lbs per fish. It was, I was assured, going to be a good season!

My arrival on 15 June 1981 coincided with heavy rain. By the Tuesday morning the river had risen appreciably and it was not to be until the Wednesday that I should have my first piscatorial encounter. That would make it 17 June again and I was to be given the same pool from which most of my big fish have been taken – the Upper Bolstad Pool. I started with my fly rod and was just hand-lining the fly in for another cast when there was a big swirl on the surface but nothing more. I cast again over the same spot, but there was no further response. Quickly, I grabbed the 'Multispin' rod already armed with a large klepper spoon. My first cast brought no offers, but I was just about to retrieve my second cast when the bait was taken with a savage pull. The fish did everything the others had done: eventually it tore off downstream and into the nearby fjord. I don't recall such a tough tussle with a fish for a long time and I began to think that it might just be the biggest fish I had ever caught. I even visualised it topping 50lbs and I have to admit to a feeling of minor disappointment when it swung the scale down to only the 40lb mark. It was, however, a hen fish – the biggest hen I had ever caught or seen before.

A day later I was up in the Rongen pool: the pool from which my host had extracted a monster of 60½lbs back in 1965. Urging me to try the prawn, my gillie bade me try a cast or two from the bank while he got some prawn tackles assembled. At my second cast with the spoon I was into something fairly solid. The fish backed away with purposeful movements of its tail. I sensed that it was another big one and it was not many moments before Inge Horvei, my young gillie for the day, and I were in the boat, contesting the odds from a more secure position. Experience of the Vosso told me that I was playing a fish in excess of 30lbs. After five minutes of tough give-and-take it is not too difficult to establish a rough estimate to within 10 or 15lbs. I began to think I might be into a 35-pounder at least. But at the end of fifteen gruelling minutes my fish seemed about ready for the gaff and it was this comparatively short time which then made me doubt my own judgement. Having duly gaffed it, Inge joyfully pronounced the fish to be over 15kg (33lbs). For the gillies, this is the magical weight beyond which they get a handsome tip.

I gave the fish a long look and commented that it could be nearer 16kg or 17kg and we left it at that. Periodically, though, I would steal a glance at the fish in the boat and make one or two guesses. Little did I know that

Arthur Oglesby with a salmon of 45lb he took from the River Vosso in June 1981.

Inge was doing the same thing and that, secretly, both of us put it a bit higher. That was to be the only fish I caught that day and some hours elapsed before we hung it on the scale at the lodge. There, the pointer quickly bounced down to the 20.5kg mark and, despite being without my pocket calculator, I knew that I had a lovely male fish of 45lbs. At that moment it was the best for the week and the second largest to be taken from the beat that year. But I was not to know then that it would be bettered on the evening after I had departed.

Meanwhile, other members of our party were bringing lovely fish back to the lodge. By a quirk of fortune for me, none were quite as large as my two, and one angler was delighted to get his first salmon – a mere minnow of 22lbs. At the time we were maintaining an average of over 28lbs per fish – an unknown event on any other river I know. But two days were to elapse before I contacted another fish and on my final full day on the river, my gillie again urged me to try the prawn.

We were back in the Rongen pool and I was casting down the head of the stream when my bait was again taken with a savage pull. The fish did everything big Vosso fish do. It fought with great tenacity for a full twenty minutes before it came near the bank. At one stage I was hopeful of beaching it unaided while my gillie used my camera, but in the end it seemed safer to gaff it – so I took the camera in one hand and the rod in the other and photographed the gillie as he gaffed a fresh-run fish of 33lbs for me. Ten minutes later we were playing another one. This was hooked near the tail of the pool and it was not long before the fish took off in full flight downstream. Mercifully, we were in the boat, and I had a repeat of my earlier hectic ride through foaming water down to the pool below. While it still made many valiant runs I was slowly able to come to terms with my fish. Then, suddenly, the gaff went home and out came another fish of exactly 33lbs. It was slightly longer and less deep than my first fish, but it was carrying long-tailed sea lice – the hallmark of another fresh salmon.

That was to be the last fish I caught in Norway during 1981, before I bade a premature farewell for my plane and home. Two days after my departure a phone call from my host gave the news of two more fish – one of 42lbs and another monster of 49½lbs. In our short week seven rods had accounted for 29 magnificent salmon. The average had been maintained in excess of 28lbs and there had been four fish of 40lbs or over. My own personal catch of four made the remarkable total weight of 68·7kg or 151·45lbs – a fabulous average of 37·86lbs per fish. Frankly, I don't ever expect to be able to do it again, but on the Vosso in June, perhaps, all things are possible.

At the end of my first successful outing on the Vosso in 1966, I strolled back to the superb Oddsbu Fishing Lodge with Odd Haraldsen. (As you may have gathered, he is a salmon angler of great competence and experience and has probably caught a higher proportion of large fish than any other living angler.) As we talked I had the thought in my mind, 'This is the fish of my lifetime. Now I shall be content!' Over the years, of course, my reactions have changed. As I have noted, my original milestone has now been passed and I have to ask myself whether it is the method or the fish which provides the deepest satisfaction. I think that the fish always predominates – but with reservations. It might well be time to consider these reservations and their development.

Frankly, I now dislike most forms of bait fishing; but not from any stupid, 'sophisticated' arguments that such methods are 'not the done thing'. I dislike gaffing my fish, but have come to realise that there must be a weight limit beyond which it is difficult to hand-tail a fish or beach it anywhere other than an ideal location. If I am to maintain purist tendencies then I might have to abandon the idea of catching a Vosso monster ever again. It would be arrogant – not to say downright stupid – of me to go to the Vosso in June armed with little more than my floating-line salmon outfit, without a gillie or his accompanying gaff. So now I accept the methods imposed on me and enjoy the challenge of adapting my tactics to suit the circumstances as I find them while having as much sport as I can.

Over the years I have found that, from the playing aspect, there are about five categories of salmon. For instance, we may go to Tweed in spring and catch fish between 6 and 10lbs. These require firm treatment but not substantial tackle: 10-12lbs test lines and leaders will do all that is required. Such fish are good fun and when fresh run can provide some spirited sport. Fish in the 15 to 20lbs bracket test us a little more. We become conscious of the weight of the fish and of the necessity for slightly stronger tackle or more delicate and prolonged play. Between 20 and 25lbs we begin to feel the mettle of a big fish. It is indeed rare for salmon over this weight to be encountered frequently in Britain. Until November 1982, when I took a 27½lb fish from the Tweed, I had never caught a salmon over 23lb in all my years of salmon fishing in this country. On Norway's Vosso river, as we have seen, such a fish is considered a tiddler.

The Vosso fish average between 26lbs and 28lbs. To maintain such an average there have to be a lot of fish which top the 30lb mark. Vosso salmon of this weight tend to be short and deep, fresh from the fjord with long-tailed sea-lice still on them. When caught on the Bolstad beat in June they have rarely been in the river for more than a few hours. They are fighting fit, having had little distance to run from the salt water. By whatever means they are caught, they offer a new and different challenge to the angler. If he has reasonable luck he might well encounter a fish topping the coveted 40lb mark, which brings another set of factors and playing problems. Then, if he is fortunate enough to hook a fish in the 50 or 60lb bracket, he will begin to wonder if he knows anything at all about playing salmon.

Playing a big salmon involves many considerations. There is the question of the length of its stay in fresh water, of water temperatures and the individual fitness of a specific fish – two salmon of the same weight are rarely alike in this respect. On my first encounter with a Vosso salmon in 1981 I had a hectic 37-minute tussle before a beautiful hen fish of 40lbs was brought to the gaff. On the following day I caught a monster of 45lbs which, despite its greater weight and strong fight, had less verve and tenacity and came to the gaff in under 20 minutes.

Some readers may have registered to their distaste that the bulk of my Norwegian salmon are all gaffed by the various gillies. Personally, I do not now carry a gaff. In the words of Hugh Falkus, it is an ugly instrument. Although I intend to kill most of the salmon I catch, I feel that a gaff so disfigures a lovely fish that I would normally rather lose one than have to resort to that method. Of course, there may come a moment when I would be glad to have a gaff on hand; but that occasion has not yet arisen in

The author preparing to beach a salmon of 28lb from the River Vosso at Bolstadoyri.

Britain, where as I said I am still trying to catch a salmon over 27lbs. I have been fishing in Norway now for sixteen years and during that time I have caught very few fish under that weight. There I have beached or hand-tailed fish up to 28lbs, but with really big fish I have been grateful for the gaff to get them out.

You may think that this is a contradiction, and perhaps you are right. If the fish and I were the only characters in the play it might be a different matter. But it is the gillie's job to assist his client. Most Norwegians have little conscience about the gaff and I would be doing my host a discourtesy if I arrogantly threw Norwegian tradition to one side, ordered my gillie out of the way, and attempted to get the fish out by my own method. Also, if you will excuse the pun, a salmon of 45lbs is a different kettle of fish from one of 27lbs. Although considered big by British standards, it is not too difficult to take a 27-pounder by the tail and lift or slide it out of the water. But, with a 45-pounder, and even the best will in the world, there are few anglers who could lift one by the wrist of the tail and hoist it out without it slipping from their grasp. In an ideal location it might be possible to slide it up a sloping beach or bank, but in many other situations there would be no way of getting such a fish out of the water other than by a large net or gaff.

Most Norwegian gillies are not content merely to gaff a fish anywhere in the body. The accepted British technique of gaffing a salmon is to put the gaff straight across the back and, in one clean movement, heave it out of the water. This method disfigures a fish badly and is not general practice in Norway: there it is a tradition that all fish are gaffed in the head. Indeed, each fish brought back to the lodge on the Vosso is inspected by all the other gillies and if gaff marks are not where they should be, there is some mild jocularity about the competence of the gillie concerned.

Many of the Vosso gillies are young and eager, vying with each other for acclaim. The loss of a big fish constitutes a personal affront and one must be ever-sensitive to the pride they take in a job well done. On the Bolstad beat of the Vosso it is traditional (at 1981 rates) for the gillies to receive a £10 tip for every fish taken over 15kg (33lbs). You may imagine their concern if a foreigner, such as myself, took it upon himself to get the better of a 45lb salmon without their help. Also, the sheer power of a Vosso fish in excess of 30lbs has to be experienced to be believed. The gillie is a vital member of the team. If the fish takes off downstream he must always be ready with the boat; and he must know the safe channels through the rapids down to the fjord or the pool below. He has a large stake in his angler's success and to deny him the ultimate pleasure of getting the fish out is to deprive him of his rightful place in the team.

Also, if I am being honest, I have to admit that the thought of beaching or hand-tailing a 45-pounder is quite daunting. In the pool where I caught my most recent fish of this weight there is a shelving grassy beach which would have been ideal for an attempt. Later on that week, when I had a

While the gillie gaffs a 33lb salmon Arthur Oglesby plays the fish with one hand and photographs it with the other.

fish of 33lbs in play in the same pool, it did occur to me to try. I had done it in the same location with two fish of 28lbs some few years ago; but it was the look of concern on my young gillie's face which induced me to take my camera from him and let him gaff the fish while I took photos with one hand and held the rod in the other. Meanwhile, I shall continue to fish without a gaff: I shall do so in the hope that one day I will encounter a fish in Britain which will really test my ability to get it out my own way.

My experiences in Norway over the past sixteen years have taught me a great deal about salmon fishing. I do not insist, blindly, therefore, in indulging in a fly-only rule. I adjust to circumstances and use the best lures for the purpose. It so happens, however, that my favourite river – the Spey – lends itself to fly fishing in all its forms while the Vosso in June does not. There is an old cliché which runs, 'When in Rome do as the Romans do'. Frankly, it is not bad advice for the angler to follow wherever he may happen to be.

Ever since the political troubles started in the north of Ireland – Ulster –
there has been a growing reluctance for British game fishermen to venture
across the Irish Sea. Coarse fishermen still go over in quantity and enjoy
some excellent sport; but there is now a fairly vast game fishing resource of
which the best is not made. The odd continental visitor takes advantage of
the situation; but many local gillies face language problems and on my
most recent visit, in 1981, I detected a sincere sadness that more British
anglers were not coming over.

In times past, of course, the salmon fishing in Ireland ranked with some
of the best to be found in what was loosely termed the British Isles.
Naturally, the true Irishman would resent the fact that Ireland is classified
with the rest of Britain. It is a fully independent State and, although the
Irish tend to have long memories, most of the present-day generation have
forgotten old enmities and there is a genuine desire to see the British
angling visitor back in force. From purely personal experience I was made
to feel more welcome than I am sometimes in my native Britain and, as a

Salmon fishing in the Ballynahinch river just below the Castle.

Grace Oglesby and Terence Wharton fishing on Lough Cloonaghlin.

guest of the Irish Tourist Board, I was shown and fished some prime salmon waters. The fact that I did not encounter any salmon on my recent visit may be attributed to the fact that it was during August 1981 when there had not been any rain for three weeks – perhaps a strange event for Ireland. I did not need to be reminded that August is usually a bad month anywhere.

I suppose that every angler has a 'wanted list'? It may be an exotic item of tackle, a species of fish or one of a particular size. It might merely be a visit to a known, legendary venue – a personal Mecca! Although I had visited Ireland before, I had never seriously wet a line there, and I had long felt that my angling education could not be complete until I went back and sampled some of its wonderful game fishing.

My immediate 'Mecca' was the Butler Arms Hotel and the fishing on Lough Currane at Waterville, County Kerry. Most salmon anglers of long experience have heard of the Butler's Pool. This is a short stretch of water connecting Lough Currane with the nearby sea. In times past it held a legendary reputation for the amount of fish it could hold and the sport it might provide. Sadly, the Butler's Pool no longer exists. A big flood in 1981 washed the dam away and there is now but a short and shallow connecting arm to the sea. This does not seem to inhibit fish running into Lough Currane, but it does mean that the pool is no longer a tourist attraction or a worthwhile fishery.

Lough Currane is noteworthy in that the salmon and sea trout fishing, other than the requisite licence dues, is absolutely free for the taking. The Waterville Angler's Club, of which a Mr Vincent O'Sullivan is the chairman, exists solely to provide boating and anchorage facilities for anyone wishing to fish on the lough. Vincent and his friend, Terence Wharton, run a gillie and boating service. And, at 1981 rates, boats may be hired for £6 per day and £12 per day with an outboard motor. If the angler wishes to have the assistance of an expert gillie included, then the total cost does not exceed £20 per day.

If we were denied the full sporting prospect of Lough Currane we were to learn something of its potential. March would seem to be the best month for salmon which may be successfully fished for from mid-February to mid-April; but there is a revival of sport in September. Sea trout also abound in the lough and it is noted for producing some of the largest sea trout in Ireland. We heard of many occasions when it is possible for an angler to take two salmon and a double-figure tally of sea trout in a day. While it is not essential for the angler to reside at the Butler Arms Hotel, by doing so he will have access to the preserved fishing on loughs Derriana, Cloonaghlin and Namona. If, however, he is content with the vast fishing resource on Lough Currane he may stay at one of the many other hotels and guest houses in the area.

Sadly, we were only able to spend one or two days at Waterville and it was not long before we were wending our way north to another exotic venue at Ballynahinch Castle in County Galway. This represented another personal 'Mecca' and as we neared our destination I was fascinated by the myriad lakes and waterways which are a great topographical feature of Connemara. The administration of the castle shows American influence; but it was while chatting with retired gillie, Frank Cummins, that I learned something of its history. It transpired that back in 1925, the late Maharajah of Nawanager, Kumar Shri Ranjitsinhji, purchased the Ballynahinch Estate and – although better known as a cricketer – was directly responsible for the erection of well over a hundred fishing weirs and casting platforms. The Maharajah was highly regarded in the area and spent a deal of his later years in residence. Fellow veteran cricketer W. G. Grace also visited the castle to sample the fine sport it could produce. And Frank Cummins told me something of the good old days when the fishing in the Ballynahinch river ranked with the best that Ireland could produce. Further bar chat with the head gillie yielded the information that, again, we were on the river at the wrong time of the year. May, June and September are the best months for salmon and the average size of the fish through the season varies between 7 and 12lbs.

Although we spent some time fishing the lower Ballynahinch water downstream of the castle, we could induce no interest in the fish. A few tartan-coloured salmon could be seen thrashing about at the tails of pools but there were none sufficiently foolhardy to take our flies. For most summer fishing, our single-handed rods proved more than adequate to

John Greene of the Irish Tourist Board fishes for salmon and sea trout in the Ballynahinch river.

Arthur Oglesby salmon fishing on the lower section of the Ballynahinch river.

cover the narrower parts of the river; wherever it broadened out, however, the current tended to become sluggish and sometimes it was necessary to resort to lough or loch-fishing tactics. Here it was desirable to have a breeze to ripple the water and to cast slightly upstream and hand-line the fly back at a varying pace. For most of the season at Ballynahinch a fly-only rule is in operation. But there are beats and sections where, at certain times, it is permissible to fish the prawn after 6 p.m.

Although our brief 1981 visit gave only a casual opportunity to sample Ireland's full potential, I should dearly love to go back at a more appropriate time. By most British, certainly Norwegian and Icelandic, standards the fishing is not expensive. As I indicated, Lough Currane is free and even the best beats on other rivers are rarely more than £20 per rod per day. Meanwhile, it is to be hoped that the political strife in the north will ease and the great sadness it all causes will be eliminated. Until then, there is a vast Irish resource waiting for the British visitor, with plenty of charming people who will give a good welcome.

The number of countries in the world where it is possible to find *salmo salar* seems to diminish. There used to be a time when the Rhine and its tributaries brought vast stocks of fish to European sources. The rivers of northern France all had runs of fish, as did those of northern Spain and Portugal. With the pollution of the Rhine the German resource was quickly ruined. The same fate befell many of the rivers in the north of France, but during the years of Spanish dictatorship, much was done by the late General Franco to nurture an otherwise diminishing resource in that country. One suspects that unless his initiative is maintained it too may go the same way, but during the time I visited some of the Spanish salmon rivers in 1971, there was ample evidence that Franco's reign had maintained a sporting resource of considerable value.

Tucked away in the north-west corner of Spain lies a vast region with magnificent scenery, lush valleys and foaming rivers. It is known as Asturias and to anglers who have fished there it is as much a byword for salmon as Perthshire, Inverness-shire, New Brunswick or Finnmark. As Spanish provinces go, however, Asturias has escaped the attention of the average tourist, and if you incline to the belief that all Spain has to offer are golden beaches, bullfights, brilliant sunshine and sherry, you are very much mistaken.

It was my good fortune to see and fish in this part of Spain in 1971, and my companion for this salmon safari was Hilton Pierpoint of Newcastle-on-Tyne. He had seen many of the rivers on an earlier visit and had thought them well worth further exploration. It was our intention to fish three of the best-known rivers as well as taking in some lake fishing for rainbow trout and mountain stream fishing for brownies. To get to the heart of Asturias we had to fly from London to Bilbao by scheduled service. A good, four-hour drive then brought us to Colombres and the San Angel Hotel. This was our overnight stopping place, but it was also handy for the Cares river where we fished later on. Our immediate destination at that time was the river Narcea, where an international salmon fishing tournament with anglers from all parts of the world was taking place.

To describe fully the breathtaking scenery we passed through on our journey would involve more superlatives than I can muster. It was truly magnificent, with the entire country framed by the high Picos de Europa, rising to some 9,000 feet – the rivers Cares, Sella and Narcea all have their sources in this high mountain country. Road surfaces varied from very good to pretty grim, so ample time had to be allowed for comfortable motoring.

When we arrived at Cornellana, we were dismayed to find the Narcea in roaring flood. Excessive snows on the high Picos were melting and the

Fly fishing for salmon on the River Sella.

Following in the footsteps of El Caudillo, Arthur Oglesby fishes for salmon on the river Sella from a casting platform used by General Franco.

river was barely fishable, except with a worm. We were shown some lovely fresh fish which had been taken a few days before our arrival, but barely troubled to wet a line ourselves.

Much information on Spanish salmon fishing potential may be gleaned from *The Atlantic Salmon – A Vanishing Species*, by Anthony Netboy. It is doubtless true that over the years Spanish salmon fishing has suffered in much the same way as that of other western nations. Rivers have been polluted wantonly and commercial interests have been ever ready to take the lion's share of the salmon. At the end of the Spanish Civil War, in 1940, only a dozen reasonably good salmon rivers remained. But General Franco, himself an ardent angler, inspired (one might imagine how a dictator interprets *inspiration*) a law in 1942 which was designed to prevent further deterioration of the inland fisheries. Its prime aim was to ban all forms of commercial netting, leaving the entire salmon resource to the sport fishermen. In later years the fishing on the top rivers came under the control of the State Tourist Bureau and was readily available to residents and foreign visitors at modest fees. It was essential, however, that beats (known as *cotos*) should be booked well in advance: as usual, costs varied depending on the beat and time of year. Hotels were not too plentiful, but if luxury was not a prerequisite there were an adequate number of smaller hotels at modest cost.

Most of the fishing on the rivers I mention was carefully controlled and maintained. Casting platforms had been built and each section of a river was under the control of a local game warden. It was necessary to take out a national fishing licence and we were recommended not to attempt to fish without the necessary licence and beat reservation. Gillies were readily available and, although few had any knowledge of English, they made excellent and conscientious guides.

Much the same tackle as could be used on the Spey or Dee was more than adequate for the rivers I saw. Fly sizes and patterns differed little from ours, but there was great enthusiasm for a weighted Mepps spoon for those who preferred spinning. For the fly-only fisherman, May and June might bring the best sport; because of the steep banks on some rivers, it is highly desirable to be able to do Spey casts. During the early months the rivers are snow-fed, but this part of Spain also produces a high rainfall, so the rivers rarely get too low. It is possible to be basking in the sunshine on the coast when ten miles inland there are those lovely soft rain showers which only a salmon fisherman can appreciate.

With the Narcea out of order, we made our way back east to visit the river Sella at Cangas de Onis. Here we fished the Sierra beat and our gillies, Ramon and Angel Sierra, were enthusiastic about our chances. Here again, however, the Sella looked too high for perfection and we fished hard in the hope that we would connect with an Asturian monster – but without much conviction. There was some excitement when we connected with a couple of big brownies, but the salmon did not want to know.

It was difficult from a brief expedition to assess Spain's ultimate fishing potential. All I can report is that the rivers looked enchanting and full of possibilities. We were, perhaps, most unfortunate that heavy rain and melting snow combined to produce big rivers, and I would dearly love to go back there another year and find these rivers at more normal height. Recorded catches from the rivers we fished left us in little doubt that the fish average 10lbs and that they are caught in sufficient numbers to make a visit there worthwhile. In June 1971 the catches since the season opened on 1 March had totalled 254 salmon from the Sella, 187 from the Narcea and 150 from the Cares and Deva.

On our way back to Colombres we took a scenic route from Covadonga down the Cares valley to Panes. Here we fished briefly at 4,000 feet in the lakes of Ernol and Ercina. Rainbows up to 12lbs had been reported from these lakes, but we caught only the smaller fish averaging around 1lb. Driving along the steep slopes of the Cares river we saw many anglers, most of whom were worming in the swollen waters. Cat-walks and casting platforms abounded and we were shown and fished from many of the places where General Franco had caught his share of salmon.

Perhaps one of the greatest advantages which Spanish salmon fishing has to offer the visitor is the opportunity to take a family holiday. Leave the family on the beach and within half-an-hour's drive the angler can be fishing on one of the named beats of a famous river. At the little port of Ribadesella, for instance, there is a first-class hotel and virgin beach, yet no more than 20 kilometres away are the middle beats of the Sella river at Arriondas and Cangas de Onis. Similarly, barely a kilometre away from the Hotel San Angel at Colombres is an unspoiled beach, while fishing on the Cares and Deva is only a short distance by car. The town of Oviedo is well placed for some of the rivers and is connected to Madrid by domestic flights. All in all, a salmon fishing holiday in northern Spain should offer a new horizon to the British salmon angler: magnificent scenery, lovely rivers and a chance of the same silvery salmon which might cost the earth in Norway or Iceland.

With a toast of *salud, pesetas y amor* we sipped our glasses of fino on our last evening there. It was true that we had not caught an Iberian salmon, but it was equally true that nowhere else could we recall such lovely scenery as yet unspoilt by the march of progress and mankind in general. I hope that it will stay that way for many years to come.

The River Sella at Cangas de Onis.

During the years leading up to 1966 it seemed that numbers of salmon entering British and Norwegian rivers were on the increase. Classic rivers like the Spey, Tweed, Tay and Dee were all producing better bags to both salmon anglers and the estuarial nets. Returns from the River Eden district of the Lancashire River Authority at the end of 1966 showed an all-time high of salmon taken from these rivers since 1945. There was a general feeling of optimism about the future. True, there was vague talk about netting on the high seas off Greenland and of an outbreak, during 1964, of an unidentified fish disease in the rivers of Ireland. But these were just wispy clouds on a distant horizon when, in Britain, all seemed serene. The angler could have his fun on well-stocked rivers, and the netsmen could reap a modest harvest without any apparent thought or worry for future stocks. During the early sixties it was not uncommon for the lower beats of the Tweed to be so full of fresh-run fish in the month of February that anglers could regularly catch double figures of salmon during the brief period of daylight on a winter's day. As winter warmed into spring, the migrating salmon would surge upstream to the middle beats and thus provide wonderful sport for the fly-fisherman. Indeed, towards the end of 1966 it was apparent that the Lune, at least, held such great stocks of fish that, should disease break out, the mortality rate would prove very heavy indeed.

I have already recounted how 1966 was a great year for me. The seasons seemed to be getting better every year. Why worry about high seas netting off Greenland, or the bumper catches being made by our coastal and estuary netsmen? There were sufficient salmon, and more, for everyone.

During October of that year, however, what had been a distant, wispy cloud on the horizon, suddenly manifested itself as an anvil-shaped cumulo-nimbus – in the form of an outbreak of disease. Small white patches, the size of an old sixpence, appeared on many of the fish being caught; and it was then realised that the Irish salmon disease, as it was then called, was showing in rivers on this side of the Irish Sea. The west coast rivers of England and southern Scotland were the first to suffer mortalities; and it was left to local river authorities to net out the dead fish and bury them in quicklime.

On the Lune, as one instance of disease-attacked rivers, somewhere in the region of ten thousand salmon were thought to have been infected. As the waters cooled with the onset of winter, quiet pools and shelving banks became littered with dead and dying fish; and by the early spring of 1967 it appeared to the casual observer that the river was devoid of life. Very soon the fresh-run springers were arriving; but within a few days of their move into fresh water the disease took hold. The entire run, it seemed, was quick to die. Other rivers too were now being affected: Tweed, Spey and

Dee all reported outbreaks and it generally became apparent that we had a plague on our hands that would, slowly but surely, thread its poison into most of the river systems of the British Isles.

A sight of the river Tweed in the November of 1967 was sufficient to make the most hardy angler despair. Hundreds of diseased and dying salmon cruised about aimlessly in the backwaters, not strong enough to complete their spawning task, apparently only awaiting their untimely and inevitable end.

Scientists seemed slow to get to work on the disease. Several labels were applied; but eventually someone came up with *ulcerative dermal necrosis* (UDN) as the best description of the malady. The initial infection was thought to be a viral one, which was followed by secondary bacterial invasion; the subsequent killer was the fungal growth on the diseased tissue. Frankly I suspect that a lot of guesswork was involved in this theory. It was observed that some diseased fish could stay alive for a long time and might even recover, while others, with only minor infected areas, would die quickly; still others would become completely covered with fungus before their eventual death. Of those fish seen and removed from the rivers, there must have been thousands unseen that were swept down to the estuaries at times of flood.

The advent of disease in our rivers seemed to make many of the apparently healthy fish more difficult to catch. This situation lasted for a few seasons and throughout the summers of 1967 and 1968, particularly, I found that I could not catch fish under conditions in which previously I should have banked on doing so. The fish gave the impression that, although unmarked with any outward sign of disease, they may well have been sickening for it.

During the long dry summer of 1969 there were few fish in our rivers and only few signs of disease. Some of us, in our flights of fancy, even pondered on the possibility of the long spell of hot weather killing the disease bugs; but it was not to be. Even as I write (spring 1982) there are many rivers which have not fully recovered from the effects of disease – and many where outbreaks still occur. It has to be admitted, however, that UDN has mercifully lost a lot of its initial virulence and one continues to hope that time will fade it out altogether.

In 1968 that excellent book by Anthony Netboy, *The Atlantic Salmon – A Vanishing Species*, appeared on the bookstalls. It left the analytical reader in little doubt just where we in Britain were bound with our destructive commercial fishing policies. During that same year it was also very obvious that something, apart from the disease, was affecting our runs of fish. Reports from rivers were very dismal, with rod and net catches down on earlier years. This brought into focus the 1965 contentions which Mr T. B. 'Happy' Fraser of the Atlantic Salmon Association of Canada put forward to publicise the dangers of high-seas fishing for salmon off the coast of Greenland. Its icy wastes have few salmon-producing rivers and it soon became obvious that, at long last, man had found one of the hitherto elusive feeding grounds of salmon while they are at sea. These self-same salmon had their origins in the rivers of Canada, Great Britain and Ireland. If the toll of commercially taken salmon continued to mount, it appeared that it would not be long before its effect would be reflected in reduced numbers returning to our rivers.

Many of us in Britain were so concerned with the disease problem that we were slow to realise the full impact of high-seas fishing; but by the spring of 1969 it was obvious that disease alone could not account for the grave shortage of fish entering our rivers. At a meeting in Warsaw during June that year a majority of the fourteen member nations of the International Commission of Northwest Atlantic Fisheries (ICNAF) voted in favour of a ban on all high-seas fishing for salmon. Those voting against the ban included Denmark and West Germany; just as the Danes and Faroese had been the principal offenders in the past, their high-seas fishing was to continue until the processes of international law had gone full circle, and an enforceable restriction was imposed in 1976.

Meanwhile, for a few of the fish entering our rivers, disease still rears its ugly head. Just how long it will flourish seems difficult to estimate. From records of the late 1800s it seems obvious that the self-same disease affected our rivers at that time. All in all it took around twelve years to abate and during some of those years it was more virulent than others. Scientists working on UDN seem no nearer a solution than they were eighty years ago: but then, even if the disease was identified and an antidote discovered, it would seem well nigh impossible to administer it to wild fish. The disease,therefore, appears to be something with which we shall have to live. But we can, and must, do something about high-seas netting, estuarial netting and excessive catches by anglers and poachers. The major blame for the initial decline in British salmon fishing may well be laid at the Danes' door. That country's fishing fleets proved very effective at virtually eliminating the tunny from the North Sea.

A study of all the classical literature on salmon angling will reveal that from the advent of salmon fishing with rod-and-line there has been a growing division between those who fish for sport and those who fish for profit. Such a situation was almost inevitable. Without doubt, the netsmen have had the right to take salmon from our coasts and estuaries long before salmon angling was even a vague possibility. This age-old right has remained and it is only in comparatively recent years – in terms of salmon fishing history – that commercial and sporting interests have conflicted. It may be interesting to examine the background to this present state of strife.

In the days before salmon angling tackle was successfully evolved it seemed perfectly natural for mankind to crop the vast harvest of salmon which ran our unpolluted rivers. In our greed, however, we eventually took too much for granted and the resource dwindled as the suitable environment for salmon was polluted or overfished. By 1861 the sense of man prevailed and the fishery laws imposed during that year were expressly designed with conservation in mind. By the turn of the century, however, the demands for salmon as a sporting resource were on the increase. Salmon angling had become a fashionable sport, even though some of our best sporting rivers were only available to the riparian owners and their personal guests. Angling pressure was never very high at this time and there was little conflict between those who fished for sport and those who fished for profit.

As far back as 1922, however, there were many far-seeing anglers who were predicting that increased commercial catches could not be sustained if the sporting resource was to have a fair crack-of-the-whip; but the status quo continued and it was only in the bad years that the angler raised his pen, dipped it in vitriol, and complained about the other lot. Quite by accident, it seemed, mankind had struck a balance between sporting and commercial interests and the correct crop to be taken. Overall stocks in the rivers at the termination of a season were generally regarded as adequate for the benefit and survival of the species.

At the end of the last war, the situation changed dramatically. Riparian owners began to see the full value of the sporting resource and certain fisheries, for the first time in their history, were let to ordinary mortals who could pay the nominal rentals involved. All around us mankind was seeking more leisure and by the mid-sixties the sport of angling in general and salmon fishing in particular was attracting more devotees – and the

The Vosso near Geitle, Norway, photographed in the 1960s when traps were frequently seen in the river.

rents were increasing. A beat that had previously accommodated two rods was slowly being made available for four rods and then six. The wealthy angler, it seemed, was prepared to pay almost any price for a chance of sport. Many rivers did produce higher catches than ever before in their history, but there was no let-up on commercial fishing and with nothing more than hit-and-miss husbandry, our advisers assumed that everything would be all right and that salmon could take the increased cropping levels without the species being placed in jeopardy.

By the mid-sixties, as I have said, there were some heavy clouds on the horizon. As far as the disease was concerned there was very little which could be done – despite attempts by biologists to isolate and contain it. We may all have moaned about an apparent lack of activity on this score, but we were faced with a *fait accompli*. On the question of high-seas netting for salmon, however, there were again many anglers who dipped their pens in the acid. But little was done by those in authority, and the apathy continued. Quite amazingly it seemed to be accepted by many of them that the poor salmon could continue to suffer the great levels of predation without stocks suffering too much. Commercial netting at home continued as before. It took a US president – and a disowned one at that – to bring about successfully an ultimate restriction in 1976 on high-seas fishing for salmon by the Danes and others in the north-west Atlantic.

Even now, Britain is the one remaining salmon-producing country not to have lifted a finger to curtail commercial fishing or impose limitations on angling methods. Where authority is challenged, back comes the stock reply: 'The Department, which is in close touch with river authorities, is satisfied that the level of salmon stocks in England and Wales gives no cause for concern from the point of view of conservation.' One is forced to wonder how this conclusion is drawn, for if reports from anglers have any semblance of truth – which indeed they do not always have – it would appear that there are some strong differences of opinion. Many rivers which produced good rod catches a few years ago are now showing fractional returns, while the returns from commercial fishing activities seem to be maintained or even increased. When, however, it is suggested that commercial fishing be limited to benefit the sporting angler, not to mention the breeding stock of fish in a river, we are told that excessive stocks in the river are not desirable. The pundits tell us that this would only result in over-cutting of the redds; that it would bring an increased risk of disease, and that the progeny of an increased spawning stock would be hard-put to find adequate rations during the two years of their infant river life before migration. There may well be some truth in any or all of these statements, but in those countries where commercial fishing has been severely curtailed, the sport resource has increased beyond the wildest expectations. Iceland and Eastern Canada are the classic examples.

At this moment there is but one organisation whose sole aim it is to

Commercial netting off Carleto-sur-Mer, Gaspe, Canada.

protect the interests of the salmon angler and the riparian owner. That is the Scottish Salmon Angling Federation, but sadly it caters only for Scotland. Those of us in the rest of Britain who regard the level of commercial exploitation to be too high have few platforms for our grievances. In more recent years the Salmon and Trout Association, and the Atlantic Salmon Trust, have highlighted some of our present-day hazards. However, as their brief is for the salmon, they have to cater for both sporting and commercial interests and cannot take sides. I serve on the committees of both organisations, but seem continually to be reminded of my father's description of a committee which he defined as 'a group of people who, as individuals, can do nothing, but that they form themselves into a committee to decide that nothing can be done'.

On reflection, perhaps that comment is a little unfair and I would not be associated with either of these groups if I did not sincerely believe that they have the interests of the salmon firmly in the vanguard of their thinking. Most of us would readily admit that angling is not the most effective way of catching fish and that if a crop has to be taken then netting is the obvious method. But which of these two methods brings the most benefit to the total economy of the country? I submit that it is not commercial fishing and that every effort should now be made to enlarge the sporting resource. It is one thing to angle unsuccessfully in a river known to be full of fish, but quite another to cast in desperation over pools where there is barely a fin to be seen. When this happens, as it did to me on the Lune in 1973 and the Spey in 1981, and we are told that the netsmen in the estuary had bonanza catches, I feel entitled to get a little indignant. If there are too few fish for me to try and catch there are too few fish left to fulfil their prime task on the spawning grounds.

In these days, therefore, when the cry is for more leisure facilities, how can these levels of commercial exploitation be justified? For how long must the angler and the conservationist suffer these netsmen – legal and illegal and mostly part-timers – and for how long will the angler subsidise the bulk of the conservation programme? I have no wish to see anyone genuinely out of work, but commercial licences could slowly be withdrawn as present holders die or retire. Is there no one in authority with the sense and initiative to see where our priorities lie?

As a self-styled pundit on matters to do with salmon fishing, you might think that the question I would be asked most frequently would relate, in some way, to tactics or techniques. Not a bit of it! Hardly a week passes without my mail bag containing at least one enquiry concerning the best *places* to catch salmon. When considering whether this chapter should be included in the book, therefore, my immediate reaction was that if the reader had nowhere to fish, he would not be reading it anyway – but then I decided that, if my aim was to help, I ought to spend some little time on this vexed question.

Frankly, while it is easy to name the best places and to suggest the best times to fish them, the facts of life are such that many of them are not available at short notice, and the overall question is a much more difficult one than any which might relate merely to tackle or techniques. I have spent a great number of years sorting the wheat from the chaff and even now it is possible to spend a whole week on a classic piece of water, at a prime time of the season, and catch nothing. If the novice angler has saved

Ken Walker of Bruce & Walker on the Tweed at Upper Floors.

his hard-earned cash for a specific week's holiday and I send him on a fool's errand, he may well dismiss both me and salmon fishing as idiotic.

As I have commented elsewhere, the only secure way of getting salmon fishing is to own a piece of good water, to live on it, and to keep guests and tenants off so that it is there for you the moment it comes into good fishing ply, with plenty of fish in the beat. You might not be able to fish it successfully every day of the season, but if you live on it long enough you will quickly learn when it will pay to fish hard or when it is preferable to stay away from the river and play golf or marbles. If you cannot own the water, the next best course it to rent a beat for the entire season, rent a house in the vicinity and stay there as long as the season lasts. If neither of these possibilities are open to you, then you must think of forming or joining a small syndicate with full season access to a piece of good water. Of course, it is important that the chosen venue is not too far from your home, so that you can be free to take advantage of your allotted period. If this is not possible either, then you might have to think of renting water for varying periods. You might have to travel a long distance to get there and the added hotel and travelling expenses must be equated with the cost of the water. If your chosen period is only for one week, the minimum let by most estates and their agents, then you might find conditions not suited to good fishing and you must expect a fishless week every so often.

Thereafter comes a long list of similar options. Most involve at least a week in an hotel, caravan or tent; fishing on hotel water, if available, or fishing on local Association water. The more remote the venue, the more likely it is to be less expensive, but highly speculative, fishing – though there are notable exceptions to this rule. Stay with the classic venues at the best times of the season, and you may expect to pay the top prices for that particular river.

My first serious attempt at salmon fishing involved a two-day visit to the Association water on the river Eden near Carlisle. We joined a veritable queue of anglers to fish a pool and during the time I was there I did see one local angler hook and land a magnificent fresh-run fish of 20lbs. A year later I tried the same venue again, but all to no avail. I then visited the Argyllshire Awe for one week for each of three years before I encountered a fish. Meanwhile, as I have commented, I caught more fish by accident while trout fishing. It was some years before my name came up for membership of the Esk Fishery Association, which had water on the Yorkshire Esk barely one hour's drive from my home. That was to see the start of my real successes, numbers-wise. I could go to the water at any time during the season. I could fish it night and day, as I wished. I established a close liaison with David Cook, the river keeper, and when he phoned to say that things were right I was in a position to down tools and get away to the river immediately. It was very important to do it *immediately*. Even the delay of a few hours could make all the difference between success and failure.

Shortly after that I was offered a rod in a three-rod syndicate on the river Lune. This involved a good ninety minutes drive from my home, but it was still possible to fish that beat every day of the season if I so chose and, with friends in the area, I was quickly advised when to come over. During 1966, by fishing odd days and weekends, particularly when advised to do so, our three rods took 195 salmon from one small beat. One member of the syndicate spent the bulk of his time abroad and the lion's share of that catch was shared between myself and the other remaining rod. Had I just rented that water for one specific week on a pre-planned basis, the chances are that I could have picked a dry spell and done little else but a deal of abortive casting.

When we come to consider the more classic rivers things get a little easier. With the death of the Countess of Seafield, I was given the opportunity of a beat on the Spey which she had previously retained for her private guests. I was offered this and adjoining water for the entire six-week period of my fishing courses in Grantown. It seemed too good to be true. I was thus able to have some fishing for guests and to have access for myself at any time during the six weeks: all this at a prime time of the season for the river Spey and that beat.

Six weeks is a long time in a fishing season. To be there in residence would give me a wonderful chance of exploiting the water to the full. Indeed, I am not diminishing such a magnificent opportunity when I relate what frequently happens, but it does give some guide to the sheer lottery aspect of it all. There are, for instance, many years when things are not quite right. It may be an especially cold spring. Oh, the fish will be there all right, but I am now past the stage when I am prepared to fish hard all day with only the odd chance. Instead, with six weeks on the water, I can afford to wait for good conditions, but you would be surprised just how few days there are in that six weeks when I really have the urge to fish hard. At the beginning of every week I have to greet the newcomers. I have to be enthusiastic about the chances and point out the varying tactics which might prove useful. However, on many of these days I would not rate my chances of catching fish to be any higher than those of the most enthusiastic novice. Enthusiasm is important, for without that one might not have the necessary diligence and fortitude to have a great chance.

During recent years I have been lucky enough to have access to the Upper Floors water of the Tweed during November. This is possibly the finest beat on the Tweed. To be offered the opportunity now of fishing there at a prime time of the season demonstrates my point that it may take a lifetime to get this sort of chance – and even then it is possible for the elements to conspire to do their worst. In 1980 we were virtually flooded off the water before we had time to have a cast, but over the same period in 1981 three anglers took 45 salmon in the week.

The angler who likes to try a new venue every year is perfectly entitled to do so provided that he does not gripe too much about his lack of sport,

Jim Bruce of Bruce & Walker on the Tweed at Upper Floors.

for he will never get to know one piece of water intimately. He will *never* (and I use that word with due reserve) be able to exploit its full potential for the simple reason that he does not give himself sufficient time to get to know it. I have been a tenant on the Castle Grant water of the Spey for nigh on fourteen years, yet there is never a year which passes when I do not learn a bit more about that water. Were I to spend a lot of time trying other venues, I might get lucky once in a while, but I would never be likely to hit much more than average luck. By concentrating on one piece of water, year after year and week after week, over the prime part of the season, there are times when I can make some excellent catches.

For the keen novice angler, therefore, and provided he can afford it, there is little to be gained by taking anything but the best. Once a good beat has been secured at a good time of the season, stay with it for at least ten years. You might find, as I frequently do, that over a ten-year period you will have two years of above-average catches, two or three years of average catches, and the rest with little or nothing at all. Towards the end of your tenancy you will know that water a lot more intimately and you will certainly be better equipped to exploit its full potential than you were when you started.

Frankly, there are few short cuts to acquiring good fishing. Much of

An aerial view of the River Spey at Castle Grant, showing Cromdale Bridge and the Manse Pool.

what is on offer through the various agencies is the residue of what is not taken by regular tenants. For this reason a lot of it may be suspect, and you might well have to take a mediocre period in order to get on the first rung of the ladder with a particular estate or agent. Most are keen to have you back again and if you stick with it you might well find that, at the first cancellation of a good period, you will be offered something better. In this respect it is important to be a competent fisherman and to have your face fit in every respect. If you fall foul of the gillie or some other individual involved, the word may get around that you are not wholly welcome. This could influence your chances of sliding into a good slot and there is no immediate and simple answer to individual problems in this respect.

Other alternatives to taking a beat on one of the classic rivers might come by seeking good Association water. Perhaps the best known in the country is to be found on the Strathspey Angling Association's water at Grantown-on-Spey. Here, seven miles of the Spey – and several more miles of the Dulnain – are put at the disposal of the visitor. During the prime season it does get heavily fished, but it possesses some delightful pools and makes a good starting point to begin an apprenticeship to salmon fishing. If you are lucky you might catch a fish during your first week; but I have to be frank and tell you that the odds are that you will not catch anything. You will have to keep coming back for more punishment, but the time will eventually come when you encounter your first salmon. If money is of little account you might well start off by seeking a rod from a regular tenant on a more private beat. Don't ask me how you discover such an opportunity. You will have to search continually and discover for yourself; discard the bad or indifferent and cherish the good, until about ten years from the start of your crusade you may have found a good niche.

Choice of river or venue must be inter-related with the time of the year you wish to fish. As I have already indicated elsewhere in the book, it is little use your choosing the finest spring beat on, say, the Tweed, if you intend to fish there in July. Conversely, there would be little point in going to a host of other rivers in February or March. There is a deal of homework to do before you can come up with a worthwhile proposition and, as it has taken me thirty years to do it for myself, I cannot do it for you. If I were to relinquish my tenancies on the beats to which I now have access, there would be a hundred-and-one applicants to take my place. It has taken a virtual lifetime to acquire them and you, unless you have the vast and unlimited resources to go out and buy your own piece of water, will have to do the same!

Presuming that life is kind and that you quickly acquire access to some reasonably good water you would be advised, as I have already noted, to stay with it for as many seasons as you can – most certainly until you have found something better. You will need to learn the water and the best way of doing that is to make firm friends with the local gillie or someone else who knows the water intimately. Although there are occasions when one can do it, it is not easy to 'read' unknown water. Even when it may be seen at drought level there is no degree of certainty that your choice of what might be good complies with the notions of the salmon. It is always a sound plan to examine the true course of a river at times of very low water. This will quickly establish the channels through which the fish run and it may give some strong clues as to where they might lie at a more normal river height. Without this opportunity, the gillie is the best bet and, as I shall demonstrate in a later chapter, he can make a very good friend or a bad enemy. Lean on him heavily, not only for information about where the fish lie, but for the best methods and tactics to adopt in the presentation of your lure or fly. For instance, it is a fairly general rule that a pool will fish better on the inside bank of any bend or curve. Even then I can think of quite a few pools where the reverse is true. Pools may fish better from one side or the other depending entirely on the height of the water. Prevailing wind direction, too, is a factor to take into account – if only to ease your casting. And there will be many unknown influences which will all take time to assess. In my view it is impossible to take a new piece of water for one week and immediately exploit it to the full. Luck alone might give a better-than-average catch; but a bit of perverse luck could just as easily send you home at the end of a week without having had a pull. No amount of reading this book, or any other, is going to solve that little problem for you!

The Harmsworth Press do publish a very useful book entitled *Where to Fish*. The Scottish Tourist Board have a similar publication for Scottish waters and there are such books as *The Haig Guide to Salmon Fishing in Scotland*, edited by David Barr: *The Great Salmon Rivers of Scotland*, by John Ashley-Cooper: *The Salmon Rivers of Scotland*, by Derek Mills and Neil Graesser. Indeed, with a little more diligent research, there are many publications which may be perused to advantage.

Suggest to an angler that he might be fishing with the wrong fly or bait and he will gladly accept your advice. Tell him that his casting and presentation are bad and you may have made a mortal enemy for life. In so many instances it is bad casting, and therefore bad presentation, that causes failure to catch fish, so some examination of these topics may not come amiss.

I do not propose to go into casting techniques at any great length. Several books have been written on this subject; and practically every book on salmon fishing gives chapter-and-verse accounts, with detailed diagrams, on how to execute the various casts. I have never been able to learn the first thing about casting techniques from a book; but for those who wish to try I can recommend two books worthy of note: *The Angler's Cast* by Captain T. L. Edwards and Eric Horsfall Turner, and *Casting*, by Captain Terry Thomas. In both instances the authors have tried to reduce detailed techniques into print: whether they have failed or succeeded is not for me to say. The attempts were sincere and carefully executed and all three of these men were first-rate anglers and top performers with any type of game fishing tackle.

My own shortcomings in casting were dramatically highlighted in 1958 by the methods of which only the late Tommy Edwards was capable. I had gone up to Grantown-on-Spey to act as photographer for Tommy and Eric, before the publication of their book. Tommy was in charge of the angling courses, run in conjunction with the Scottish Council of Physical Recreation by Nigel Grant – then of the Palace Hotel. At the end of my photographic session, I thought it an opportune moment to seek Tommy's opinion on my casting techniques. At the end of an hour, I was left in no doubt that in the nicest way Tommy could put it – which was not always the nicest way – I was well below the required standard! I learnt a lot that first year and was surprised and delighted when, the following year, I was invited to attend the Grantown courses as one of Tommy's assistants. From that time on it was to be an annual event. Over the years, until his death in 1968, I was to learn from Tommy not only how to improve my own casting techniques, but also the intricacies of passing on that knowledge to other people. Following his death it was a great honour for me to be asked to take his place as chief instructor at Grantown. Even now I continue to learn, since all my assistants are very competent casters and anglers; and in quieter moments we pick each other's brains and discuss techniques.

Following various changes of ownership of the Palace Hotel, I eventually moved my headquarters to the Seafield Lodge Hotel in Grantown-on-Spey. This proved to be an ideal move and with Nigel Grant again in control as 'mine host' it was to become the most appropriate place for our operations. Additionally, Nigel quickly established Seafield Lodge as a prime residence for anglers visiting the district. Currently my courses are based there, and any reader wishing to attend is invited to get full particulars from Mr Grant or myself. Included in the package is access to the seven-mile stretch of Association water. Among the guest personalities currently available are such names as Hugh Falkus and Alastair Perry. Hugh needs little introduction from me and I will remind you that it was Alastair Perry who, in 1969, achieved a British record tournament cast of 63 metres with a double-handed salmon fly rod.

Apart from fancy casts like the Spey, double Spey and roll, the basic fly-casting action is fairly straightforward. Most novices quickly learn the primary techniques and at the end of a week are certainly sufficiently competent to be let loose on a river. Most troubles arise when contrary winds make conditions difficult; or, after the novices have perfected their techniques standing on a river bank or platform, they attempt the same performance when immersed up to their armpits in breast-waders. Like everything else in sport, it is all a question of timing; it frequently happens that the timing of the power stroke has to be varied slightly, depending on the angler's height above water level. Every good forward cast must start with a good back cast. A common fault with salmon fly-fishermen, using a double-handed rod, is for the backward cast to be started too late. At the start, the rod point should be well below the horizontal, if water levels permit; and the backward cast should be initiated early so that the full

Casting practice on Arthur Oglesby's casting school at Grantown on Spey. Visitors may try out all types of Bruce & Walker game fishing rods.

power may be applied to drive the line and fly, in as tight a loop as is manageable, over the angler's head, and up into the air at a position on the dial of one o'clock.

Attempts to raise the rod point before starting the backward cast must be checked, since there is then a grave danger of driving the fly into the ground or the water behind. Even if such a back cast is successful, there is every possibility that the forward power stroke will come too early. The line will then extend well above the water level and be subjected to any contrary winds before it comes into contact with the water surface. Such a cast can be highly desirable when shooting a lot of line with a following wind; but for contrary wind situations, it must be considered bad practice.

Another common fault which will take the power out of a cast, and restrict its potential distance, is circling. In effect this means that the angler has lifted his fly from a downstream position and then causes the line to make a circling motion as it is delivered to its new position across the current. Invariably the line does not extend fully; and if there is any suspicion of downstream wind, the line alights with a very pronounced downstream belly. We have already examined the disadvantages of this in our chapters on tactics; and if the downstream belly can be half-eliminated before the cast is completed, only a slight 'mend' need be thrown into the line to make it straighten and the fly itself move correctly in the water in the early stages after delivery. On streamy water, of course, it is quite feasible to make an initial circling cast; then to lift the line again to ensure a tight loop over the rod tip in a straight backward movement. This leads to a good and straight delivery of the final forward cast. On gliding water, of course, such double manipulation may well cause water disturbance and frighten the fish. With a short line some elimination of this circling can be avoided if, before the angler lifts the line into his initial back cast, he merely points the rod in the direction the new cast is to go. It is sometimes troublesome in excessive wind conditions; but is normally the correct style. Many anglers try to aerialise too much line. It is far better to have full control of a comparatively short lifted length of line, and then to release some hand-held backing as the forward cast extends fully.

Basic casting faults with a double-handed salmon fly-rod generally involve:

1.   Starting the backward cast with the rod above the horizontal or at too high an angle to get the best lift. The back cast does not then discharge the line fully, to stay high in the air; and as the backward power stroke reaches its ultimate extreme, instead of being extended straight behind, the line tends to be partially coiled. The effect of this is a clumsy bundle of line on the forward stroke.

2.   Imparting a circling motion to the line, instead of keeping the backward and forward casts in exactly the same plane, with a tight loop over the tip of the rod.

3.   Pushing the rod forward violently, without smooth flexing during

the power application. Pushing does nothing whatever to extend the distance of the cast, and only serves to kill the flex of the rod. It is the smooth, swinging, pendulum-action of the rod which gives the power, and any excessive drive or push at the end only results in a jerky and ineffective action.

Although I emphasise the desirability of a tight loop, there are many competent casters who have developed a fetish for it. Indeed, it *is* highly desirable to achieve good distance, and is a technique much used by tournament casters. The snag, in practical fishing terms, is that if too tight a loop is thrown there is a grave danger of the fly catching on the leader and introducing what is loosely termed a 'wind knot'. In many instances it would be more appropriately labelled as a 'bad casting knot'. The answer here is to open up the loop a little by widening the power arc of the cast. Technically this might impose a slight limit on the ultimate distance which may be cast, but in practice I have found that insignificant. The best way I can describe this method of eliminating wind knots, is for the angler to lower his rod point after the power stroke in the fore-cast has been applied. If the rod is lowered to the horizontal, as the cast and fly are *en route* to their destination, the loop will turn over without the fly fouling up on the leader and thus introducing the knot. It is a precise action on the part of the angler, and not the most simple technique to consign to print. It does not matter how many wind knots there are on the leaders of the tournament casters; but it is of immense importance to the angler if he wishes to draw a successful conclusion with a fighting salmon. Wind knots reduce the practical strength of a leader by about 50 per cent.

The initial requirements of a good cast are that the line should go back in as tight a loop as possible without inducing the wind knot problem. It is still essential to make the rod do the work and there are too many fishermen who tend to use sheer, brute strength rather than exercise the rod correctly. The rod needs to be flexed at only two points, but these two applications of power must be equal. It is no good merely *waving* the rod back and *flicking* it forward – or vice versa. As it is impossible to put down in print exactly what a good cast should look like, I suggest that those novices keen to learn should seek out one of the top professional casting instructors – or come on my fishing course. For a few pounds they will see at first-hand what they themselves can achieve with thorough practice.

I am still amazed how an angler will spend a small fortune in hiring a beat on a classic river, and yet make no effort to ensure that his casting techniques are as near perfect as he can make them. Without a shadow of doubt, the main cause of angling failure, under ideal fishing conditions, is due to indifferent technique. The general casting standards in Britain are abysmally low; and this alone could well account for indifferent fish-catching results. There is no magical requirement for good casting. It is basically a mathematical operation and, once mastered, is capable of adaptation to cover all contingencies. It was the lack of good professional

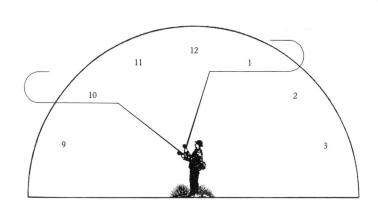

Fig. 12   The main arcs of power with a fly rod.

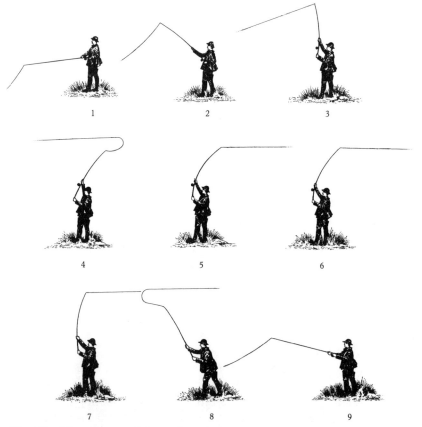

Fig. 13   The sequence of the good overhead cast. The lift is commenced at 1 and carried on to 3. A slight drift and pause is permitted between 4 and 5. Then the return power should be applied between 6, 7 and 8, bringing the rod down to 9 as the cast straightens out.

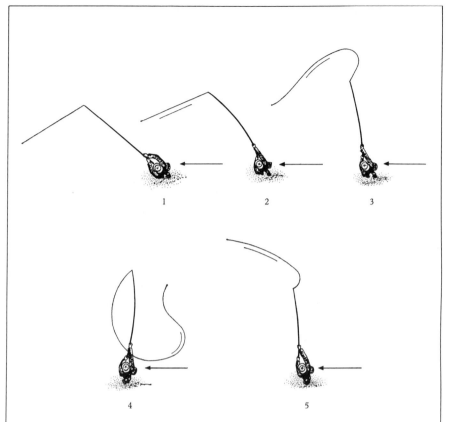

Fig. 14   *Circling is very bad technique. The line is lifted from the downstream position, and becomes circled as it is delivered to the new position. This will not produce a good lay down on the line, and will restrict distance.*

Fig. 15   *In the normal cast the rod should have a pendulum action near the body. Any form of pushing and leaning in the final fore-cast only kills the spring of the rod and reduces distance.*

instruction which first prompted the formation of the Association of Professional Game Angling Instructors (APGAI) in 1969. The conception was good, but the birth of the association was a little painful: we were not without our critics! The founding of the association was, however, a sincere attempt to raise the standards of game fishing generally; and the passage of time has shown its ultimate value. Few golfers have reached any great standard of perfection without having had, at some time in their career, a few lessons from the club professional. We live in the age of professionalism in sport of all types; but there is still an element of taboo in the angling world against the professional. It is a widely held contention that angling is a solitary, contemplative sport and, as such, should not be tarnished with anything that smacks of professionalism. With the greater modern demands for fishing, and the fact that there are more participants in this sport than in any other, I should have thought it high time that standards were improved – even if only for the benefit of those who fish behind the clumsy angler!

No matter what the old diehards may think to the contrary, it has to be stated that the modern, well-designed, carbon fibre rod has brought great

When the Spey cast is properly executed (and this one is not quite), disturbance is confined to a small area near to and upstream of the angler.

benefit to the salmon angler. In times past, with split-cane or fibreglass, it was only possible to make rods lighter by making them shorter. The trend to shortness continued throughout the early seventies. Indeed, as I have already noted, there is much satisfaction to be gained from using a short rod at the appropriate time; but for a big river in the spring they lack that quality of 'water command'. Now, it is possible to have a 15-foot carbon rod weighing no more than a 10-foot cane rod. My young son, Mark, at the age of eight, could even handle a 17½-foot carbon rod with some measure of success. The ease with which these longer carbon rods lift a long line and the presentation they offer in throwing that line a long way makes them invaluable. You may think that in many situations a long cast is not desirable. I can assure you, though, that on a big river like the Spey, and particularly on hard-fished water, a long cast might make all the difference between success and failure.

Where the new and longer carbon rods really score is in their ability to perform the Spey cast. There are anglers, I know, who continue to pour scorn on it. One writer continually asserts that it is disturbing to the water. Frankly, I have grave doubts that he can do it correctly. What is more, it seems unlikely that he has ever seen anyone else do it with finesse. The old notion of a Spey cast, and one frequently referred to even by casting instructors, is that it is a roll cast with a change of direction. Initially, it does pay to have some knowledge of the roll cast for it can be a useful method of either lifting a sunk line to the surface or of rolling a slack line into a tight or straight one. Generally, the roll cast involves a slow lift of the rod so that the line stays on the water. Then, when the rod is lifted high and just past the vertical, a sharp forward snap of the rod drives the line out again to its original position. Most times this cast does disturb the water in which it is manoeuvred and it is not easy to change direction by any meaningful amount. But, having practised that sharp, snap of the rod, the angler would be well advised to forget that such a roll will be the final movement of his Spey cast. It might bear great similarity to it, but there is a subtle and important modification to be made.

Assume that the angler is wading – an important consideration for achieving a good Spey cast – and that he is on the left bank, i.e. the river flowing from his right to his left. The current will take the fly down until it is on the dangle. In order to get the fly out to its new position the angler merely lifts his rod point to the near vertical: he does this slowly to keep the line on the water, but as he reaches the topmost position he turns the whole of the top of his body, above the waist, and simultaneously switches all the line downstream of him into a position on the water slightly upstream of him and into a semi-circle as shown in the figure. Then, instead of doing a final roll cast out to the new position (an act which might have got Spey casting its bad name), the angler brings the rod point a little further back and makes a cast high into the air. The execution of this final movement is best likened to a cast with a spinning rod. When done correctly the line sails out high into the air and alights on the water with no more disturbance than a well-executed overhead cast. Of course, there is some initial slight water disturbance immediately upstream of the angler, where he made his line alight on the water in its semi-circle prior to casting. But this is over water which has already been fished and, in general use, there is little chance of it disturbing the fish the angler hopes to catch – possibly thirty yards away and out in mid-stream.

Using the 15-foot 'Walker' rod (by Bruce and Walker) I have found that, provided the wind is not unhelpful, it is possible to throw an entire 30-yard line with minimum effort. Indeed, experiments with a 35-yard prototype Spey-casting line convince me that even greater distances are occasionally possible in suitable wind conditions. It is very important to have a helpful wind to achieve the ultimate, and there will be days when the angler has to resort to normal methods.

Nowadays, under normal casting conditions, I find myself using the Spey cast for practically all my double-handed fly fishing. It is less tedious than overhead casting for the simple reason that the caster only applies power in one direction. Also, it removes all thought for bank or overhead obstruction, and the angler may fish down any piece of water without concentrating on anything other than presenting his fly to the fish. An additional quality of the Spey cast is that the angler's fly never leaves the water for a back cast. This being so, it is never likely to hit a rock or a tree behind the angler so that the point of the hook is removed without his knowledge.

For best manipulation of the Spey cast it is important to be wading. This removes any tendency for the mid-manoeuvre of the cast to foul up the line on the bank. It also keeps most of the line on or near the water upstream of the angler and in a perfect place for it to be cast out high and long. With practice it is possible to shoot an appreciable amount of line. With a double-tapered line care must be taken not to lift the line with the narrow, back taper outside the rod point. This should be hand-lined in until the thick, belly portion of the line is outside the rod point – then the remainder is easily shot if the angler aims his cast sufficiently high to take all the line out before the front section lands on the water. I cannot emphasise too strongly the importance of making a high final cast. This is the very essence of a good Spey cast, which is thus quite unlike the roll cast in its correct execution. It is, of course, impossible to convey to you on paper the subtle points which might transform an indifferent Spey caster into an expert. I have recently completed a film on casting for Bruce and Walker Limited, entitled *Fly Casting*, and specifically using carbon fibre rods – though the principles involved may be utilised with rods of any similar action and construction. The film demonstrates the tenuous differences between the achievement of mediocrity and excellence. The principal Spey-casting sequences – executed by Eric Robb, a gillie on the No. 2 Castle Grant beat of the Spey – demonstrate better than any words just

Limbering up with the 15ft Walker carbon rod before a coaching session on the Spey.

how useful this cast is and just how much utter nonsense is written about it and many other forms of cast. (The film should be available to *bona fide* angling clubs from Bruce and Walker by the time this book is in print. It can also be obtained on videotape from Video Image Productions at the address given in the Preface.)

The double Spey cast is another form of cast for use primarily by the right-handed fisherman fishing from the right bank. Both the Spey and double Spey may be executed from either bank provided that the angler changes hands accordingly. I will not go into tedious detail on this, but all I can emphasise is that, for the bulk of my double-handed salmon fly fishing, I now use one of these casts.

Many of the faults which are applicable to double-handed casting may be witnessed when anglers use a single-handed rod. One sees anglers waving their rods about, not allowing any rod action to develop. Some anglers have too much wrist action while others rely too much on elbow and forearm movement. Even some of our top casters and instructors have become wedded to the notion that wrist action is undesirable. For the really competent and very strong caster I do think that wrist action

Fig. 16

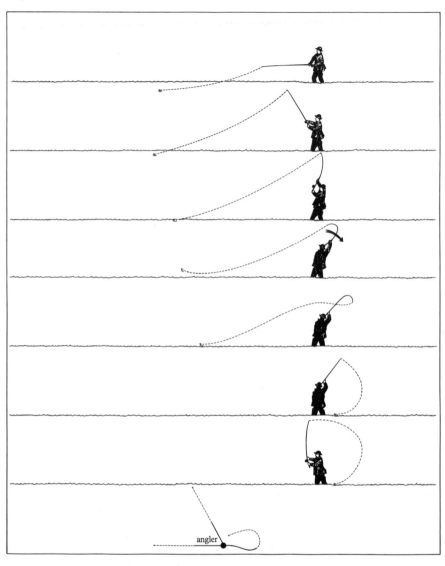

assumes less importance; but I am of the firm opinion that its correct use should be taught to novices. When writing on this topic in their book, *The Angler's Cast*, Edwards and Horsfall Turner noted, 'The point we stress, heterodox though it may be to accepted opinion, is that wrist action is by far the *most important* factor in any single-handed cast. If the sceptic has any doubt on this point, let him pick up a hammer and drive a nail into a piece of wood. Does he hold the hammer with stiff wrist and forearm? Of course not: he breaks the stroke at the wrist and causes acceleration of the hammer head by a sort of flick. That, precisely, is the action of the single-handed cast, fly or bait.'

Fig. 17

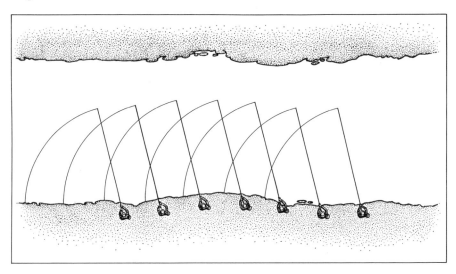

Casting techniques with spinning tackle, while not so painful to watch as bad fly-casting styles, are still pretty bad in general. The modern casting reel, be it fixed-spool or multiplier, is comparatively easy to use. With power applied at the right moment, the bait will invariably alight at a reasonable point on the water. Here again, precise timing is all-important; and it is the power of the rod, and not that awkward push, which transmits itself into the weight of the bait to send it hurtling out over the water. As with fly fishing, many anglers want to push at the final cast. They must realise that this very act kills correct rod action, and drastically reduces potential distance. With a little practice, the spinner should be made to land in a precise area of water; and subsequent casts should be so controlled that the bait travels the same distance, and in the same direction, as achieved by earlier ones.

Good casting is not an art. It is purely a craft that can be quickly learned by any able-bodied person. There is no magic in it; but reasonable standards must be learnt and can only be reached by developing a thorough understanding of what is happening – and why. An hour with a competent professional instructor will do more for the indifferent performer than reading a hundred thousand words in print!

There can be no doubt that in order to fish at full potential there are many rivers, such as the Spey, where breast-waders are essential, particularly if fly fishing is the angler's main choice. There are, of course, many big rivers where the use of a boat becomes necessary; and there are also quite a lot of rivers where neither is desirable.

Some anglers have a phobia about deep wading. It is perfectly true that in heavy water it is not without its moments of tension, or even danger. The use of a wading stick is generally advised and should be a great help – though care must be taken that its use does not lead the angler into parts of the river where he should not be. Most of my worried moments have come when I have relied on a wading stick to get me out to an awkward place. I may then have stumbled and faltered, and had the added curse of my shooting-line fouling around the stick. Nowadays, I do not use a wading stick, preferring to go quietly on my way down a pool, making sure that each step has a firm foothold before transferring my weight. I rarely get into serious difficulty, but like all anglers, I have had the occasional ducking. The most notable occurred when I was deep wading the River

Arthur Oglesby wades too deep in the River Tengs, Norway, and is given a good fright and a thorough soaking.

Tengs in Norway. Suddenly I ran out of river bed and needless to say a cameraman was on hand to take a picture of my plight. I must confess to a feeling of near panic; but I quickly got control of myself and let the current swing me on to a shelf of gravel. As senility approaches, I expect the day will come when I will feel more comfortable with a stick.

Some writers argue that waders should not be too tight around the waist. Frankly, I don't think that it matters at all. If the angler is deep wading, all the air is expelled from the waders by water pressure; and, if disaster befalls, it seems to me merely a question of keeping one's head above water and letting the current carry one down. All the time, of course, one should be able to make slight arm movements to edge closer towards the bank.

Much ventilation was given to this topic in the film *Salmo – The Leaper* which has been screened on BBC Television's *World About Us* series. The producer and star performer, Hugh Falkus, ably demonstrated that it is panic which drowns, and that if the angler keeps his head – no matter what his apparel or wading style – he will emerge alive even if exceedingly wet. This film alone is known to have saved the lives of at least nine anglers: people who saw the film, noted the drill, and later wrote to Falkus following an unplanned immersion in deep water. It is essential to lie on one's back with the feet going downstream first. This way the angler will not hit his head on a protruding rock or stone. It is also important to keep the arms moving *in the water*. As Falkus dramatically points out in his commentary: 'Mouth open, with a cry for help, and water rushes in. Arms up, in gesticulation, and the body sinks.'

Like everything else in fishing, confidence in wading is only achieved by doing it constantly. When my wife first took up salmon fishing she was like a nervous kitten. Nowadays, however, she will think little of wading across smaller streams on her own; and although she uses a wading stick on rivers like the Spey, she is not frightened of going in deep. The greatest care must be taken when the angler is working his way down a shelving run of gravel, with deep water on either side. It may well be easy enough to wade down; but when the time comes to get out, it will be sheer hard work to walk back upstream against the current. There may also be the hazard of the gravel shifting, when a few unpleasant moments may occur. I well recall one instance when I was fishing with a friend on the river Spey. We went our separate ways. Some two hours later he appeared on the opposite bank. 'How did you get across?' I shouted. 'I waded across', he replied, with, unknown to me, a broad grin on his face. Walking downstream, I found the place where I presumed he had crossed. I started to do so, and eventually made it; but not before I had seen all my sins flash before me a thousand times. I would not have gone back across there, at that height of water, for all the money in the world. Upon reaching my friend, I learnt that he had been pulling my leg. He had walked down to a bridge and crossed that way.

While deep wading can be well-nigh essential in order to fish some pools correctly, there may just be a slight danger of wading so deep that the angler disturbs the salmon in their lies. For this reason alone it is very important to know your river. Eventually you will find a route down the water which will bring the best water coverage, and wading without tears! Care must also be taken when wading in rivers subject to rapid rises of water. I have known occasions when there has been barely time to get out before the flood hits. It can be pretty frightening.

Over on that section of the Lune where I used to fish regularly, it was customary to wade across the river before starting fishing. The river fished best from the opposite bank from that on which the cars were easily parked; and it was only very high water which made it impossible to wade across. I well recall one instance when I had waded over to do some night sea trout fishing. In the space of an hour the river rose quite rapidly, but in the darkness I failed to observe this until it was too late. I had a long walk that night! Moreover, I trod on many a sleeping cow until I finally stumbled into a small village. Once there, a kindly soul who was just leaving the village pub (it was 1 a.m.) gave me a lift round by the nearest bridge and back to my car.

Wading, therefore, is not without its hazards; but it must be done on occasions to be in with a chance of a fish. There are, of course, many rivers which do not lend themselves to wading, since they are too deep, or where any form of wading might only frighten the fish and do little or nothing to extend the useful casting range. Wade only when compelled to do so by the conditions; and use a little forethought before committing yourself to the water!

While on this topic, it has to be pointed out that on the bigger rivers it can vastly influence your effective casting range. Of course not all fish lie at the other side of the river, and the angler may well find that the bulk of his fish are hooked at his side of the stream. Even then the deep-wading angler is better able to cover the lies at his side of the river. He can hang the fly or make it move more slowly by being positioned immediately upstream of where the fish might take. Hugh Falkus contends, and I have no reason to argue with him, that deep wading will usually catch him more fish than standing near the bank. The more his body is immersed, the less there is above water to frighten the fish – for it is the movement above the surface which proves the more alarming. Most fish are accustomed to seeing odd bits of junk, such as large fertiliser bags and so on, submerged and floating down the current. It is my view as well that they pay little attention to a pair of slowly-moving legs. It is nearly always what they see above the water which frightens them most. Indeed, I well recall an occasion when Falkus and I were fishing the same pool together. He had gone down ahead of me with a floating line and I came down behind him with a sinking one. My fly was within mere inches of his feet when he saw a salmon take it and my rod bend into action. That fish was duly landed –

The author with a salmon of 20lb from the Bolstad pool of the Vosso. Note the method of tailing.

and, incidentally, the entire episode was filmed by the *World About Us* film crew. I will concede that the fish might have followed my fly from its original lie, but there is little doubt that while doing so it was completely unconcerned about my companion's legs and feet.

The playing of a fish sometimes poses problems for novices. The fact is that there can be no hard-and-fast rule in salmon fishing. A freshly-hooked fish has a few definite ideas of its own; and it may take some time before the angler is the complete master of the situation.

No matter by which method you have hooked a fish, it is a long way from being safely on the bank; and many a hard-earned catch has been lost through careless handling. In the first few seconds following firm hooking, you may quite casually put your rod over your shoulder and wade or walk to the nearest vantage point to play your fish. Make sure that the reel can run freely if the fish wants to take line; and take care not to let any slack line offer a chance of it gaining its freedom. You should aim to get slightly downstream of the fish, so that it is not only fighting against your tackle but against the current as well. Attempts to hang on while the fish flounders downstream should be discouraged. In this movement it can 'lean' on your tackle so to speak, and thus get assistance to swim against the current. Don't be in too great a hurry to hustle it out of the deep and fast water. It is in this part of the river that most of the steam will be taken out of it. Many fish are lost through over-anxiousness; and time spent in keeping a steady strain on the fish, while it fights the current, is well spent. A minute of play to each pound weight is a rough guide to the time it should take you to play out your salmon; but bear in mind that in the early stages the fish has not seen you, nor has it felt in any real danger. (Mind you, there is no definite rule for weight against playing time: I have played a fish of 45lbs to a standstill in under twenty minutes and have taken the same time with one of only 10lbs.) It is only during the final moments of play that the fish will make some desperate bid for freedom. If you intend to gaff it, wait until it is lying on its side before striking the gaff home. If, on the other hand, there is a shelving gravel beach handy, you may draw the fish to the side, get hold of it firmly by the tail and slide it up the beach. This method of handling is not completely safe unless you are certain that the fish is played out. Any form of over-anxiety at this stage may well send you home with a tale of the big one that got away! This brings me to the general question of landing salmon; and during March 1969 I wrote the following article for *The Shooting Times and Country Magazine*:

'Remarkably few salmon fishermen venture very far these days without the comforting feel of a gaff beside them. Indeed, there are many who would feel an air of nakedness without such a weapon on hand. There are, of course, a few occasions when the use of a gaff can save an otherwise embarrassing situation. But, in my opinion, it is used much too widely; and for many occasions when it would be perfectly simple to beach or tail the fish out by hand . . .

In my early days of salmon fishing, of course, the gaff was always by my side; and in the great excitement and anxiety to have the fish ashore it was inevitably stabbed into the fish's vitals at the very first opportunity. "Let's get the fish out at all costs", was the simple creed of those early days. My reasoning was not hard to comprehend. I had spent a long time fishing. Every salmon hooked was like a piece of elusive jade, to be snatched from its environment by the quickest means known and available. I think, for this reason, that the novice is to be excused for his reliance on the gaff; but it might pay to ponder on the inevitable feeling of anxiety which the possession of a gaff automatically bestows on the angler who continually relies on one.

'I should think that, in nine cases out of ten, the angler who is unaccompanied by a gillie invariably attempts to gaff his fish before it is fully played out. He looks round furtively, and there is no one on hand to help. With great trepidation, he makes ready with his gaff; and, as sure as fate, will have an early stab as the fish swims past on one of its final passes before being fully played out. With a bit of luck he may well get the gaff home and come lunging ashore with his prize. The fish will doubtless be dripping blood and stabbed through the vitals wherever fate planned the gaff should strike. With normal luck he may well miss the first time – and even the second and third. By now he is getting anxious and in danger of completely losing any of the sound reasoning that led to the successful playing of the fish in the first place. He desperately wants it out; and it is at this stage that he is quite likely to do something so irrational that, in a fraction of a second, fish and line part company. The doleful angler is then left with memories of a big one that got away! Rarely would the angler dream of blaming himself; and the size of the fish and its immense strength, gradually grow in proportion to the number of times the story of its loss is related to friends! It has happened to me; and I have witnessed it happen to others, who were completely rational human beings. They appeared to be driven from the rational to panic when they saw the fish, just beyond or just within their grasp – so near or yet so far! If only they had forgotten the gaff and had tried to steer the fish during play to some convenient place where they could have beached it conveniently when it was completely played out. If at the eleventh hour, no such place emerged, and the fish was lying on its side, it would be a simple matter to lower the gaff and place it into the gills of the fish so that it would do the least damage and would not cause unsightly effect. There are, however, occasions when the use of a gaff is both sensible and desirable but there are also many more occasions when its use is not necessary.

'For all my normal salmon fishing I do not now carry a gaff. I go without one in the faint hope that one day I might hook such a big fish in British waters that I would wish that I had one to hand. I have, however, already conceded that I have been glad to have some of my very large Norwegian fish gaffed by the gillie, but I have never really been put to the test on any British river. When fishing on a river with a shelving gravel beach it is but a simple matter to wait until the fish is fully played out and then pick it up by the tail. Alternatively, if it is a bigger-than-average fish, it is comparatively easy to slide its head onto the beach and then push it uphill by the tail. It is quite remarkable how even a big fish will respond to being pushed head first up the gravel, when there might be a chance of losing it if it were picked up bodily by the tail. In such a situation the fish might merely kick and gain its freedom from even a tight grip. I have used the beaching technique with fish up to 28lbs in Norway and have hand-tailed several up to 20lbs without great difficulty.

'Quite frequently it is convenient to net a salmon. The main proviso is that the net be large enough to take the fish and that a friend is on hand to help. The net should be lowered into the water and only when the head of the fish is over the rim should the assistant lift it. It is generally a mistake to net a fish tail first.

'Before the beaching or tailing techniques become acceptable to the angler, however, there has to be a basic change of philosophy. No longer must the successful *killing* of the fish be the sole objective. There must be a personal reappraisal of what really matters in a day's sport with the salmon. Is the killing of the greatest number of fish still the prime objective? Or is it the maximum pleasure of the sport to be derived from hooking and playing the fish? When the angler comes into the second category, he may well have to pay for his experience by the loss of a few fish; and it would indeed be sad if a lost fish happened to be one of the really big ones.

'It was in the spring of 1967 that I firmly resolved to fish thereafter without a gaff. In terms of fish caught that year, it cost me something. It was a season during which, for me, fish were hard to come by. I lost the first three by stupid tactical errors on my part. On the first occasion, I tried to beach the fish on part of the river covered with chain-link gabions. One of the hooks on the triangle was showing outside the mouth of the fish, and quickly caught in the chain-link. The fish unhooked itself with great alacrity and was back into the water like a flash. Similarly stupid tactics caused the loss of the other two; and I almost went back on my resolve! A few days later, however, I had my tenacity of purpose rewarded when I beached a lovely fish of 22lbs I had taken on a small fly. I did not use the gaff again that year; and have not, personally, carried a gaff since.

'This does not mean that I shall never again allow another to gaff my fish. If ever I hook that 60-pounder in Norway it would all be a different tale. On the general question of gaffs, however, an amusing incident comes to mind. Some years ago I was fishing with a friend who decried the use of the gaff on *every* occasion. The river was carrying extra water and was running down like thick coffee. For some obscure reason I was attempting to fish while my friend stood close by. We were both up to our knees in water when, in a startled whisper, my friend, pointing to his feet, said, "Look at this". Glancing down I saw the broad expanse of a salmon's tail. The fish had literally come and lain over his feet as it paused in its upstream migration. "Now's the chance to show me your tailing technique!" I jokingly said to my friend – whereupon he quietly lowered his hand and made a sudden grab around the tail of the fish. There was a violent cascade of spray. The fish came half out of the water – and then about 12lbs of untamed fury was let loose. The result was inevitable. Within split seconds it was back in the river, as though the devil himself were after it; and it quickly tore across the surface and into deep water. My chum was soaked; but complained, with a huge grin, that he did not consider that a fair test! Fair enough!'

Shortly after publication of this article on landing salmon, I received a letter thus:

Dear Sir,
Further to your article on gaffing. Tailing with one's hand is most effective and very easy. However, I was surprised to see a photo showing you holding the salmon the wrong way. When tailing salmon with your hand, always have your thumb and forefinger towards the tail. With your little finger towards the tail, as in the picture, your fish is much more likely to slip through your hands. With large fish, or when my hands are cold, I always put a wet handkerchief in my hand before tailing the fish, as this greatly increases 'grip' and reduces 'slip'. Never try this method with sea trout, as they have no 'bone' in their tails and slip through one's hand.
Yours faithfully,
T.T.

My subsequent commentary was as follows:

'I was not aware that anyone had established a right and wrong way of tailing salmon; just as there is, as yet, no stipulated method for picking up a pint of beer. One does it a certain way out of habit, or for most comfort and effectiveness. I have read very contradicting reports on this question of tailing; and I came to the conclusion, many years ago, that it did not matter. I have tailed fish by both methods. I have seen very many experienced anglers also tail their fish out by both methods; some have a preference for T.T.'s way, others for mine. It is not a matter about which I would like to pontificate. T.T. is certainly clear on the question of sea trout – although there are ways of getting these fish out by hand without too much trouble. There are also times, with really big salmon, when it pays to beach them. This can easily be done by pushing the fish, head first, up the bank. The rod is pointed in the direction the fish is required to go and the fish is pushed up by the tail. Under all these circumstances I think that my grip would be the more effective and comfortable.

'On the question of sea-trout: I have always been under the impression that these fish were anatomically the same as salmon, except that they are much thicker around the 'wrist' of the tail and therefore slip out of one's hand much more readily. One of the old rules of fish recognition (between salmon and sea trout) for those who could not readily tell the difference, was to pick the fish up by the tail to see if it slipped. If it stayed then it was a salmon; but if it slipped out of one's grip, it was presumed to be a sea trout. Like many rules, it was not infallible; but it was a good guide.

'Since this statement about my tailing methods, I have been at pains to pick the brains of as many experienced salmon anglers as I could. At the Knockando salmon hatchery on the river Spey I was shown a selection of colour slides of salmon being trapped for artificial spawning and noted carefully that all the fish handled by the bailiffs were tailed after my own fashion. Angling film shows reveal that Hugh Falkus, and a host of other notable fishermen, also tail their fish my way; but the American expert, Lee Wulff, tails them out after the fashion of T.T. My vast library of angling photographs has depicted many anglers tailing out salmon. I can find only one which shows fish being tailed in any style other than my own.

'In order to test the matter further I put the question to a doctor. He readily accepted the adaptability of the human hand; but after some thought felt that my way might produce the better grip. I must confess that I am still left wondering and would certainly never be so bold as to say whether there is a right and wrong way of doing the job. I think that every angler must find the best way to suit himself, depending upon the size of his hand and the strength of his grip.'

Matters to do with all these aspects of wading, playing, gaffing or tailing salmon will be determined by the venues or preferences of the individual angler. Those who sit in a boat on Tweed or Tay may well never have cause to wade or to land their own fish. Others, like myself, may feel slightly cheated if they have not had full involvement in the entire operation. Until anglers know the water, however, they would do well to serve an apprenticeship under a competent gillie or boatman. Let us now move on to give closer examination to the entire question of gillies and boatmen.

According to my dictionary the spelling is 'gillie' and not 'ghillie'. He is defined as either an attendant on a highland chief; a servant who carries the chief across streams; or one who attends a sportsman in the Scottish Highlands. In general usage the term 'gillie' has come to mean a guide or servant in the specialised sense of salmon fishing; and the writer who commented, 'they are a dour lot!' was not far from the truth.

Gillies come in several shapes and sizes, and have varying degrees of affluence. Some are part-timers, with limited knowledge of their beat of the river. Others know literally every stone and every conceivable lie, under every condition or height of water. The good ones are like rare jade; but the bad ones can well spoil an otherwise enjoyable outing.

In general, however, I must confess that gillies *are* a dour lot. It does not need great powers of reflection to find the causes for such an outlook. The man who turns to gillieing for his livelihood is usually a native of the area. He knows the river intimately and has become accustomed to the perfect conditions when the best sport is likely to be had. Small wonder that the edge is taken off his enthusiasm when he has an indifferent angler fishing a period of the season which is not likely to produce much sport. While I have often felt it a strain to have a bad gillie, it must be infuriating for a good gillie to be burdened with a bad angler.

A gillie is only important to me during the period I am fishing a new water. If he is up to his job, he will tell me the best lies, and can give facts about the water which, fishing alone, I would take years to find out for myself. Although he was not a gillie, I well recall being eternally grateful to David Cook on the little Yorkshire Esk. He taught me more about the river in a year than I could have learned in ten years by myself. Nowadays I rarely need the services of a gillie to land a fish, and I am still sufficiently agile to carry my own tackle. Moreover, there are times when I dislike the presence of a gillie, particularly if I sense some form of resentment at the way I am doing things.

Gillies' habits differ greatly from one river to another. Many of those I know on the Scottish Dee refuse to wear waders. The head gillie of one famous beat was very indignant years ago when I refused to let him gaff a 20lb fish I was bringing in, because it was obvious that unless he could wade away from the shallows it would take me ages to play the fish out so that he could gaff it dry-shod. 'Give me the gaff ', I said, 'and I'll gaff it'. 'What am I here for then?' was his quick retort. 'I don't know', I replied. 'But unless you clothe yourself adequately to gaff my fish, I would rather do it myself.' He handed the gaff over and I duly brought the fish ashore. He was a bit sullen for the rest of the day, but I respected his knowledge of the water and a more friendly relationship was luckily established during the rest of the week.

There is a subtle difference between gillies and boatmen. When fishing a river like the Tweed a good boatman is fairly essential for success – at least on the lower beats of the river. As with gillies, there are good boatmen and bad ones; but most have long experience of the water and their enthusiasm waxes and wanes with the experience of their angler and the chances of sport. My old Tweed boatman was a good barometer of the sport to be expected. If I arrived full of enthusiasm and he appeared indifferent, I guessed that the chances were minimal; if, however, he was raring to go and hustling me to get ready, it was a good bet that we would have a few fish that day.

I know of few gillies who do not have a taste for whisky. One of my acquaintance, on a West Highland river, could down a bottle without batting an eye. The only noticeable difference at the end of the day was that his Spey-casting became a bit tatty. On one occasion everything looked to be going smoothly until the fly circled over his head and removed his hat. Suddenly he was base-over-apex in some swirling water. But he was quickly ashore and another dram soon put him right.

The great feature about Norwegian gillies is their youth. In many hamlets the younger generation are away at schools; but the short fishing season of that country almost coincides with school or college vacations and the young men are back at home with time on their hands. Small wonder that they use the period to earn some extra money and, with their agility and nimbleness, they make excellent assistants on those violent waters. It seems a point of honour for all Norwegian gillies to gaff the fish in the head. The market value of fish gaffed in the body is lower, and it is only when a really big fish has to be taken from dangerous water that these gillies will forsake their commercial principles.

If not all gillies are perfect, neither are the anglers who fish with them. A good angler will listen to the advice of a gillie and will weigh that advice against his own experience. Although I have a wide experience in salmon fishing, I always make a point of consulting the gillie or boatman. Usually the advice is worth taking and after a few years on a beat or portion of river, the angler and the gillie usually build up a mutual respect and friendship for each other. It is important, I think, to let your gillie know at the outset just what you would like from him. On a river like the Dee, for instance, all I could ask of my gillie is that he position himself unseen so that he can peer into the clear water and give me information about any response to my fly. Although the day might come, I do not yet require a burden-bearer and·I have sufficient experience of tailing my own fish to look after this job myself.

A good gillie on a strange water, however, is still a gem; and to get the best from him he should be treated with respect, courtesy and as a fellow sportsman.

Photograph overleaf: David Cook prepares to gaff a salmon on the Yorkshire Esk near Grosmont.

Throughout the preceding chapters we have examined the various types of tackle which the all-round salmon angler may well require to see him through a season. There are few ways to short-circuit the vast amount of tackle required if the angler wishes to give himself the best chance. We have seen the desirability of at least three rods for differing types of fly fishing and a similar number of rods for every aspect of spinning. Such a comprehensive outfit is not entirely necessary, however, and if I had to limit myself to three only, I think that I should opt for the 15-foot 'Walker' rod by Bruce and Walker to cope with all my floating and sunk-line operations in the early spring and late autumn; the 10-foot 'Multispin' carbon rod by the same maker and the 10-foot 'Light Line' carbon rod for all single-handed fly fishing purposes. Let me emphasise again that this latter rod is not recommended by the makers for salmon fishing. It is essentially a trout fly rod – and an excellent one at that – but I like to use it for salmon. Provided that the angler always remembers that it is primarily a trout rod, and does not demand too much of it, he will have a delightful outfit. For more demanding single-handed situations the angler may be better advised to use the 10½-foot 'Salmon and Sea Trout' rod by Bruce and Walker. This is a tough, yet light, rod capable of casting a long line and killing a good fish.

While I have a decided preference for the carbon rods made by Bruce and Walker, I do not wish to imply that there are no other good rods on the market. However, I am now fully convinced that carbon is the best rod-making material we have ever had and I would not recommend a newcomer to consider anything else. Of course they are not cheap and some are not so well-designed as they might be. It is one thing to have a carbon rod, and quite another to have one which has been well-designed and thoroughly tested through the prototype stage. I know that Bruce and Walker do this thorough testing because I have been involved in it.

There is a widespread belief that carbon is more prone to breakage than other rod-making materials. During the testing of some prototypes in 1975 it is true that I did manage to break some. The points of fracture gave good clues to the points of weakness. A year later Bruce and Walker gave me a set of rods with the specific request that I try to break them in normal fishing situations. I gave some of those rods more hard work than they might ever expect in the lifetime of the average angler. Some were bounced up and down on the roof rack of my car for two months, fished with every day, and called upon to cope with the ultimate in casting and playing conditions. I could not break them in any normal fishing circumstance, and the only one of the original set to break was one which fell off the roof of my car in the spring of 1981 when I had forgotten to lock it in and was travelling at 60 mph.

All that being said, it is just as easy to break a carbon rod as it is to break one of any other material. I have seen anglers break them when they have tried to lift too long a sunken line. I have seen them snap when the angler has been tugging and heaving to remove a bait or fly which has got stuck in a tree or on the bottom of the river. But I have never seen one break while a fish was in play or when the angler was casting correctly and within the limits of such a rod – whether made of carbon or anything else.

When choosing a rod it is important to see that it has action through to the butt. Some glass and carbon fibre rods do have a tendency towards 'tippiness'. They are perfectly adequate for playing fish, but as the angler primarily wants a good casting tool, some fall short of perfection. Of course, I am not suggesting that you want a floppy rod. It should have some 'steel' about it and there are anglers who like a 'fast' action in preference to a 'slow' actioned rod. Recognising this, Bruce and Walker have made varied types of rods to suit their customers. For instance, Ken Walker has a distinct preference for a fairly stiff action; while Jim Bruce likes a softer one. Rather than squabble about which rods to market, they did the sensible thing commercially and brought out the 'Bruce' and the 'Walker' range. Time alone will tell if they adhere to this formula for marketing their best rods, but it makes sound sense to me. I have a slight preference for the 'Walker' range, but then I am a fairly strong chap and can still get the best from these 'faster' rods. My wife shows a preference for the 'Bruce' range and demonstrates more than adequate competence at casting and playing fish with one. From sales research, however, it would appear that the 15-foot 'Walker' quickly established itself as a market leader in double-handed salmon fly rods: and, although I now possess nigh on fifty assorted fishing rods, that one remains my favourite for double-handed salmon fly fishing.

Quite apart from choosing the right fly rod for your purpose, it is very important to match the rod with a suitable line. Most modern fly rods have the Association of Fishing Tackle Makers (AFTM) number engraved near the rod handle. This is supposed to be the number of the best line suited to the rod. Some makers – Bruce and Walker are an example – give a range of line sizes which the rod will handle comfortably and then leave the final choice to the discretion of the angler. In theory there should be only one line which suits any rod best; but carbon does permit some variation. The original AFTM formula involved the front 10 yards (30 feet) of line outside the rod point. When the rod functioned perfectly with this length of line of a specific size it was said to be correctly 'loaded' and that size of line was nominated. However, it is easily seen that if a rod handles 10 yards of No. 11 line perfectly, it might not be so well matched when the angler asks the rod to aerialise 20 yards. In the latter instance it might be better that a No. 9 or No. 10 line had been chosen.

My own preference, particularly when fishing strong water in the spring, is to use as heavy a line as the rod will comfortably take. For me, with my 15-foot 'Walker', this means a No. 11 double-taper line. And, as I have already pointed out, on suitable days I can Spey-cast the entire 30 yards of line. Such a heavy line might not be suitable, tactically, for the lower water of late spring and summer. At this time of the year, therefore, I put on a No. 9 line and get that little bit more delicate presentation.

Code numbers for lines are fairly straightforward. A DT-10-F line is simply a double-tapered No. 10 floating line; while WF-8-S conveys that it is a weight-forward (forward-taper) No. 8 sinker. DT-9-F/S is merely a double-tapered No. 9 floating line with a sinking tip.

The choice of line size, therefore, is largely dictated by the rod we wish to use. Whether we go for sinkers or floaters, double-taper or forward-taper is again something of a matter for preference or where and how we are going to fish. The 'Kingfisher' silk lines had great merit when they were available. They could be greased to make them float or rubbed down with detergent to make them sink. These lines tended to be less bulky, weight for weight, than plastic floating lines; but it was sometimes a little tedious to be continually greasing them throughout a day's floating-line fishing. Invariably, too, some of the grease got on to the leader and may well have caused the fly to skate. They were, however, extremely nice lines to use.

Of the fully floating and sinking lines, the *AirCel* and the *WetCel* are among the most popular makes imported into Britain. Other favourites are lines made by the Cortland Company; but like several other makes they are generally imported from America. The British Masterline Company presents a wide choice and the market is well covered.

If we rule out silk lines there is, as we have seen in all the chapters on fly fishing, a great need to have both floaters and sinkers on hand to cope with the changing conditions throughout a season. It is not really possible to make a floating line sink effectively, nor to make a sinking line float. Having made this point, however, it must be emphasised that all floating lines are not as buoyant as the makers would have us believe. If there is any suggestion of an eddy in the water, it will often make the line sink; but for general purposes they float effectively enough provided that they are cleaned periodically and any scum is removed. Furthermore, dirty water with surface scum has a tendency to make these lines sink; but in good streamy water they work very effectively and must be considered a boon to the salmon fisherman.

Many of these lines come in various colours and we have already examined occasions when it might pay to use a darker-coloured line than the more normal white one. Generally speaking, though, floating lines are white (but are available in brown or light green) and the sinking ones dark green. Most times this facilitates easy recognition.

The choice between forward-taper or double-taper for floating-line fishing is a little more difficult to determine. Much depends upon the type of water to be fished. Because I fish a wide variety of rivers I like to have both types of line on hand to cope with differing techniques. For a medium-sized river there is a lot to be said for a forward-taper line. The line is so constructed that the bulk of the weight or diameter is in the forward section. This portion is therefore the maximum amount which may be aerialised. The rest of the line, with much smaller diameter than the forward section, is designed to be 'shot' when the final cast is made. This leads to an ultimate distance beyond which it is very difficult to cast. Techniques for using a line of this type involve hand-lining the back section of line through the rings and then, as the forward cast is made, the hand-held line is released so that it may be taken out more easily by the heavy forward section. As I have noted, it is virtually impossible to aerialise more than the forward section; and there is a limit to the amount which may be shot. Because of the small diameter of this back taper, it does shoot much more readily than would be the case with a double-taper line. *It is, however, virtually impossible to do any form of worthwhile Spey or roll casting with a forward-taper line.*

With a double-taper line it is quite possible to aerialise a great deal more than would be possible with the forward-taper variety. It does not shoot so readily, but has a decided advantage when any form of Spey or roll cast is required. The final choice must of course remain with the angler. For personal preference I tend to use the forward-taper line on small rivers or in summertime with a single-handed rod; and the double-taper line for the Spey, Tay or Tweed. There are, as we have seen, great merits in the shooting-head system for sunk-line fishing. Indeed, the same technique may be used with a floating head; but it is then much more difficult to make any meaningful 'mends' in the line. The method does find great favour with some anglers.

On the question of sinking lines there is little comment to make. My own, definite, preference is for the double-taper variety on the simple basis that I get two lines for the price of one. There is little point in having the forward-taper variety when the normal double-taper line may be cut in two and one section then spliced to monofilament backing. Anyway, it is not possible to lift a lot of drowned line so that the forward-taper principle is still involved. Even then it may well be found that the half-portion (15 yards) of shooting head is a little too much. For this reason I invariably cut 3 yards off the belly portion of the line to leave me a working 12 yards which is spliced to the monofilament backing. This latter type of line should be of fairly substantial diameter, since it will bear the brunt of the casting work. Casting with very heavy flies will also subject it to harsh treatment. For this reason I tend to opt for backing of about 25lbs test and then splice it with a needle knot to the heavy back-taper of the line. Great care must be taken with this knot or the occasion will come when you suddenly see your fly-line rocket off into orbit. This happened to me on one occasion, but luckily my gillie found it on the bed of the river! After this I increased the security of the knot by applying a bit of plastic cement.

With this type of fishing it is a good plan to pre-stretch the backing before starting to cast and some distinct advantage may be gained by using oval section monofilament, as already described. When wound on the reel, normal monofilament backing quickly develops a coil. If it is not pre-stretched there will be a grave danger of bunching and an inevitable snarl-up into the butt ring once a hefty cast is made. With a bit of practice some remarkably long casts may be made with this technique; but it is true to say that they are more easily accomplished from a boat or bank, where the backing will be laid on a clear surface, than from a deep-wading position in which the water inevitably imposes drag on the pulled-off backing. If the current is strong, this drag is substantially increased, and reduces the distance of the cast considerably.

Perhaps the most surprising feature about many talented salmon fishermen is their very limited range of knotting techniques. There are several very good knots which have been evolved since the advent of nylon monofilament. Descriptions of most knots may be found in many tackle catalogues; but the illustrations in Fig. 18 are a simple diagrammatic guide to the knots I require most frequently. Although we may purchase ready-made leaders, the knot at Fig. 18a will make a perfect loop in any ordinary piece of nylon. This may be attached to our fly line with the figure-of-eight knot as shown in Fig. 18b. The best junction is achieved by a nail knot (Fig. 18e) and all we then need is a suitable knot with which to tie on our fly. The Turle knot (Fig. 18d) is my favourite and I have rarely felt the need for another. The water knot proves ideal for joining short lengths of nylon and is most useful for tying in a dropper fly for loch or stillwater fishing. Another very useful attachment is the half-blood knot (Fig. 18g). This should not be used when fly fishing, since it may well cause the fly to hinge and not fish in the correct manner. It is, however, the most used knot for attaching a spinning bait or swivel to monofilament line. A more sophisticated version of this is the tucked half-blood knot; but I rarely bother with this refinement and cannot recall ever losing a fish because the standard version has let me down.

Rod rings pose another interesting problem. There is still a tendency to opt for the flashy, agate types. These are perfectly satisfactory until they crack. The short margins of the crack then cause serious fraying damage to monofilament line. I like big, open bridge-rings, with a large ring at the butt and plenty of space in all the others to enable the shooting-head and backing to move smoothly with a minimum of friction. Some years ago, when trying out a rod by an overseas maker, I was surprised to note that the rings were so narrow that the knot joining my backing to the line would not pass through the tip ring. Little wonder that some rods do not shoot line as readily as others, or that fish get lost through line knots jamming in the rings. Of course, there have to be limits in this sort of thing; but I think that it pays to go for the largest rings which look in harmony with the rod. All spinning rods should be fitted with a good-sized butt ring, particularly

Fig. 18a Double-loop Knot.
The loop for a level nylon fly-leader;
the line being attached with a figure
of eight knot as in 18b.

Fig. 18b

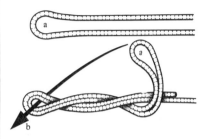

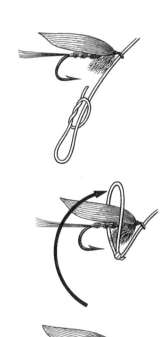

Fig. 18c The Blood Knot.

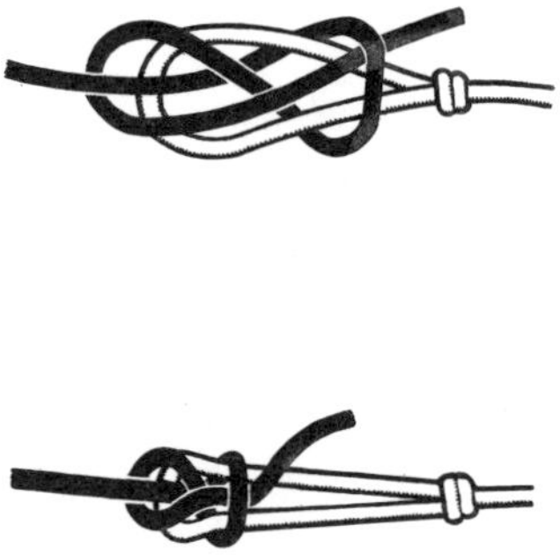

Fig. 18d The Turle Knot.

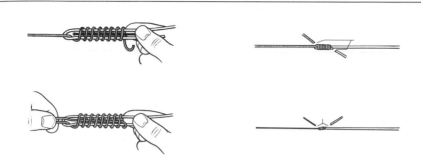

Fig. 18e The Nail Knot.
Although the Nail Knot simply cuts through a vacuum-finished silk line it is extremely useful with today's tough, plastic-coated fly lines. The harder the knot is pulled, the better it holds, so it is no longer necessary to knot a fly line to a leader loop.

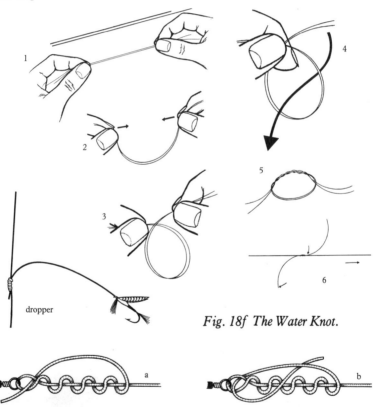

Fig. 18f The Water Knot.

Fig. 18g The Half-Blood Knot.
A and B are variations of the Half-Blood Knot commonly used to tie monofilament nylon to a hook, swivel or spinner mount. I prefer method A, which I have used for many years and never yet known to slip, but the Tuck Knot (B) can give extra security when an unusually large-eyed swivel or hook is being used.

if the rod is expressly designed for use with a fixed-spool reel. It is also important to have the ring standing well off from the rod if line friction is not to be caused by the line hitting the rod as well as the ring. The line, when cast, comes off in loops and even with the largest ring some bunching is inevitable. This causes friction and restricts distance potential.

Reel-fittings and seatings are also bones of contention. It is time that the AFTM adopted standards which eliminate reels flopping about on the rod or being so tight that it is difficult, or even impossible, to get the fittings over the spade end of the reels. A good supply of strong adhesive tape accompanies me on all my fishing trips since I find on occasion that the required reel will not fit the rod in hand, and it then has to be bound on.

Most fly rods have a 'fly keeper' ring just above the butt. Frankly, I find them a curse. They are not in the best place to 'keep' a fly. The hook or hooks are still exposed and can easily catch in clothing or flesh. Also the small ring has an irritating habit of being in the way when backing line is being shot – quite frequently it snarls round the fly-keeper ring and has to be disentangled. A much better place to 'keep' the fly is underneath the forward reel mounting. If the fly is merely single-hooked then the entire hook is covered, both protected from damage and unable to inflict damage. Multi-hooked flies pose more problems in this respect, but they are no more hazardous or vulnerable there than in the standard keeper ring. A compromise location may be found for the hook to be lodged round one of the line guards on the reel.

In spinning, I have already highlighted the importance of having the weight figure stamped on a bait. This is something which could well be

The fly keeper ring is not a good place to store flies. Hooks can too readily catch in clothing or flesh.

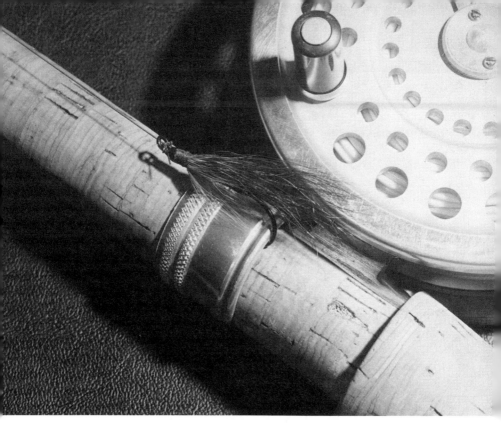

A better fly keeper ring is to be found under the front reel seat. This can cover double hooked flies, but does leave a third of trebles exposed.

done to advantage for the angler. It would also be desirable if spinner manufacturers were to take up the challenge of producing a certain length of bait in three alternative weights, with a wide variety of size and weight permutations on which the angler could base his choice. With this type of guide the angler would be better equipped to face a season's fishing.

Apart from these minor grumbles, I think that it is fair to suggest that the British tackle industry is now providing the angler with better products than ever before. Tournament casting did much to bring the need for improvements to the notice of both manufacturers and anglers and, although a lot of tournament tackle is as far removed from practical angling needs as a racing car is from a stately saloon, the tournament world has been the proving ground for a lot of useful ideas. 'Race bred' is a much used term in car advertisements and I think that we could apply the term 'tournament bred' to some of our tackle and techniques. We owe quite a lot to the tournament world for present-day rod action and casting techniques.

As I have already commented elsewhere in this book, there is a great deal of satisfaction to be derived from catching salmon on flies which the angler has tied himself. I make no great claim to expertise in fly-tying, but I have tied flies since the late forties; and while few of my flies would catch fishermen, I am pleased to record that they do catch a few fish. I am under few illusions that my flies are any better than other, professionally-dressed, ones. The snag is that, nowadays, a well-tied salmon fly may cost a small fortune in the shops; and if the angler is to have a useful range of patterns and sizes he might well have to invest a large sum of money on these items alone.

In order to make flies that conform to the old recipes, a great deal of material preparation and dexterity are required. I would not presume to be able to tie such a fly to the high standard of the professional dresser. Therefore, I avoid traditional patterns and seek only to make flies of the most simple materials and to construct them so that they will stand a deal of hard work and not fall apart at the first cast. In order to do this I may break some of the rules of the craft. I have had no tuition in fly-dressing, but have just picked it up from watching other people – which is not, in fact, the best way to learn. My flies, however, must have *some* merit if they continue to catch fish, and this is the only yardstick I set them against. For this reason I have now discarded all flies with feather-wing dressings. Instead I go for hair-wing flies, relying on the movement of the flowing fibres to represent small fish or large insects. My flies have to look as though they come alive in a current of flowing water. Unless they do this, even though they might contain the most beautiful feathers and have cost the earth to buy, I discard them out of hand. I have a large collection of such rejects. They are all mounted in a beautiful bound leather hold-all and are most attractive. They have been tied exquisitely, but they will never find a place on my leader.

The trouble with some of the bigger, traditional flies is not their basic inability to raise and hook fish, but their general inability to retain the fish on the hook during the tense and frantic moments of play. There is too much leverage with the large, old-fashioned flies and I rarely fish with anything more than a No. 4 treble, double or single-hook fly. When conditions demand larger flies than this I tend to rely, almost exclusively, on the tube type with an articulated treble-hook at the tail.

For small flies I rely on the most simple dressing. The selected hook is placed in a vice and the shank covered lightly with clear Bostik. A few turns of binding silk are then spun on to the shank and wound down to the point where the tail will finish. A length of fine tinsel wire is then bound in, followed by a split length of marabou silk. The tying silk is then taken to the head of the fly, and the body silk is bound round the shank until it is locked into position at the head. Following this, the tinsel is wound round in open spirals until it too is tied in position at the head of the fly. It is fairly important to bind in the tinsel in a different direction to that taken by the body silk, so that it helps to keep the silk bound in if a fish should cut the silk at any time. A few hackle fibres are then taken from a suitable feather and bound in underneath the eye of the hook. All that is then left to do is to select some squirrel or bucktail winging of suitable colour and tie this on top of the shank. The whole is then bound in with tying silk and a further addition of clear Bostik. A final whip-knot completes the dressing and the knot is layered with black enamel to give a professional finish to the head.

Big flies on tubes are even more simple to dress. I now rarely bother with any body materials, but tie in the various colours of bucktail winging and finish off as before. The place at which the triangle of hooks are to extend should be carefully assessed and the fibres allowed to extend beyond the length of the tube so that they will give some masking to the hooks. I am not a great advocate of having the fibres extending much further than the hook position, since there is a possibility that the fish might nip the end of the fly without coming into contact with the hook. There are those who argue that this does not matter; and that if a fish takes the fly, it will take it with a 'bang'. If, however, anyone has seen the way a salmon sometimes plays with a shrimp, they will feel as apprehensive as I do about fishing with flies with long hackles beyond the hooks.

In my glass tank of flowing water it was quite surprising to note how the triangle hook has a vague resemblance to the caudal fin of a small fish. Thus I feel that it does not matter greatly if it is a little bare. If the fish attempts to take the fly properly, there should be little doubt about a good hook-hold. It is well to make sure that the strength of the treble is in keeping with the width of its gape. I have lost many a good fish through having the hook straighten out, or break at the shank.

On most of my big flies I like plenty of dressing; but on the very small ones it is sometimes difficult to keep the dressing sufficiently sparse. As I have already indicated, I am not greatly concerned with pattern, but I do like to have a wide variety of sizes, with further variables on the amount of dressing those sizes contain. I suggest a bit of experimentation, even if you are ashamed to show your flies to more talented fly-dressing friends. The only yardstick by which they should be judged is whether they catch fish!

With advancing old age I tend to regard fly-tying as a bit of a chore. Most of my salmon fly requirements are now filled by Esmond Drury or by Riding Bros, who make some excellent flies.

Although I have visited North America a few times and have fished for the big game species in the Gulf of Mexico and off the Atlantic seaboard, I have never wet a line in the Atlantic salmon-producing rivers of the northernmost eastern states nor in the prolific rivers of Gaspe, Newfoundland and Labrador. I cannot comment, therefore, from first-hand experience; but I am in regular communication with many North American anglers – some noted ones – and have come to learn that, while their salmon are basically the same as ours, they frequently adopt slightly different tactics to catch them.

It must be stated at the outset that most of the worthwhile salmon fishing in the North American continent lies within the boundaries of Canada. This east coast fishing must not be confused with fishing on the Pacific coast where the salmon are of a different species. The Atlantic salmon are mainly concentrated along the north and south shores of the Gulf of St Lawrence, Labrador and Newfoundland. The provinces of Quebec, New Brunswick and Nova Scotia offer some of the finest fishing for Atlantic salmon anywhere in the world; but it is closely controlled and much of it is in the hands of small, wealthy American syndicates.

Perhaps the river with the greatest reputation is the Restigouche. This, along with several other legendary rivers, has its home in the Gaspe peninsula and is world-renowned for its fine fishing, as are the Grand Cascapedia, the Matapedia, the Kedgwick, Upsalquitch and the Matane. Further south there is the well-know Miramichi river; and on the northern shores of the St Lawrence, in the province of Quebec, lies a vast territory with many fine, though lesser-known, rivers. The Natashquan, Moisie, Romaine and Etamamiou are very fine; and the Moisie is said to hold larger salmon than any water in that area.

While many of the salmon waters are virtually closed to visitors, there are quite a few rivers (or sections of rivers) where fishing is free on the payment of licence dues. Many of the rivers of Newfoundland and Nova Scotia come into this category. Controls vary from province to province. Most New Brunswick rivers are leased to 'outfitters'; and there are Crown waters, available for a fee to non-residents, and free to residents of the province. Quebec has many rivers leased to private clubs and 'outfitters'; and for fishing certain rivers, such as the Matane, only a licence is required since they are set aside for public use.

'Outfitters' are individuals or small companies who lease the fishing from the government agency and sub-let a rod or rods. Normally they provide a full package deal with lodge accommodation near the fishing site; float-plane transportation, and guides and canoes. The season, generally, is over the three months from June to August. Fly fishing *only* is allowed by law and there are many rivers where it is quite common to fish the dry fly. One reason why Canadian salmon take the dry fly is that they are usually fished for during the warmer months and at a time when they are comparatively fresh run. Many of the rivers abound with smaller salmon and grilse, and these fish have usually not had long, static periods of inactivity in the water to become stale and potted.

Limit bags are in force on all rivers. Taking a general view, the floating line methods as founded in this country are in general practice; and for many years the flies and tackle popular at home found great favour. For the past several years, however, North American anglers have rightly tended to regard our traditional flies as over-dressed and have come to favour the hair-wing flies which are now becoming so popular over here. Sizes are usually No. 6 to No. 8 singles or doubles, with similarly dressed patterns to those used in the UK. As a compromise between traditional floating line and dry-fly methods, some anglers tie a fly onto their leader with a final 'riffling' or half-hitch, as mentioned elsewhere.

North American anglers demonstrate a general tendency to use single-handed rods, usually around 8 to 10 feet long. A few old-timers on the Grand Cascapedia, however, still seem to cling to their double-handed rods, though I suspect that the advent of carbon fibre might induce more to take advantage of the wonderful extra 'water command' a double-handed rod gives. It must be realised, however, a lot of fishing is done from canoes, where casting a long line, or Spey-casting, is not required. With little bank vegetation to hamper overhead casting other waters are easily waded.

Serious enquiries for fishing in Canada may be directed to The Atlantic Salmon Association, 1434 St Catherine Street West, 109 Montreal, Quebec, Canada H3G 1R4.

Fishing on the Miramachi river, New Brunswick, Canada.

The foregoing chapters represent a distillation of virtually all that I know about salmon and the craft of catching them. Sadly, most of it seems to have a tinge of history about it; and some salmon waters where I used to enjoy such wonderful sport, in the golden years, lack a lot of the lustre they once had. What lies in store for the salmon angler of the future, therefore? This is a tough question. I should need a computerised crystal ball and some of the Almighty's perception to be able to look very far ahead. The rods of our forefathers were long and cumbersome; and the 17-footers of bygone days have all rotted away or are treasured possessions as family heirlooms. Rarely are they used for fishing nowadays. Instead, until the blessed advent of carbon fibre, we witnessed a trend to shorter and lighter rods. We were much influenced by the Americans in this respect and it was refreshing – and rather revealing – to note that when carbon fibre began to make its full impact, we immediately saw or rediscovered the great advantage of the longer rod, particularly when it did not prove to be so heavy as those monsters of yesteryear.

Some anglers think that the trend to shorter rods will continue and that the double-haul cast, so popular nowadays when used with a single-handed rod on our still waters and reservoirs, will ultimately be in more general use on our salmon rivers. Had it not been for carbon fibre, this might well have been the case. With carbon, however, we can afford to make our rods longer. In fact, even with trout rods, the trend to shortness has been reversed. As I have already pointed out, the long rod has a great deal to commend it; and the longer the rod, in theory the greater the distance which may be achieved in Spey-casting. I suspect that it will now be a long time before rods of a length much less than 10 feet will make their full impact on the classic rivers of Scotland – particularly in the early spring.

We have already noted many changes in the materials used for rod construction. When I was a boy, greenheart was still a popular material. Then came the slow change to split-cane and thence to fibreglass. Now there is a definite and sensible swing to carbon fibre. One wonders where it all might end. There is vague talk of boron, but I am assured by those who know that it has little, if anything, to offer over carbon. From my schoolboy days I seem to recall that the element carbon had an atomic weight of 12. It does not seem likely that, in the foreseeable future, we are going to find another material which can be lighter than carbon and still remain a solid.

Nylon monofilament will doubtless be with us for a long time; and we may expect diameters to decrease as test strength increases. Doubtless, also, we will see minor changes (I avoid the word 'improvement') in fly design. In the past, I think that we reached the ultimate in smallness and

I am strongly of the opinion that for fishing on the classic rivers – except in very low water or summer – only rarely do we need flies smaller than size 10. We may expect both fly and spinning reels to stay much as they are for some time yet; but we may well expect refinements in the form of slipping clutches, geared re-winds or fully automatic reels. Sadly, I don't expect to see any immediate advance in spinning or spoon bait design; but it would be nice, as I have said, if the manufacturers made a range of baits of variable sizes and weights *with the weights stamped on the bait.*

If there is to be little change in tackle within the next decade, there should be some decisive action in changing the law on salmon fishing generally. Although all anglers will concede that angling is a very ineffective method of catching salmon, the balance of catches between the sporting angler and the commercial fisherman is not fair. A fish sent to Billingsgate, or its new equivalent, from commercial sources does little to benefit the economy of the area in which it was taken. A fish caught by a visiting angler, on the other hand, brings all the side benefits to the local community in which it was caught. The visitor gives employment to the hotel trade and the other ancillary businesses associated with it. There is employment for gillies and general benefit to shops and other firms which operate in the area. Additionally, the fair-minded angler will never denude river stocks below an acceptable level, although it has to be admitted that there are a growing number of anglers who, having paid a high rental, seek to catch all they can get by whatever means are at their disposal.

Sadly, there is an increasing trend for *all* exploiters of the salmon resource to take all they can get without much thought for the future. Disease and Danish netting were the first main clouds on the horizon. Now, we know that a high level of exploitation is undertaken here at home. The amount of legal and illegal netting which goes on around our coasts is reaching astronomical proportions. The entire aspect of salmon fishery management is still too much of a hit-and-miss affair. And, although there are several vociferous minorities banging the drum, there are very few in authority who are taking the slightest bit of notice. Most of those able to wield power lurk behind their desks, furtively watching the calendar for their retirement date and their pension. Of course, all aspects of salmon fishing are a bit of a political hot potato. The left wing suggest that the 'rich' are seeking to rob the 'poor' of their livelihood – their entitlement to net – in order to have better sport for the 'rich'. The affluent right, on the other hand – if there are any left in this highly-taxed society – and sensible conservationists, claim that the 'poor' should be inhibited somewhat in order to provide a more profitable resource for the total economy of the country and better facilities for the visiting angler, who will bring that prosperity.

Many other nations have seen the wisdom of developing the sporting resource at the expense of the commercial fisherman. Socialist Iceland is a classic example. Changes are also coming to Norway, but we in Britain seem to continue to lean in favour of the commercial fisherman. On a beat of the Lune which I used to fish regularly we could expect a reasonable catch from April through to the end of the season: in 1966, as I have already noted, we took 195 salmon from that small beat. My latest information is that in 1981 it produced only one salmon for the entire season.

With an intiative which started in Norway a few years ago, much is now being done to breed and rear salmon in an artificial environment. The extent of this may be gauged from the fact that in 1971 the total fish-farm salmon harvest in Norway was 100 tons. In 1980, it had reached 4,150 tons, while 15,000 tons has been estimated as a target within easy reach by 1985. Projections for 1990 are 30,000 to 50,000 tons. Should that figure be achieved – the Norwegians are confident that it will be – salmon from their fish farms will become a major influence in the world's salmon food industry. Much is also happening in Britain in this direction and, while I do not have any figures, it may be permissible to indulge in a minor bout of optimism. If fish farming for salmon does take off in a big way, it might just be that present commercial fishing on the high seas and around our estuaries will cease to be profitable and that the high capital and overhead expenses involved will not bring an adequate return. Let us do all that we can to hasten that day!

Meanwhile, there is still too much indiscriminate cropping. One angler who wrote to me in 1980 – a serving officer in the Royal Air Force – reported that the high-definition radar systems on some planes can detect nylon nets up to fifteen miles in length off the north-west coast of Ireland. Many anglers also know of the increasing concern demonstrated by some authorities over the virtual piracy at sea where increasing numbers of boats are illegally taking all the salmon they can get. Some fishery protection vessels have even been challenged and damaged. The unemployment of the early eighties is doing little but encourage people to flout the law. Of course, it is one thing making a law and quite another securing its enforcement: but there is much that could be done if there was a sincere desire to do it. Sadly, the salmon angler does not yet have an organisation with sufficient teeth to bite in the right places and the general apathy continues.

Yet another threat to our sport is posed by those groups of individuals who classify fishing with other field sports and claim that it is cruel. Already, the thin end of a fairly broad wedge is being pointed at those who hunt and shoot. At the moment, of course, it is not politically expedient to include the angler in this frontal attack. There are too many anglers for any political party to ignore and we might have a slight lull in which to take a deep breath before the full attack is leased against us. But come our way it will!

Meanwhile, for a reason best known to those who seek to bring a ban on hunting and shooting, there is some difference in the ethics of killing game and catching fish. Frankly, this strange dichotomy escapes me. I fail to understand why such organisations as the RSPCA and others can salve their consciences on this question. I suspect that the real snag lies in the fact that people are badly informed and too emotional. They see deer and rabbits as little Bambi's or bunnies, and cannot equate them with rats. The fact that all are capable of great damage and that the deer and the rabbit are preferable as meat does not seem to matter: the 'anti' would quickly exterminate the rat, but is all too keen to pamper the deer and the rabbit. Fish don't bring out these emotions in people, but surely they are all God's creatures and deserve the same respect?

From the early teaching in the Bible (Genesis Chapter 9) it is perfectly plain that man was intended to hunt and eat meat and fish. Primitive man must have spent 90 per cent of his waking moments hunting for food. This instinct is still deeply rooted in many of us and no great sin is involved in demonstrating a desire to catch or shoot our own fish and meat. Most people casually accept their meat and fish from the butcher and fishmonger. Do they show any concern for the welfare of these animals and fish while they are still alive? Ethically and morally the responsible sportsman who hunts and fishes and spends his time and money protecting the environment in which wildlife thrives, has the greatest entitlement to eat animal flesh and fish. He is concerned for their future well-being as a species. Indeed, it is a well-observed fact that when game is scarce – as on some grouse moors from time to time – shooting is abandoned or restricted. The true sportsman is essentially a disciplined conservator and he only takes when nature or good husbandry gives an excess.

Sadly, the same may not be said of most coarse fishermen. They do not require their catch as food. Most are content to catch fish and put them back. At first sight this may seem a commendable aspect, but one is forced to ask if it is morally right to bait and entice a creature merely for fun? Of course, the game fisherman has the advantage over the shooting man in that he can select the fish he will keep and eat and thus conserve those which are too small or out of condition, or will prove beneficial to the fishery later on. The shooting man, on the other hand, has little time to decide whether he will pull the trigger on a bird or beast which might be better spared. The firing of the shot is the final act, but the angler does have a period of grace for discretion – provided that the fish is unharmed and can be returned to the water in good condition if the need arises.

Whatever other motives may be involved with those who hunt, shoot or fish for sport, there is no better group to defend the interests of the wildlife they seek. Stripped of the right to hunt, shoot or fish, it would not be long before all our wildlife was in great jeopardy. With a free rein the poacher would recognise even fewer ethics and game wildlife could be predicted to cease within about five years. Because of the political influences we have examined, we may expect that angling will be the last sport to come under fire; but we have already had a stern warning of what a socialist government with a big majority might do. The hunting of elephants has been banned in many African countries for several years. Is it not a little ironic that, due entirely to unrestricted poaching and a lack of adequate policing, elephants are now a threatened species?

Perhaps another cloud which looms large on the horizon is the increasing demand which will be made upon our water authorities for industrial and urban water supply. We may expect the population expansion to continue. And, with many of our rivers already suffering abstraction, we may well expect the decline in content and flow to continue. Another problem that may confront us is acid rain. I have already heard of one west coast river which, with a south-east wind, collects rainfall from the midlands. Following such a rainstorm in 1980 an entire migration of salmon and sea trout were known to perish – and this after they had been in *fresh water* for only a few days.

The whole future of our migratory fish stocks seems to hang in a precarious balance. The salmon are faced with overwhelming odds and, if mankind does not offer some respite in the very near future, they could just pass into history as the greatest, but extinct, fish once sought by the sporting angler.

INDEX